Fourth Edition

# Race and Ethnicity in the United States

### Richard T. Schaefer
*DePaul University*

PEARSON
Prentice
Hall

Upper Saddle River, NJ 07458

Library of Congress Cataloging-in-Publication Data

Schaefer, Richard T.
  Race and ethnicity in the United States / Richard T. Schaefer. — 4th ed.
     p. cm.
  ISBN 0-13-173326-5
1. Minorities United States. 2. prejudices United States. 3. United States Ethnic reltios.
4. United States—Race relation. I. Title.
  E184.A1S25 2006
  305.800973—dc22

2006021005

**Editorial Director:** Leah Jewell
**Publisher:** Nancy Roberts
**Editorial Assistant** Lee Paterson
**Marketing Manager:** Marissa Feliberty
**Production Liaison:** Fran Russello
**Permissons Specialist:** Victoria Putman
**Manufacturing Buyer:** Brian Mackey
**Cover Design:** Kiwi Design
**Cover Illustration/Photo:** Diana Ong/Super Stock
**Director, Image Resource Center:** Melinda Patelli
**Manager. Rights and Permission:** Zina Arabia
**Manager, Visual Research:** Beth Brenzel
**Manager, Cover Visual Research & Permission:** Karen Sanatar
**Image Permission Coordinator:** Joanne Dippel
**Photo Researcher:** Beaura Ringrose
**Project Management:** Jan Pushard/Pine Tree Compositon
**Composition:** Laserwords
**Printer/Binder:** Courier Companies, Inc.

Credits and acknowledgments borrowed from other sources and reproduced, with permission, in
this texbook appear on appropriate page within text (or on page 232).

Pearson Education LTD.
Pearson Education Singapore, Pte. Ltd
Pearson Education, Canada, Ltd.
Pearson Education—Japan
Pearson Education Australia PTY, Limited

Pearson Education North Asia Ltd
Pearson Educación de México, S.A. de C.V.
Pearson Education Malaysia, Pte. Ltd
Pearson Education, Upper Saddle River, New Jersey

10  9  8  7  6  5  4  3  2  1
ISBN 0-13-173326-5

*To my mother and in memory of my father*

# Contents

# Preface

"Minorities Majority" read first-page newspaper headlines in Fall 2004, when the Census Bureau released its annual population estimates. Now in 280 counties, Whites who are not Hispanic are outnumbered by Latinos, African Americans, Asian Americans, Native American tribal members, and others. However, do these groups wield the power in all these counties? In any of these counties? Does the United States' becoming more diverse signify a significant advancement in the quality of life of people of color relative to gains made by White Americans? These are the real questions; however, rarely are they asked and almost never are they answered. Some people who have not followed these trends seemed stunned that in 2003, Orange County, surf 'n sun capital of southern California and home of Disneyland, now has minority majority. Nor should one have been surprised that in the wake of Hurricane Katrina 2005 New Orleans poor were overwhelmingly African American. Although these events may not signify a major shift in social inequality among groups, they do underscore the importance of being familiar with the nature of race and ethnicity in the United States.

Race and ethnicity are an important part of the national agenda. Race is not a static phenomenon, and although it has always been a part of the social reality, specific issues may change over time, but they continue to play out against a backdrop of discrimination that is rooted in the social structure and changing population composition, as influenced by immigration patterns and reproduction patterns.

We continue to be reminded about the importance of the social construction of many aspects of racial and ethnic relations. What constitutes a race in terms of identity? What meaning do race and ethnicity have amid the growing number of interracial marriages and marriages across cultural boundaries? Beyond the spectrum of race and ethnicity, we see the socially constructed meaning attached to all religions as members debate who is the "true" keeper of the faith. The very issue of national identity is also a part of the agenda. The public and politicians alike ask, "How many immigrants can we accept?"

and "How much should be done to make up for past discrimination?" We are also witnessing the emergence of race, ethnicity, and national identity as global issues.

## Changes in the Fourth Edition

As with all previous editions, every line, every source, and every number have been rechecked for its currency. We pride ourselves on providing the most current information possible to document the patterns in intergroup relations in the United States.

Relevant scholarly findings in a variety of disciplines, including economics, anthropology, and communication sciences, have been incorporated. The feature "Listen to Our Voices" appears in every chapter. Three of these selections have been updated as indicated in bold:

**Listen to Our Voices**

- Problem of the Color Line, W. E. B. DuBois (Chapter 1)
- **Pendulum Swings on Civil Rights, James Zogby (Chapter 2)**
- **Of Race and Risk, Patricia J. Williams (Chapter 3)**
- **Imagining Life without Illegal Immigrants, Dean E. Murphy (Chapter 4)**
- When the Boats Arrived, Diane Glancy (Chapter 5)
- Gangsters, Gooks, Geeks, Geishas, Helen Zia (Chapter 6)

This edition includes a new feature entitled "Research Focus" that highlights the relevant research on a topic touched upon in each of the first five chapters.

**Research Focus**

- **Measuring Multiculturalism (Chapter 1)**
- **What's in a Name? (Chapter 2)**
- **Discrimination in Job Seeking (Chapter 3)**
- **How Well Are Immigrants Doing? (Chapter 4)**
- **Measuring the Importance of Religion (Chapter 5)**

Another new feature is the addition of an Internet Resource Directory at the conclusion of the book that offers current, relevant Internet sites.

The fourth edition includes the following additions and changes:

- New key terms such as bilingualism (Chapter 5), English immersion (Chapter 5), bilingual education (Chapter 4), intelligent design (Chapter 5), cultural capital (Chapter 6), and social capital (Chapter 6)

- The section on race is now revamped and titled "Does Race Matter" to emphasize that race is socially constructed (Chapter 1).
- A new U.S. map has been added showing minority–majority states (Chapter 1).
- A new section on low-wage labor emphasizes that a large proportion of racial and ethnic minorities are among the working poor (Chapter 3).
- A new U.S. map showing percentage of foreign born by state has been added (Chapter 4).
- A section on bilingual education has been added (Chapter 5)
- A new coverage of Pierre Bourdieu's culture capital and social capital has been added as a part of new section "The Persistence of Equality" (Chapter 6).

In addition, tables, figures, maps, and political cartoons have been updated.

## Features to Aid Students

Several features are included in the text to facilitate student learning. A Chapter Outline appears at the beginning of each chapter and is followed by Highlights, a short section alerting students to important issues and topics to be addressed. To help students review, each chapter ends with a summary Conclusion. The Key Terms are highlighted in bold when they are first introduced in the text and are listed with page numbers at the end of each chapter. The Intergroup Relations Continuum first presented in Chapter 1 is repeated again in Chapter 5 to reinforce major concepts while addressing the unique social circumstances of individual racial and ethnic groups.

In addition, there is an end-of-book Glossary with full definitions referenced to page numbers. This edition includes both Review Questions and Critical Thinking Questions. The Review Questions are intended to remind the reader of major points, whereas the Critical Thinking Questions encourage students to think more deeply about some of the major issues raised in the chapter. *Internet Connections—Research Navigator™* exercises allow students to do some critical thinking and research on the Web. An Internet Resource Directory has been expanded to allow access to the latest electronic sources. An extensive illustration program, which includes maps and political cartoons, expands the text discussion and provokes thought.

## Ancillary Materials

The ancillary materials that accompany this textbook have been carefully created to enhance the topics being discussed.

## For the Instructor

**Instructor's Manual with Tests** (*0-13-173328-1*)   This carefully prepared manual includes chapter overviews, key term identification exercises, discussion questions, topics for class discussion, audiovisual resources, and test questions in both multiple-choice and essay format.

**TestGEN-EQ** (*0-13-173327-3*)   This computerized software allows instructors to create their own personalized exams, to edit any or all of the existing test questions, and to add new questions. Other special features of this program include random generation of test questions, creation of alternate versions of the same test, a scrambling question sequence, and test preview before printing.

**ABC News/Prentice Hall Video Library DVD for Race and Ethnic Relations** (*0-13-189067-0*)   Selected video segments from award-winning ABC News programs such as *Nightline, ABC World News Tonight*, and *20/20* accompany topics featured in the text. An Instructor's Guide accompanies the DVD. Please contact your Prentice Hall representative for more details.

## For the Student

**Companion Website™**   In tandem with the text, students can now take full advantage of the World Wide Web to enrich their study of material found in the text. This resource correlates the text with related material available on the Internet. Features of the Web site include chapter objectives, study questions, census updates, and links to interesting material and information from other sites on the Web that can reinforce and enhance the content of each chapter. Address: www.prenhall.com/schaefer

**The New York Times/Prentice Hall eThemes of the Times**   *The New York Times* and Prentice Hall are sponsoring eThemes of the Times, a program designed to enhance student access to current information relevant to the classroom. Through this program, the core subject matter provided in the text is supplemented by a collection of timely articles downloaded from one of the world's most distinguished newspapers, *The New York Times*. These articles demonstrate the vital, ongoing connection between what is learned in the classroom and what is happening in the world around us. Access to **The New York Times/Prentice Hall eThemes of the Times** is available on the Schaefer Companion Website™.

**Census 2000 CD-ROM, Second Edition** (0-13-192911-9).   Capturing the rich picture of our nation drawn by Census 2000, this CD-ROM brings related census data into your classroom in a rich, multimedia format. It uses files taken directly from the Census Bureau Web site, organizes them around your course, and offers teaching aids to support student learning. This updated CD-ROM can be packaged with *Race and Ethnicity in the United States, Fourth Edition*. Please see your local Prentice Hall representitive for details.

**Research Navigator™.**  Research Navigator™ can help students to complete research assignments efficiently and with confidence by providing three exclusive databases of high-quality scholarly and popular articles accessed by easy-to-use search engines.

- **EBSCO's ContentSelect™ Academic Journal Database**, organized by subject, contains 50–100 of the leading academic journals for sociology. Instructors and students can search the online journals by keyword, topic, or multiple topics. Articles include abstract and citation information and can be cut, pasted, e-mailed, or saved for later use.
- ***The New York Times* Search-by-Subject™ Archive** provides articles specific to Sociology and is searchable by keyword or multiple keywords. Instructors and students can view full-text articles from the world's leading journalists writing for *The New York Times.*
- **Link Library** offers editorially selected "best of the web" sites for Sociology. Link Libraries are continually scanned and kept up to date, providing the most relevant and accurate links for research assignments.

Gain access to Research Navigator™ by using the access code found in the front of the brief guide called *The Prentice Hall Guide to Research Navigator™ (0-13-243753-8).* The access code for Research Navigator™ is included with every guide and can be packaged for no extra charge with *Race and Ethnicity in the United States, Fourth Edition.* Please contact your Prentice Hall representative for more information.

**TIME Special Edition Sociology** (*0-13-154734-8*): Prentice Hall and *TIME Magazine* are pleased to offer you and your students a chance to examine today's most current and compelling issues in an exciting new way. **TIME Special Edition: Sociology** offers a selection of twenty *TIME* articles on today's most current issues and debates in sociology. **TIME Special Edition** provides your students the full coverage, accessible writing, and bold photographs that *TIME* is known for. Available as a package option with *Race and Ethnicity in the United States, Fourth Edition*, it is perfect for discussion groups, in-class debates, or research assignments. Please see your local Prentice Hall representative for more information.

*10 Ways to Fight Hate* brochure (*0-13-028146-8*) Produced by the Southern Poverty Law Center, the leading hate-crime and crime-watch organization in the United States, this brochure walks students through ten steps that they can take on their own campus or in their own neighborhood to fight hate every day.

## Acknowledgments

The fourth edition benefited from the thoughtful reaction of my students in classes. Data analysis of the General Social Survey and Census Bureau data sets were provided by my faculty colleague Kiljoong Kim of DePaul University. Faculty colleagues Blackhawk Hancock and Monique Payne provided helpful comments on the new section covering social and cultural capital. Rachel Hanes, a student at DePaul, assisted with special tasks related to the preparation of the manuscript.

The fourth edition was improved by the suggestions of Deborah Brunson, University of North Carolina–Wilmington; Jac D. Bulk, University of Wisconsin–La Crosse; Efren N. Padilla, California State University–Hayward; and Kristen M. Wallingford, Davidson College.

I would also like to thank my editor, Nancy Roberts, for developing this edition. She has been a true colleague in this endeavor.

The truly exciting challenge of writing and researching has always been for me an enriching experience, mostly because of the supportive home I share with my wife, Sandy. She knows so well my appreciation and gratitude, now as in the past and in the future.

Richard T. Schaefer
*schaeferrt@aol.com*
*www.schaefersociology.net*

# About the Author

Richard T. Schaefer grew up in Chicago at a time when neighborhoods were going through transitions in ethnic and racial composition. He found himself increasingly intrigued by what was happening, how people were reacting, and how these changes were affecting neighborhoods and people's jobs. In high school, he took a course in sociology. His interest in social issues caused him to gravitate to more sociology courses at Northwestern University, where he eventually received a B.A. in sociology.

"Originally as an undergraduate I thought I would go on to law school and become a lawyer. But after taking a few sociology courses, I found myself wanting to learn more about what sociologists studied, and fascinated by the kinds of questions they raised," Dr. Schaefer says. "Perhaps the most fascinating and, to me, relevant to the 1960s was the intersection of race, gender, and social class." This interest led him to obtain his M.A. and Ph.D. in sociology from the University of Chicago. Dr. Schaefer's continuing interest in race relations led him to write his master's thesis on the membership of the Ku Klux Klan and his doctoral thesis on racial prejudice and race relations in Great Britain.

Dr. Schaefer went on to become a professor of sociology. He has taught sociology and courses on multiculturalism for thirty years. He has been invited to give special presentations to students and faculty on racial and ethnic diversity in Illinois, Indiana, Missouri, North Carolina, Ohio, and Texas.

Dr. Schaefer is author of *Racial and Ethnic Groups,* Tenth Edition (2006, Prentice Hall). Dr. Schaefer is also the author of the tenth edition of *Sociology* (2007), the seventh edition of *Sociology: A Brief Introduction* (2008), and the third edition of *Sociology Matters* (2008). His articles and book reviews have appeared in many journals, including *American Journal of Sociology, Phylon: A Review of Race and Culture, Contemporary Sociology, Sociology and Social Research, Sociological Quarterly,* and *Teaching Sociology.* He served as president of the Midwest Sociological Society from 1994–1995. In recognition of his achievements in undergraduate teaching, he was named Vincent de Paul Professor of Sociology in 2004.

# 1 Understanding Race and Ethnicity

1

{ HIGHLIGHTS }

Minority groups are subordinated in terms of power and privilege to the majority, or dominant, group. A minority is defined not by being outnumbered but by five characteristics: unequal treatment, distinguishing physical or cultural traits, involuntary membership, awareness of subordination, and in-group marriage. Subordinate groups are classified in terms of race, ethnicity, religion, and gender. The social importance of race is derived from a process of racial formation; its biological significance is uncertain. The theoretical perspectives of functionalism, conflict theory, and labeling offer insights into the sociology of intergroup relations.

Immigration, annexation, and colonialism are processes that may create subordinate groups. Other processes such as expulsion may remove the presence of a subordinate group. Significant for racial and ethnic oppression in the United States today is the distinction between assimilation and pluralism. Assimilation demands subordinate-group conformity to the dominant group, and pluralism implies mutual respect between diverse groups.

Only a few years into the twenty-first century two events shook the country in different ways—the attacks of 9/11 and the devastation left by Hurricane Katrina in 2005.

In the wake of the September 11, 2001, terrorist attacks in the United States, Alexandr Manin, a citizen of Kazakhstan, joined the military in October

2001. He was not joining some far-flung military effort of his country of birth: The 25-year-old from Brooklyn was joining the U.S. Marine Corps. A legal permanent resident, Alexandr can join the U.S. military even though he is not a citizen. His decision is not that unusual. Thousands of immigrants join each year. Some do it for the training or employment possibilities, but others are motivated by allegiance to their new country. As Alexandr said, "It doesn't matter that America is not my country; New York is my city, and what happened shook my life. I feel patriotic, and I have this itch now to go sooner" (Chen and Sengupta 2001, A1).

Hurricane Katrina destroyed more than an enormous part of the Gulf Coast. In its wake people were asking questions of the President if the slow response was due the presence of large numbers of poor and Black residents left homeless. Rap star Kanye West weighed in and said that "George Bush doesn't care about Black people." The President denounced such criticism, declaring, "When those Coast Guard choppers . . . were pulling people off roofs, they didn't check the color of a person's skin." Yet the nation was split on this view with 66 percent of African Americans feeling the response would have been faster if the victims had been White compared to only 26 percent of Whites holding that view.

Yet Katrina proved to be more than a Black-White issue. The Asian American community expressed concern over the neglect it saw in assisting Vietnamese Americans who lived in the rural Gulf Coast—themselves only a generation removed from having experienced upheaval during the Vietnam War. Native Americans nationwide reached out to help Gulf Coast reservations whose rebuilding, they felt, was being ignored by the government. And finally, the mayor of New Orleans expressed concern that many of the people arriving to help rebuild the city were Latino and that the first housing likely to be created would be for White residents. The mayor declared that the Almighty wanted the rebuilding metropolis to become a "chocolate" city (Bush 2005; Bustillo 2006; Pew Research Center 2005).

So, in the United States, with its diverse racial and ethnic heritage and new immigrants, is it only major events that bring out social concerns?

- In October 2005, an Elgin high school that is over one-third Hispanic had an assembly in celebration of Mexican Independence Day. A senior refused to stand, fearing that since he was in the process of enlisting that honoring another nation's anthem might jeopardize his military status.
- Earlier that same year, residents of Danbury, Connecticut, were seeking to ban volleyball in their parks. Actually, it was "ecuavolley," a form of the game beloved by Ecuadorian Americans. Played in their backyards, it attracts families and friends and often brings a hundred people together. The Latino community became enraged when the local government, unable to figure out how to ban the sport, tried to convince the federal government to "raid" the backyards looking for illegal immigrants.

- What about trying to stop the sale of methamphetamines? Sounds rea-sonable, but when in Georgia agents found they now had arrested their forty-ninth convenience store clerk—all of whom were recent Indian immigrants—they realized their "trap" was poorly planned. Undercover agents went to the stores asking for cold medicine containing the chem-icals, matches, and camping fuel to "finish up a cook." The arrested clerks all stated later that they had merely felt he meant the customer was doing some kind of barbecue and denied that they were assisting in the setting up a meth lab.

- Further north, it was a different immigrant group that attracted unwanted attention. Lewiston, Maine, is also adjusting. In this old New England town, hundreds of Somalis arrived seeking work and affordable housing thousands of miles from their African hometowns, which were torn apart by civil strife and famine. Residents expressed alarm over this in-flux, prompting the mayor to send a letter to all the Somalis already in Lewiston to discourage friends and relatives from relocating there. The pace of Somalis, many of them U.S. citizens, resettling to Lewis-ton slowed significantly amidst the furor (C. Jones 2003, Malone 2005; Thornburgh 2005; Zernike 2005).

Relations between racial and ethnic groups are not like relations between family members. The history of the United States is one of racial oppres-sion. It goes well beyond a mayor in Maine or people made homeless by a natural disaster in the Gulf Coast. Episodes of a new social identity devel-oping, as in the case of Alexandr Manin, are not unusual, but that does not mean that the society is not structured to keep some groups of people down and extend privileges automatically to other groups based on race, ethnicity, or gender.

People in the United States and elsewhere are beginning to consider that the same principles that guarantee equality based on race or gender can apply to other groups who are discriminated against. There have been grow-ing efforts to ensure that the same rights and privileges are available to all people, regardless of age, disability, or sexual orientation. These concerns are emerging even as the old divisions over race, ethnicity, and religion con-tinue to fester and occasionally explode into violence that envelops entire nations.

The United States is a very diverse nation, as shown in Table 1.1. Accord-ing to the 2000 census, about 17 percent of the population are members of racial minorities, and about another 13 percent are Hispanic. These percent-ages represent almost one of three people in the United States, without counting White ethnic groups. As shown in Figure 1.1, between 2000 and 2100 the population in the United States is expected to rise from 30 percent Black, Hispanic, Asian, and Native American to 60 percent. Although the composition of the population is changing, the problems of prejudice, dis-crimination, and mistrust remain.

**Table 1.1  Racial and Ethnic Groups in the United States, 2000**

| Classification | Number in Thousands | Percentage of Total Population |
|---|---|---|
| Racial Groups | | |
| Whites (includes 16.9 million White Hispanic) | 211,461 | 75.1 |
| Blacks/African Americans | 34,658 | 12.3 |
| Native Americans, Alaskan Native | 2,476 | 0.9 |
| Asian Americans | 10,243 | 3.6 |
| Chinese | 2,433 | 0.9 |
| Filipinos | 1,850 | 0.7 |
| Asian Indians | 1,679 | 0.6 |
| Vietnamese | 1,123 | 0.4 |
| Koreans | 1,077 | 0.4 |
| Japanese | 797 | 0.2 |
| Other | 1,285 | 0.5 |
| Ethnic Groups | | |
| White ancestry (single or mixed) | | |
| Germans | 42,842 | 15.2 |
| Irish | 30,525 | 10.8 |
| English | 24,509 | 8.7 |
| Italians | 15,638 | 5.6 |
| Poles | 8,977 | 3.2 |
| French | 8,310 | 3.0 |
| Jews | 5,200 | 1.8 |
| Hispanics (or Latinos) | 35,306 | 12.5 |
| Mexican Americans | 23,337 | 8.3 |
| Central and South Americans | 5,119 | 1.8 |
| Puerto Ricans | 3,178 | 1.1 |
| Cubans | 1,412 | 0.5 |
| Other | 2,260 | 0.8 |
| TOTAL (ALL GROUPS) | 281,422 | |

Note: Percentages do not total 100 percent, and subheads do not add up to figures in major heads because of overlap between groups (e.g., Polish American Jews or people of mixed ancestry, such as Irish and Italian).

Source: Brittingham and de la Cruz 2004; Bureau of the Census 2003a; Grieco and Cassidy 2001; Therrien and Ramirez 2001; United Jewish Communities 2003.

# What Is a Subordinate Group?

Identifying a subordinate group or a minority in a society seems to be a simple enough task. In the United States, the groups readily identified as minorities—Blacks and Native Americans, for example—are outnumbered by non-Blacks

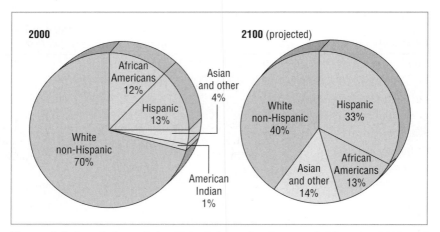

**Figure 1.1** Population of the United States by Race and Ethnicity, 2000 and 2100 (Projected)
According to projections by the Census Bureau, the proportion of residents of the United States who are White and non-Hispanic will decrease significantly by the year 2050. By contrast, there will be a striking rise in the proportion of both Hispanic Americans and Asian Americans.
*Source*: Bureau of the Census 2004b.

and non-Native Americans. However, **minority group** is not necessarily the result of being outnumbered. A social minority need not be a mathematical one. A minority group is a subordinate group whose members have significantly less control or power over their own lives than do the members of a dominant or majority group. In sociology, minority means the same as subordinate, and dominant is used interchangeably with majority.

Confronted with evidence that a particular minority in the United States is subordinate to the majority, some people respond, "Why not? After all, this is a democracy, so the majority rules." However, the subordination of a minority involves more than its inability to rule over society. A member of a subordinate or **minority group** experiences a narrowing of life's opportunities—for success, education, wealth, the pursuit of happiness—that goes beyond any personal shortcoming he or she may have. A minority group does not share in proportion to its numbers what a given society, such as the United States, defines as valuable.

Being superior in numbers does not guarantee a group control over its destiny and ensure majority status. In 1920, the majority of people in Mississippi and South Carolina were African Americans. Yet African Americans did not have as much control over their lives as Whites, let alone control of the states of Mississippi and South Carolina. Throughout the United States today are counties or neighborhoods in which the majority of people are African

American, Native American, or Hispanic, but White Americans are the dominant force. Nationally, 50.8 percent of the population is female, but males still dominate positions of authority and wealth well beyond their numbers.

A minority or subordinate group has five characteristics: unequal treatment, distinguishing physical or cultural traits, involuntary membership, awareness of subordination, and in-group marriage (Wagley and Harris 1958):

1. Members of a minority experience unequal treatment and have less power over their lives than members of a dominant group have over theirs. Prejudice, discrimination, segregation, and even extermination create this social inequality.

2. Members of a minority group share physical or cultural characteristics that distinguish them from the dominant group, such as skin color or language. Each society has its own arbitrary standard for determining which characteristics are most important in defining dominant and minority groups.

3. Membership in a dominant or minority group is not voluntary: People are born into the group. A person does not choose to be African American or White.

4. Minority-group members have a strong sense of group solidarity. William Graham Sumner, writing in 1906, noted that people make distinctions between members of their own group (the in-group) and everyone else (the out-group). When a group is the object of long-term prejudice and discrimination, the feeling of "us versus them" often becomes intense.

5. Members of a minority generally marry others from the same group. A member of a dominant group often is unwilling to join a supposedly inferior minority by marrying one of its members. In addition, the minority group's sense of solidarity encourages marriage within the group and discourages marriage to outsiders.

While "minority" is not about numbers, there is no denying that the majority is diminishing in size relative to the growing diversity of racial and ethnic groups. In Figure 1.2 we see that more and more states have close to a majority of non-Whites or Latinos and that several states have already reached that point today.

## Types of Subordinate Groups

There are four types of minority or subordinate groups. All four, except where noted, have the five properties previously outlined. The four criteria for classifying minority groups are race, ethnicity, religion, and gender.

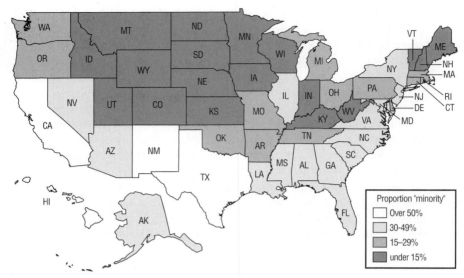

**Figure 1.2** Race and Ethnic Presence by State (Projected)
According to projections by the Census Bureau, the proportion of residents of the United States who are White and non-Hispanic will decrease significantly by the year 2050. By contrast, there will be a striking rise in the proportion of both Hispanic Americans and Asian Americans.
*Source*: 2004 data released in 2005 by Bureau of the Census 2005b.

## Racial Groups

The term **racial group** is reserved for minorities and the corresponding majorities that are socially set apart because of obvious physical differences. Notice the two crucial words in the definition: *obvious* and *physical*. What is obvious? Hair color? Shape of an earlobe? Presence of body hair? To whom are these differences obvious, and why? Each society defines what it finds obvious.

In the United States, skin color is one obvious difference. On a cold winter day when one has clothing covering all but one's head, however, skin color may be less obvious than hair color. Yet people in the United States have learned informally that skin color is important, and hair color is unimportant. We need to say more than that. In the United States, people have traditionally classified and classify themselves as either Black or White. There is no in-between state except for people readily identified as Native Americans or Asian Americans. Later in this chapter we will explore this issue more deeply and see how such assumptions have very complex implications.

Other societies use skin color as a standard but may have a more elaborate system of classification. In Brazil, where hostility between races is less than in the United States, numerous categories identify people on the basis of skin color. In the United States, a person is Black or White. In Brazil, a variety of terms, such as *cafuso, mazombo, preto,* and *escuro,* are applied to describe various combinations of skin color, facial features, and hair texture. What makes differences obvious is subject to a society's definition.

The designation of a racial group emphasizes physical differences as opposed to cultural distinctions. In the United States, minority races include Blacks, Native Americans (or American Indians), Japanese Americans, Chinese Americans, Arab Americans, Filipinos, Hawaiians, and other Asian peoples. The issue of race and racial differences has been an important one, not only in the United States but also throughout the entire sphere of European influence. Later in this chapter we will examine race and its significance more closely. We should not forget that Whites are a race, too. As we will consider in Chapter 5, who is White has been subject to change over time as certain European groups were felt historically not to deserve being considered White, but over time, partly to compete against a growing Black population, the whiting of some European Americans has occurred.

Some racial groups may also have unique cultural traditions, as we can readily see in the many Chinatowns throughout the United States. For racial groups, however, the physical distinctiveness and not the cultural differences generally prove to be the barrier to acceptance by the host society. For example, Chinese Americans who are faithful Protestants and know the names of all the members of the Baseball Hall of Fame may be bearers of American culture. Yet these Chinese Americans are still part of a minority because they are seen as physically different.

## Ethnic Groups

Ethnic minority groups are differentiated from the dominant group on the basis of cultural differences, such as language, attitudes toward marriage and parenting, and food habits. **Ethnic groups** are groups set apart from others because of their national origin or distinctive cultural patterns.

Ethnic groups in the United States include a grouping that we call Hispanics or Latinos, which includes Mexican Americans, Puerto Ricans, Cubans, and other Latin Americans in the United States. Hispanics can be either Black or White, as in the case of a dark-skinned Puerto Rican who may be taken as Black in central Texas but be viewed as a Puerto Rican in New York City. The ethnic group category also includes White ethnics, such as Irish Americans, Polish Americans, and Norwegian Americans.

The cultural traits that make groups distinctive usually originate from their homelands or, for Jews, from a long history of being segregated and prohibited from becoming a part of the host society. Once in the United States, an immigrant group may maintain distinctive cultural practices through associations, clubs, and worship. Ethnic enclaves such as a Little Haiti or a Greektown in urban areas also perpetuate cultural distinctiveness.

Ethnicity continues to be important, as recent events in Bosnia and other parts of Eastern Europe have demonstrated. Almost a century ago, African

## LISTEN TO OUR VOICES

## Problem of the Color Line

*W. E. B. Du Bois*

In the metropolis of the modern world, in this the closing year of the nineteenth century, there has been assembled a congress of men and women of African blood, to deliberate solemnly upon the present situation and outlook of the darker races of mankind. The problem of the twentieth century is the problem of the color line, the question as to how far differences of race—which show themselves chiefly in the color of the skin and the texture of the hair—will hereafter be made the basis of denying to over half the world the right of sharing to their utmost ability the opportunities and privileges of modern civilization. . . . civilization.

To be sure, the darker races are today the least advanced in culture according to European standards. This has not, however, always been the case in the past, and certainly the world's history both ancient and modern, has given many instances of no despicable ability and capacity among the blackest races of men.

In any case, the modern world must remember that in this age when the ends of the world are being brought so near together the millions of black men in Africa, America, and Islands of the Sea, not to speak of the brown and yellow myriads elsewhere are bound to have a great influence upon the world in the future, by reason of sheer numbers and physical contact. If now the world of culture bends itself towards giving Negroes and other dark men the largest and broadest opportunity for education and to have a beneficial effect upon the world and hasten human progress. But if, by reason of carelessness, prejudice, greed and injustice, the black world is to be exploited and ravished and degraded, the results must be deplorable, if not fatal—not simply to them, but to the high ideals of justice, freedom and culture which a thousand years of Christian civilization have held before Europe. . . .

Let the world take no backward step in that slow but sure progress which has successively refused to let the spirit of class, of caste, of privilege, or of birth, debar from life, liberty and the pursuit of happiness a striving human soul.

Let not color or race be a feature of distinction between white and black men, regardless of worth or ability. . . .

Thus we appeal with boldness and confidence to the Great Powers of the civilized world, trusting in the wide spirit of humanity, and the deep sense of justice of our age, for a generous recognition of the righteousness of our cause.

*Source*: Du Bois [1969a]. From pp. 20–21, 23, in An ABC of Color, by W. E. B. Du Bois. Copyright 1969 by International Publishers.

American sociologist W. E. B. Du Bois, addressing an audience in London, called attention to the overwhelming importance of the color line throughout the world. In "Listen to Our Voices," we read the remarks of Du Bois, the first Black person to receive a doctorate from Harvard, who later helped to organize the National Association for the Advancement of Colored People (NAACP). Du Bois's observances give us a historic perspective on the struggle for equality. We can look ahead, knowing how far we have come and speculating on how much further we have to go.

## Religious Groups

Association with a religion other than the dominant faith is the third basis for minority-group status. In the United States, Protestants, as a group, outnumber members of all other religions. Roman Catholics form the largest minority religion. Chapter 5 focuses on the increasing Judeo-Christian-Islamic diversity of the United States. For people who are not a part of the Christian tradition, such as followers of Islam, allegiance to the faith often is misunderstood and stigmatizes people. This stigmatization became especially widespread and legitimated by government action in the aftermath of the 9/11 attacks.

Religious minorities include such groups as the Church of Jesus Christ of Latter-day Saints (the Mormons), Jehovah's Witnesses, Amish, Muslims, and Buddhists. Cults or sects associated with such practices as animal sacrifice, doomsday prophecy, demon worship, or the use of snakes in a ritualistic fashion would also constitute minorities. Jews are excluded from this category and placed among ethnic groups. Culture is a more important defining trait for Jewish people worldwide than is religious dogma. Jewish Americans share a cultural tradition that goes beyond theology. In this sense, it is appropriate to view them as an ethnic group rather than as members of a religious faith.

## Gender Groups

Gender is another attribute that creates dominant and subordinate groups. Males are the social majority; females, although more numerous, are relegated to the position of the social minority. Women are considered a minority even though they do not exhibit all the characteristics outlined earlier (e.g., there is little in-group marriage). Women encounter prejudice and discrimination and are physically distinguishable. Group membership is involuntary, and many women have developed a sense of sisterhood. Women who are members of racial and ethnic minorities face a special challenge to achieving equality. They suffer from double jeopardy because they belong to two separate minority groups: a racial or ethnic group plus a subordinate gender group.

Given the diversity in the nation, the workplace is increasingly a place where intergroup tensions may develop.
*Source*: © Tribune Media Services, Inc. All rights reserved. Reprinted with permission.

### Other Subordinate Groups

This book focuses on groups that meet a set of criteria for subordinate status. People encounter prejudice or are excluded from full participation in society for many reasons. Racial, ethnic, religious, and gender barriers are the main ones, but there are others. Age, disabilities, and sexual orientation are among the factors that are used to subordinate groups of people.

## Does Race Matter?

We see people around us—some of whom may look quite different from us. Do these differences matter? The simple answer is no, but because so many people have for so long acted as if difference in physical characteristics as well as geographic origin and shared culture do matter, distinct groups have been created in people's minds. Race has many meanings for many people. Often these meanings are inaccurate and based on theories discarded by scientists generations ago. As we will see, race is a socially constructed concept (Young 2003).

## Biological Meaning

The way the term race has been used by some people to apply to human beings lacks any scientific meaning. We cannot identify distinctive physical characteristics for groups of human beings the same way that scientists distinguish one animal species from another. The idea of **biological race** is based on the mistaken notion of a genetically isolated human group.

Even among past proponents who believed that sharp, scientific divisions exist among humans, there were endless debates over what the races of the world were. Given people's frequent migration, exploration, and invasions, pure genetic types have not existed for some time, if they ever did. There are no mutually exclusive races. Skin color among African Americans varies tremendously, as it does among White Americans. There is even an overlapping of dark-skinned Whites and light-skinned African Americans. If we grouped people by genetic resistance to malaria and by fingerprint patterns, Norwegians and many African groups would be of the same race. If we grouped people by some digestive capacities, some Africans, Asians, and southern Europeans would be of one group and West Africans and northern Europeans of another (Leehotz 1995; Shanklin 1994).

Biologically there are no pure, distinct races. For example, blood type cannot distinguish racial groups with any accuracy. Furthermore, applying pure racial types to humans is problematic because of interbreeding. Despite continuing prejudice about Black–White marriages, a large number of Whites have African American ancestry. Scientists, using various techniques, maintain that the proportion of African Americans with White ancestry is between 20 and 75 percent. Despite the wide range of these estimates, the mixed ancestry of today's Blacks and Whites is part of the biological reality of race (Herskovits 1930, 15; Roberts 1955).

Even the latest research as a part of the Human Genome Project mapping human DNA has only served to confirm genetic diversity with differences within traditionally regarded racial groups (e.g., Black Africans) much greater than that between groups (e.g., between Black Africans and Europeans). Research has also been conducted to determine whether personality characteristics such as temperament and nervous habits are inherited among minority groups. Not surprisingly, the question of whether races have different innate levels of intelligence has led to the most explosive controversy (Bamshad and Olson 2003).

Typically, intelligence is measured as an **intelligence quotient (IQ)**, the ratio of a person's mental age to his or her chronological age, multiplied by 100, where 100 represents average intelligence and higher scores represent greater intelligence. It should be noted that there is little consensus over just what intelligence is, other than as defined by such IQ tests. Intelligence tests are adjusted for a person's age, so that 10-year-olds take a very different test from someone aged 20. Although research shows that certain learning strategies can improve a person's IQ, generally IQ remains stable as one ages.

A great deal of debate continues over the accuracy of these tests. Are they biased toward people who come to the tests with knowledge similar to that of the test writers? Consider the following two questions used on standard tests.

1. Runner: marathon (A) envoy: embassy, (B) oarsman: regatta, (C) martyr: massacre, (D) referee: tournament.
2. Your mother sends you to a store to get a loaf of bread. The store is closed. What should you do? (A) return home, (B) go to the next store, (C) wait until it opens, (D) ask a stranger for advice.

Both correct answers are B. But is a lower-class youth likely to know, in the first question, what a regatta is? Skeptics argue that such test questions do not truly measure intellectual potential. Inner-city youths often have been shown to respond with A to the second question because that may be the only store with which the family has credit. Youths in rural areas, where the next store may be miles away, are also unlikely to respond with the designated correct answer. The issue of culture bias in tests remains an unresolved concern. The most recent research shows that differences in intelligence scores between Blacks and Whites are almost eliminated when adjustments are made for social and economic characteristics (Brooks-Gunn, Klebanov, and Duncan 1996; Herrnstein and Murray 1994, 30; Kagan 1971; Young 2003).

The second issue, trying to associate these results with certain subpopulations such as races, also has a long history. In the past, a few have contended that Whites have more intelligence on average than Blacks. All researchers agree that within-group differences are greater than any speculated differences between groups. The range of intelligence among, for example, Korean Americans is much greater than any average difference between them as a group and Japanese Americans.

The third issue relates to the subpopulations themselves. If Blacks or Whites are not mutually exclusive biologically, how can there be measurable differences? Many Whites and most Blacks have mixed ancestry that complicates any supposed inheritance of intelligence issue. Both groups reflect a rich heritage of very dissimilar populations, from Swedes to Slovaks and Zulus to Tutus.

In 1994, an 845-page book unleashed a new national debate on the issue of IQ. The latest research effort of psychologist Richard J. Herrnstein and social scientist Charles Murray (1994), published in *The Bell Curve,* concluded that 60 percent of IQ is inheritable and that racial groups offer a convenient means to generalize about any differences in intelligence. Unlike most other proponents of the race–IQ link, the authors offered policy suggestions that include ending welfare to discourage births among low-IQ poor women and changing immigration laws so that the IQ pool in the United States is not diminished. Herrnstein and Murray even made generalizations about IQ levels among Asians and Hispanics in the United States, groups subject to even more intermarriage. It is not possible to generalize about absolute differences between groups, such as Latinos versus Whites, when almost half of Latinos in the United States marry non-Hispanics.

Years later, the mere mention of "the bell curve" signals to many the belief in a racial hierarchy with Whites toward the top and Blacks near the bottom. The research present then and repeated today points to the difficulty in definitions: What is intelligence, and what constitutes a racial group, given generations, if not centuries, of intermarriage? How can we speak of definitive inherited racial differences if there has been intermarriage between people of every color? Furthermore, as people on both sides of the debate have noted, regardless of the findings, we would still want to strive to maximize the talents of each individual. All research shows that the differences within a group are much greater than any alleged differences between group averages.

All these issues and controversial research have led to the basic question of what difference it would make if there were significant differences. No researcher believes that race can be used to predict one's intelligence. Also, there is a general agreement that certain intervention strategies can improve scholastic achievement and even intelligence as defined by standard tests. Should we mount efforts to upgrade the abilities of those alleged to be below average? These debates tend to contribute to a sense of hopelessness among some policymakers who think that biology is destiny, rather than causing them to rethink the issue or expand positive intervention efforts.

Why does such IQ research re-emerge if the data are subject to different interpretations? The argument that "we" are superior to "them" is very appealing to the dominant group. It justifies receiving opportunities that are denied to others. For example, the authors of *The Bell Curve* argue that intelligence significantly determines the poverty problem in the United States. We can anticipate that the debate over IQ and the allegations of significant group differences will continue. Policymakers need to acknowledge the difficulty in treating race as a biologically significant characteristic.

## Social Construction of Race

If race does not distinguish humans from one another biologically, why does it seem to be so important? It is important because of the social meaning people have attached to it. The 1950 (UNESCO) Statement on Race maintains that "for all practical social purposes 'race' is not so much a biological phenomenon as a social myth" (Montagu 1972, 118). Adolf Hitler expressed concern over the "Jewish race" and translated this concern into Nazi death camps. Winston Churchill spoke proudly of the "British race" and used that pride to spur a nation to fight. Evidently, race was a useful political tool for two very different leaders in the 1930s and 1940s.

Who are we in terms of race or ethnicity? These concepts in the United States are socially constructed and while most of the time we think we correctly identify people around us, sometimes we cannot.

Race is a social construction, and this process benefits the oppressor, who defines who is privileged and who is not. The acceptance of race in a society as a legitimate category allows racial hierarchies to emerge to the benefit of the dominant "races." For example, inner-city drive-by shootings have come to be seen as a race-specific problem worthy of local officials cleaning up troubled neighborhoods. Yet schoolyard shoot-outs are viewed as a societal concern and placed on the national agenda.

People could speculate that if human groups have obvious physical differences, then they could have corresponding mental or personality differences. No one disagrees that people differ in temperament, potential to learn, and sense of humor. In its social sense, race implies that groups that differ physically also bear distinctive emotional and mental abilities or disabilities. These beliefs are based on the notion that humankind can be divided into distinct groups. We have already seen the difficulties associated with pigeonholing people into racial categories. Despite these difficulties, belief in the inheritance of behavior patterns and in an association between physical and cultural traits is widespread. It is called **racism** when this belief is coupled with the feeling that certain groups or races are inherently superior to others. Racism is a doctrine of racial supremacy, stating that one race is superior to another (Bash 2001; Bonilla-Silva 1996).

We questioned the biological significance of race in the previous section. In modern complex industrial societies, we find little adaptive utility in the presence or absence of prominent chins, epicanthic folds of the eyelids, or the comparative amount of melanin in the skin. What is important is not that people are genetically different but that they approach one another with dissimilar perspectives. It is in the social setting that race is decisive. Race is significant because people have given it significance.

Race definitions are crystallized through what Michael Omi and Howard Winant (1994) called racial formation. **Racial formation** is a sociohistorical process by which racial categories are created, inhibited, transformed, and destroyed. Those in power define groups of people in a certain way that depends on a racist social structure. The Native Americans and the creation of the reservation system for Native Americans in the late 1800s is an example of this racial formation. The federal American Indian policy combined previously distinctive tribes into a single group. No one escapes the extent and frequency to which we are subjected to racial formation.

In the southern United States, the social construction of race was known as the "one-drop rule." This tradition stipulated that if a person had even a single drop of "Black blood," that person was defined and viewed as Black. Today children of biracial or multiracial marriages try to build their own identities in a country that seems intent on placing them in some single, traditional category.

## Sociology and the Study of Race and Ethnicity

Before proceeding further with our study of racial and ethnic groups, let us consider several sociological perspectives that provide insight into dominant–subordinate relationships. **Sociology** is the systematic study of social behavior and human groups and therefore is aptly suited to enlarge our understanding of intergroup relations. There is a long, valuable history of the study of race relations in sociology. Admittedly, it has not always been progressive; indeed, at times it has reflected the prejudices of society. In some instances, scholars who are members of racial, ethnic, and religious minorities, as well as women, have not been permitted to make the kind of contributions they are capable of making to the field.

### Stratification by Class and Gender

All societies are characterized by members having unequal amounts of wealth, prestige, or power. Sociologists observe that entire groups may be assigned less or more of what a society values. The hierarchy that emerges is called stratification. **Stratification** is the structured ranking of entire groups of people that perpetuates unequal rewards and power in a society.

Much discussion of stratification identifies the **class**, or social ranking, of people who share similar wealth, according to sociologist Max Weber's classic definition. Mobility from one class to another is not easy. Movement into classes of greater wealth may be particularly difficult for subordinate-group members faced with lifelong prejudice and discrimination (Gerth and Mills 1958).

Recall that the first property of subordinate-group standing is unequal treatment by the dominant group in the form of prejudice, discrimination, and segregation. Stratification is intertwined with the subordination of racial, ethnic, religious, and gender groups. Race has implications for the way people are treated; so does class. One also has to add the effects of race and class together. For example, being poor and Black is not the same as being either one by itself. A wealthy Mexican American is not the same as an affluent Anglo or as Mexican Americans as a group.

Public discussion of issues such as housing or public assistance often is disguised as discussion of class issues, when in fact the issues are based primarily on race. Similarly, some topics such as the poorest of poor or the working poor are addressed in terms of race when the class component should be explicit. Nonetheless, the link between race and class in society is abundantly clear (Winant 1994).

Another stratification factor that we need to consider is gender. How different is the situation for women as contrasted with men? Returning again to the first property of minority groups—unequal treatment and less control—treatment of women is not equal to that received by men. Whether the issue is jobs or poverty, education or crime, the experience of women typically is more difficult. In addition, the situations faced by women in such areas as health care and welfare raises different concerns than it does for men. Just as we need to consider the role of social class to understand race and ethnicity better, we also need to consider the role of gender.

## Theoretical Perspectives

Sociologists view society in different ways. Some see the world basically as a stable and ongoing entity. They are impressed by the endurance of a Chinatown, the general sameness of male–female roles over time, and other aspects of intergroup relations. Some sociologists see society as composed of many groups in conflict, competing for scarce resources. Within this conflict, some people or even entire groups may be labeled or stigmatized in a way that blocks their access to what a society values. We will examine three theoretical perspectives that are widely used by sociologists today: the functionalist, conflict, and labeling perspectives.

**Functionalist Perspective**  In the view of a functionalist, a society is like a living organism in which each part contributes to the survival of the whole. The **functionalist perspective** emphasizes how the parts of society are structured to maintain its stability. According to this approach, if an aspect of social life does not contribute to a society's stability or survival, it will not be passed on from one generation to the next.

It seems reasonable to assume that bigotry between races offers no such positive function, and so we ask, why does it persist? Although agreeing that racial hostility is hardly to be admired, the functionalist would point out that it serves some positive functions from the perspective of the racists. We can identify five functions that racial beliefs have for the dominant group.

1. Racist ideologies provide a moral justification for maintaining a society that routinely deprives a group of its rights and privileges.
2. Racist beliefs discourage subordinate people from attempting to question their lowly status; to do so is to question the very foundations of the society.
3. Racial ideologies not only justify existing practices but also serve as a rallying point for social movements, as seen in the rise of the Nazi party.
4. Racist myths encourage support for the existing order. Some argue that if there were any major societal change, the subordinate group would suffer even greater poverty, and the dominant group would suffer lower living standards (Nash 1962).
5. Racist beliefs relieve the dominant group of the responsibility to address the economic and educational problems faced by subordinate groups.

As a result, racial ideology grows when a value system (e.g., that underlying a colonial empire or slavery) is being threatened.

There are also definite dysfunctions caused by prejudice and discrimination. **Dysfunctions** are elements of society that may disrupt a social system or decrease its stability. There are six ways in which racism is dysfunctional to a society, including to its dominant group.

1. A society that practices discrimination fails to use the resources of all individuals. Discrimination limits the search for talent and leadership to the dominant group.
2. Discrimination aggravates social problems such as poverty, delinquency, and crime and places the financial burden of alleviating these problems on the dominant group.
3. Society must invest a good deal of time and money to defend the barriers that prevent the full participation of all members.
4. Racial prejudice and discrimination undercut goodwill and friendly diplomatic relations between nations. They also negatively affect efforts to increase global trade.
5. Social change is inhibited because change may assist a subordinate group.
6. Discrimination promotes disrespect for law enforcement and for the peaceful settlement of disputes.

That racism has costs for the dominant group as well as for the subordinate group reminds us that intergroup conflict is exceedingly complex (Bowser and Hunt 1996; Feagin, Vera, and Batur 2000; Rose 1951).

**Conflict Perspective**   In contrast to the functionalists' emphasis on stability, conflict sociologists see the social world as being in continual struggle. The **conflict perspective** assumes that the social structure is best understood in terms of conflict or tension between competing groups. Specifically, society is a struggle between the privileged (the dominant group) and the exploited (the subordinate groups). Such conflicts need not be physically violent and may take the form of immigration restrictions, real estate practices, or disputes over cuts in the federal budget.

The conflict model often is selected today when one is examining race and ethnicity because it readily accounts for the presence of tension between competing groups. According to the conflict perspective, competition takes place between groups with unequal amounts of economic and political power. The minorities are exploited or, at best, ignored by the dominant group. The conflict perspective is viewed as more radical and activist than functionalism because conflict theorists emphasize social change and the redistribution of resources. Functionalists are not necessarily in favor of inequality; rather, their approach helps us to understand why such systems persist.

Those who follow the conflict approach to race and ethnicity have remarked repeatedly that the subordinate group is criticized for its low status. That the dominant group is responsible for subordination is often ignored. William Ryan (1976) calls this an instance of **blaming the victim**: portraying the problems of racial and ethnic minorities as their fault rather than recognizing society's responsibility.

The recognition that many in society fault the weak rather than embrace the need for restructuring society is not new. Gunnar Myrdal, a Swedish social economist of international reputation, headed a project that produced the classic 1944 work on Blacks in the United States, *The American Dilemma*. Myrdal concluded that the plight of the subordinate group is the responsibility of the dominant majority. It is not a Black problem but a White problem. Similarly, we can use the same approach and note that it is not a Hispanic problem or a Haitian refugee problem but a White problem. Myrdal and others since then have reminded the public and policymakers alike that the ultimate responsibility for society's problems must rest with those who possess the most authority and the most economic resources (Hochschild 1995; Southern 1987).

**Labeling Approach**   Related to the conflict perspective and its concern over blaming the victim is labeling theory. **Labeling theory**, a concept introduced by sociologist Howard Becker, is an attempt to explain why certain people are viewed as deviant and others engaging in the same behavior are not. Students of crime and deviance have relied heavily on labeling theory. According to labeling theory, a youth who misbehaves may be considered and treated as a delinquent if she or he comes from the "wrong kind of family." Another youth, from a middle-class family, who commits the same sort of misbehavior might be given another chance before being punished.

The labeling perspective directs our attention to the role negative stereotypes play in race and ethnicity. The image that prejudiced people maintain of a group toward which they hold ill feelings is called a stereotype. **Stereotypes** are unreliable generalizations about all members of a group that do not take individual differences into account. The warrior image of Native American (America Indian) people is perpetuated by the frequent use of tribal names or even terms such as "Indians" and "Redskins" as sports team mascots. In Chapter 2, we will review some of the research on the stereotyping of minorities. This labeling is not limited to racial and ethnic groups, however. For instance, age can be used to exclude a person from an activity in which he or she is qualified to engage. Groups are subjected to stereotypes and discrimination in such a way that their treatment resembles that of social minorities. Social prejudice exists toward ex-convicts, gamblers, alcoholics, lesbians, gays, prostitutes, people with AIDS, and people with disabilities, to name a few.

The labeling approach points out that stereotypes, when applied by people in power, can have very negative consequences for people or groups identified falsely. A crucial aspect of the relationship between dominant and subordinate groups is the prerogative of the dominant group to define society's values. U.S. sociologist William I. Thomas (1923), an early critic of racial and gender discrimination, saw that the "definition of the situation" could mold the personality of the individual. In other words, Thomas observed that people respond not only to the objective features of a situation (or person) but also to the meaning these features have for them. So, for example, a lone walker seeing a young Black man walking toward him may perceive the situation differently than if the oncoming person is an older woman. In this manner, we can create false images or stereotypes that become real in their social consequences.

In certain situations, we may respond to negative stereotypes and act on them, with the result that false definitions become accurate. This is known as a **self-fulfilling prophecy**. A person or group described as having particular characteristics begins to display the very traits attributed to him or her. Thus, a child who is praised for being a natural comic may focus on learning to become funny to gain approval and attention.

Self-fulfilling prophecies can be devastating for minority groups (Figure 1.3). Such groups often find that they are allowed to hold only low-paying jobs with

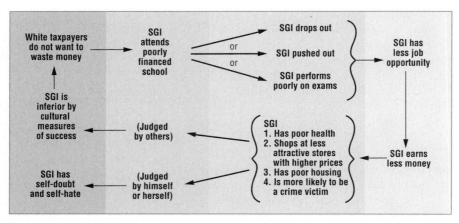

**Figure 1.3** Self-Fulfilling Prophecy
The self-validating effects of dominant-group definitions are shown in this figure. The subordinate-group individual (SGI) attends a poorly financed school and is left unequipped to perform
jobs that offer high status and pay. He or she then gets a low-paying job and must settle for a
standard of living far short of society's standards. Because the person shares these societal standards, he or she may begin to feel self-doubt and self-hatred.

little prestige or opportunity for advancement. The rationale of the dominant
society is that these minority people lack the ability to perform in more important and lucrative positions. Training to become scientists, executives, or physicians is denied to many subordinate-group individuals, who are then locked
into society's inferior jobs. As a result, the false definition becomes real. The
subordinate group has become inferior because it was defined at the start as inferior and was therefore prevented from achieving the levels attained by the
majority.

Because of this vicious circle, a talented subordinate-group person may
come to see the worlds of entertainment and professional sports as his or
her only hope for achieving wealth and fame. Thus, it is no accident that
successive waves of Irish, Jewish, Italian, African American, and Hispanic
performers and athletes have made their mark on culture in the United
States. Unfortunately, these very successes may convince the dominant
group that its original stereotypes were valid—that these are the only
areas of society in which subordinate-group members can excel. Furthermore, athletics and the arts are highly competitive areas. For every Michael
Jordan and Jennifer Lopez who makes it, many, many more will end up
disappointed.

# The Creation of Subordinate-Group Status

Three situations are likely to lead to the formation of a subordinate-group–dominant-group relationship. A subordinate group emerges through migration, annexation, and colonialism.

## Migration

People who emigrate to a new country often find themselves a minority in that new country. Cultural or physical traits or religious affiliation may set the immigrant apart from the dominant group. Immigration from Europe, Asia, and Latin America has been a powerful force in shaping the fabric of life in the United States. **Migration** is the general term used to describe any transfer of population. **Emigration** (by emigrants) describes leaving a country to settle in another; **immigration** (by immigrants) denotes coming into the new country. From Vietnam's perspective, the "boat people" were emigrants from Vietnam to the United States, but in the United States they were counted among this nation's immigrants.

Although people may migrate because they want to, leaving the home country is not always voluntary. Conflict or war has displaced people throughout human history. In the twentieth century, we saw huge population movements caused by two world wars; revolutions in Spain, Hungary, and Cuba; the partition of British India; conflicts in Southeast Asia, Korea, and Central America; and the confrontation between Arabs and Israelis.

In all types of movement, even the movement of a U.S. family from Ohio to Florida, two sets of forces operate: push factors and pull factors. Push factors discourage a person from remaining where he or she lives. Religious persecution and economic factors such as dissatisfaction with employment opportunities are possible push factors. Pull factors, such as a better standard of living, friends and relatives who have already emigrated, and a promised job, attract an immigrant to a particular country.

Although generally we think of migration as a voluntary process, much of the population transfer that has occurred in the world has been involuntary. The forced movement of people into another society guarantees a subordinate role. Involuntary migration is no longer common; although enslavement has a long history, all industrialized societies today prohibit such practices. Of course, many contemporary societies, including the United States, bear the legacy of slavery.

Migration has taken on new significance in the twenty-first century partly due to **globalization**. Globalization refers to the worldwide integration of government policies, cultures, social movements, and financial markets through trade and the exchange of ideas. The increased movement of people and money across borders has made the distinction between temporary and permanent migration less meaningful. Although migration has always been fluid, in today's global economy, people are connected across societies culturally and economically like they have never been before. Even after they have relocated, people maintain global linkages to their former country and with a global economy (Richmond 2002).

## Annexation

Nations, particularly during wars or as a result of war, incorporate or attach land. This new land is contiguous to the nation, as in the German annexation of Austria and Czechoslovakia in 1938 and 1939 and in the U.S. Louisiana Purchase of 1803. The Treaty of Guadalupe Hidalgo that ended the Mexican-American War in 1848 gave the United States California, Utah, Nevada, most of New Mexico, and parts of Arizona, Wyoming, and Colorado. The indigenous peoples in some of this huge territory were dominant in their society one day, only to become minority-group members the next.

When annexation occurs, the dominant power generally suppresses the language and culture of the minority. Such was the practice of Russia with the Ukrainians and Poles, and of Prussia with the Poles. Minorities try to maintain their cultural integrity despite annexation. Poles inhabited an area divided into territories ruled by three countries but maintained their own culture across political boundaries.

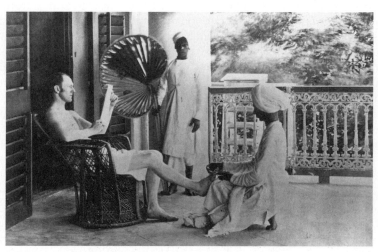

Colonialism in India and elsewhere established for generations a hierarchical relationship between Europeans and much of the rest of the world. Pictured here is a British officer being fanned and pampered by two Indian attendants.

## Colonialism

Colonialism has been the most common way for one group of people to dominate another. **Colonialism** is the maintenance of political, social, economic, and cultural dominance over people by a foreign power for an extended period (Bell 1991). Colonialism is rule by outsiders but, unlike annexation, does not involve actual incorporation into the dominant people's nation. The long control exercised by the British Empire over much of North America, parts of Africa, and India is an example of colonial domination.

Societies gain power over a foreign land through military strength, sophisticated political organization, and investment capital. The extent of power may also vary according to the dominant group's scope of settlement in the colonial land. Relations between the colonial nation and the colonized people are similar to those between a dominant group and exploited subordinate groups. The colonial subjects generally are limited to menial jobs and the wages from their labor. The natural resources of their land benefit the members of the ruling class.

By the 1980s, colonialism, in the sense of political rule, had become largely a phenomenon of the past, yet industrial countries of North America and Europe still dominated the world economically and politically. Drawing on the conflict perspective, sociologist Immanuel Wallerstein (1974) views the global economic system of today as much like the height of colonial days. Wallerstein has advanced the **world systems theory**, which views the global economic system as divided between nations that control wealth and those that provide natural resources and labor. Many of the ethnic, racial, and religious conflicts noted at the beginning of the chapter are exacerbated by the limited economic resources available in developing nations. In addition the presence of massive inequality between nations only serves to encourage immigration generally and more specifically the movement of many of the most skilled from developing nations to the industrial nations.

A significant exception to the end of foreign political rule is Puerto Rico, whose territorial or commonwealth status with the United States is basically that of a colony. The nearly 4 million people on the island are U.S. citizens but are unable to vote in presidential elections unless they migrate to the mainland. In 1998, 50 percent of Puerto Ricans on the island voted for options favoring continuation of commonwealth status, 47 percent favored statehood, and less than 3 percent voted for independence. Despite their poor showing, proindependence forces are very vocal and enjoy the sympathies of others concerned about the cultural and economic dominance of the U.S. mainland (Navarro 1998; Saad 1998).

Colonialism is domination by outsiders. Relations between the colonizer and the colony are similar to those between the dominant and subordinate peoples within the same country. This distinctive pattern of oppression is called **internal colonialism**. Among other cases, it has been applied to the plight of Blacks in the United States and Mexican Indians in Mexico, who are colonial peoples in their own country. Internal colonialism covers more than simple economic oppression. Nationalist movements in African colonies struggled to achieve political and economic independence from Europeans. Similarly, some African Americans also call themselves nationalists in trying to gain more autonomy over their lives (Blauner 1969, 1972).

## The Consequences of Subordinate-Group Status

There are several consequences for a group of subordinate status. These differ in their degree of harshness, ranging from physical annihilation to absorption into the dominant group. In this section, we will examine six consequences of subordinate-group status: extermination, expulsion, secession, segregation, fusion, and assimilation. Figure 1.4 illustrates how these consequences can be defined.

### Extermination

The most extreme way of dealing with a subordinate group is to eliminate it. Today the term **genocide** is used to describe the deliberate, systematic killing of an entire people or nation. This term is often used in reference to the Holocaust, Nazi Germany's extermination of 12 million European Jews and other ethnic minorities during World War II. The term **ethnic cleansing** was introduced into the world's vocabulary as ethnic Serbs instituted a policy intended to "cleanse"—eliminate—Muslims from parts of Bosnia. More recently, a genocidal war between the Hutu and Tutsi people in Rwanda left 300,000 school-age children orphaned (Chirot and Edwards 2003).

However, genocide also appropriately describes White policies toward Native Americans in the nineteenth century. In 1800, the American Indian population in the United States was about 600,000; by 1850 it had been reduced to

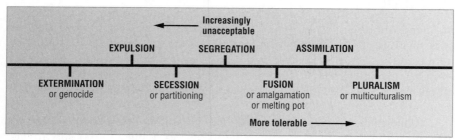

**Figure 1.4** Intergroup Relations Continuum
The social consequences of being in a subordinate group can be viewed along a continuum ranging from extermination to forms of mutual acceptance such as pluralism.

250,000 through warfare with the U.S. Army, disease, and forced relocation to inhospitable environments.

## Expulsion

Dominant groups may choose to force a specific subordinate group to leave certain areas or even vacate a country. Expulsion, therefore, is another extreme consequence of minority-group status. European colonial powers in North America and eventually the U.S. government itself drove almost all Native Americans out of their tribal lands into unfamiliar territory.

More recently, Vietnam in 1979 expelled nearly 1 million ethnic Chinese from the country, partly as a result of centuries of hostility between the two Asian neighbors. These "boat people" were abruptly eliminated as a minority within Vietnamese society. This expulsion meant that they were uprooted and became a new minority group in many nations, including Australia, France, the United States, and Canada. Thus, expulsion may remove a minority group from one society; however, the expelled people merely go to another nation, where they are again a minority group.

## Secession

A group ceases to be a subordinate group when it secedes to form a new nation or moves to an already established nation, where it becomes dominant. After Great Britain withdrew from Palestine, Jewish people achieved a dominant position in 1948, attracting Jews from throughout the world to the new state of Israel. In a similar fashion, Pakistan was created in 1947 when India was partitioned. The predominantly Muslim areas in the north became Pakistan, making India predominantly Hindu. Throughout this century, minorities have repudiated dominant customs. In this spirit, the Estonian, Latvian, Lithuanian, and Armenian peoples, not content to be merely tolerated by the majority, all seceded to form independent states after the demise of the Soviet Union in 1991. In 1999, ethnic Albanians fought bitterly for their cultural and political recognition in the Kosovo region of Yugoslavia.

Some African Americans have called for secession. Suggestions dating back to the early 1700s supported the return of Blacks to Africa as a solution to racial problems. The settlement target of the American Colonization Society was Liberia, but proposals were also advanced to establish settlements in other areas. Territorial separatism and the emigrationist ideology were recurrent and interrelated themes among African Americans from the late nineteenth century well into the 1980s. The Black Muslims, or Nation of Islam, once expressed the desire for complete separation in their own state or territory within the present borders of the United States. Although a secession of Blacks from the United States has not taken place, it has been proposed.

## Segregation

**Segregation** is the physical separation of two groups in residence, workplace, and social functions. Generally, the dominant group imposes segregation on a subordinate group. Segregation is rarely complete, however; intergroup contact inevitably occurs even in the most segregated societies.

Sociologists Douglas Massey and Nancy Denton (1993) wrote *American Apartheid,* which described segregation in U.S. cities based on 1990 data. The title of their book was meant to indicate that neighborhoods in the United States resembled the segregation of the rigid government-imposed racial segregation that prevailed for so long in the Republic of South Africa.

Analyzing the 2000 census results shows little change despite growing racial and ethnic diversity in the nation. Sociologists measure racial segregation using a segregation index or index of dissimilarity. The index ranges from 0 to 100, giving the percentage of a group that would have to move to achieve even residential patterns. For example, Atlanta has an index of 65.6 for Black–White segregation, which means that about 66 percent of either Blacks or Whites would have to move so that each small neighborhood (or census tract) would have the same racial balance as the metropolitan area as a whole. In Figure 1.5, we give the index values for the most and least segregated metropolitan areas among the 50 largest in the nation with respect to the Black–White racial divide.

Overall, the least segregated metropolitan areas tend to be those with smallest African American populations. For Latinos, the separation patterns are similar, with the highest patterns of isolation occurring in the cities with

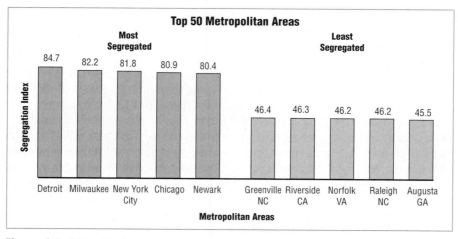

**Figure 1.5** White-Black Segregation, 2000
*Source*: From "Ethnic Diversity Grows, Neighborhood Integration Lags Behind." Reprinted by permission of John Logan, Brown University, *http://www.s4.brown.edu.*

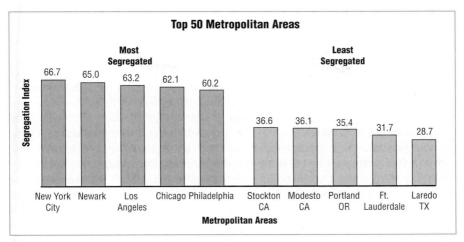

**Figure 1.6** White-Latino Segregation, 2000
*Source*: From "Ethnic Diversity Grows, Neighborhood Integration Lags Behind." Reprinted by permission of John Logan, Brown University *http://www.s4.brown.edu.*

the larger number of Hispanics (Figure 1.6). There has been little change in overall levels of racial and ethnic segregation from 1990 to 2000. Similarly, Asian–White segregation remains high and showed little change during the 1990s (Lewis Mumford Center 2001).

This focus on metropolitan areas should not cause us to ignore the continuing legally sanctioned segregation of Native Americans on reservations. Although the majority of our nation's first inhabitants live outside these tribal areas, the reservations play a prominent role in the identity of Native Americans. Although it is easier to maintain tribal identity on the reservation, economic and educational opportunities are more limited in these areas segregated from the rest of society.

The social consequences of residential segregation are significant. Given the elevated rates of poverty experienced by racial and ethnic minorities, their patterns of segregation mean that the consequences of poverty (dismal job opportunities, poor health care facilities, delinquency, and crime) are much more likely to be experienced by even the middle-class Blacks, Latinos, and tribal people than it is by middle-class Whites (Massey 2004).

Given segregation patterns, many Whites in the United States have limited contact with people of other racial and ethnic backgrounds. In one study of 100 affluent powerful White men looking at their experiences past and present, it was clear they had lived in a "white bubble"—neighborhoods, schools, elite colleges, and workplaces overwhelmingly White. The continuing pattern of segregation in the United States means our diverse population grows up in very different nations. (Feagin and O'Brien 2003).

## Fusion

**Fusion** occurs when a minority and a majority group combine to form a new group. This combining can be expressed as A + B + C → D where A, B, and C represent the groups present in a society, and D signifies the result, an ethno-cultural-racial group sharing some of the characteristics of each initial group. Mexican people are an example of fusion, originating as they do out of the mixing of the Spanish and indigenous Indian cultures. Theoretically, fusion does not entail intermarriage, but it is very similar to **amalgamation**, or the process by which a dominant group and a subordinate group combine through intermarriage into a new people. In everyday speech, the words fusion and amalgamation are rarely used, but the concept is expressed in the notion of a human **melting pot**, in which diverse racial or ethnic groups form a new creation, a new cultural entity (Newman 1973).

The analogy of the cauldron, the "melting pot," was first used to describe the United States by the French observer Crèvecoeur in 1782. The phrase dates back to the Middle Ages, when alchemists attempted to change less valuable metals into gold and silver. Similarly, the idea of the human melting pot implied that the new group would represent only the best qualities and attributes of the different cultures contributing to it. The belief in the United States as a melting pot became widespread in the early twentieth century. This belief suggested that the United States had an almost divine mission to destroy artificial divisions and create a single kind of human. However, the dominant group had indicated its unwillingness to welcome such groups as Native Americans, Blacks, Hispanics, Jews, Asians, and Irish Roman Catholics into the melting pot. It is a mistake to think of the United States as an ethnic mixing bowl. Although there are superficial signs of fusion, as in a cuisine that includes sauerkraut and spaghetti, most contributions of subordinate groups are ignored (Gleason 1980).

Marriage patterns indicate the resistance to fusion. People are unwilling, in varying degrees, to marry outside their own ethnic, religious, and racial groups. Surveys show that 20 to 50 percent of various White ethnic groups report single ancestry. When White ethnics do cross boundaries, they tend to marry within their religion and social class. For example, Italians are more likely to marry Irish, who are also Catholic, than they are to marry Protestant Swedes.

There is only modest evidence of a fusion of races in the United States. Racial intermarriage has been increasing, and the number of interracial couples immigrating to the United States has also grown. In 1980, there were 167,000 Black–White couples, but by 2004 there were 413,000. Among couples in which at least one member is Hispanic, marriages with a non-Hispanic partner account for 27 percent. Taken together interracial and Hispanic–non-Hispanic couples account for 7.2 percent of married couples today (Bureau of the Census 2005a, 51; Lee and Edmonston 2005).

Faced with new laws restricting rights of noncitizens, people representing countries from around the world participate in naturalization ceremonies in Seattle, Washington, on the Fourth of July, 1997.

## Assimilation

**Assimilation** is the process by which a subordinate individual or group takes on the characteristics of the dominant group and is eventually accepted as part of that group. Assimilation is a majority ideology in which A + B + C → A. The majority (A) dominates in such a way that the minorities (B and C) become indistinguishable from the dominant group. Assimilation dictates conformity to the dominant group, regardless of how many racial, ethnic, or religious groups are involved (Newman 1973, 53).

To be complete, assimilation must entail an active effort by the minority-group individual to shed all distinguishing actions and beliefs and the unqualified acceptance of that individual by the dominant society. In the United States, dominant White society encourages assimilation. The assimilation perspective tends to devalue alien culture and to treasure the dominant. For example, assimilation assumes that whatever is admirable among Blacks was adapted from Whites and that whatever is bad is inherently Black. The assimilation solution to Black–White conflict is the development of a consensus around White American values.

Assimilation is very difficult. The person must forsake his or her cultural tradition to become part of a different, often antagonistic culture. Members of the subordinate group who choose not to assimilate look on those who do as deserters.

Assimilation does not occur at the same pace for all groups or for all individuals in the same group. Assimilation tends to take longer under the following conditions:

- The differences between the minority and the majority are large.
- The majority is not receptive or the minority retains its own culture.
- The minority group arrives over a short period of time.
- The minority-group residents are concentrated rather than dispersed.
- The arrival is recent, and the homeland is accessible.

Assimilation is not a smooth process (Warner and Srole 1945).

Assimilation is viewed by many as unfair or even dictatorial. However, members of the dominant group see it as reasonable that people shed their distinctive cultural traditions. In public discussions today, assimilation is the ideology of the dominant group in forcing people how to act. Consequently, the social institutions in the United States, such as the educational system, economy, government, religion, and medicine, all push toward assimilation, with occasional references to the pluralist approach.

## The Pluralist Perspective

Thus far, we have concentrated on how subordinate groups cease to exist (removal) or take on the characteristics of the dominant group (assimilation). The alternative to these relationships between the majority and the minority is pluralism. **Pluralism** implies that various groups in a society have mutual respect for one another's culture, a respect that allows minorities to express their own culture without suffering prejudice or hostility. Whereas the assimilationist or integrationist seeks the elimination of ethnic boundaries, the pluralist believes in maintaining many of them.

There are limits to cultural freedom. A Romanian immigrant to the United States could not expect to avoid learning English and still move up the occupational ladder. To survive, a society must have a consensus among its members on basic ideals, values, and beliefs. Nevertheless, there is still plenty of room for variety. Earlier, fusion was described as $A + B + C \rightarrow D$ and assimilation as $A + B + C \rightarrow A$. Using this same scheme, we can think of pluralism as $A + B + C \rightarrow A + B + C$, where groups coexist in one society (Manning 1995; Newman 1973; Simpson 1995).

In the United States, cultural pluralism is more an ideal than a reality. Although there are vestiges of cultural pluralism—in the various ethnic neighborhoods in major cities, for instance—the rule has been for subordinate groups to assimilate. Yet as the minority becomes the numerical majority, the ability to live out one's identity becomes a bit easier. African Americans, Hispanics, and Asian Americans already outnumber Whites in 9 of the 10 largest cities (Figure 1.7). The trend is toward even greater diversity. Nonetheless, the cost of cultural integrity throughout the nation's history has been high. The various Native American tribes have succeeded to a large extent in maintaining their heritage, but the price has been bare subsistence on federal reservations.

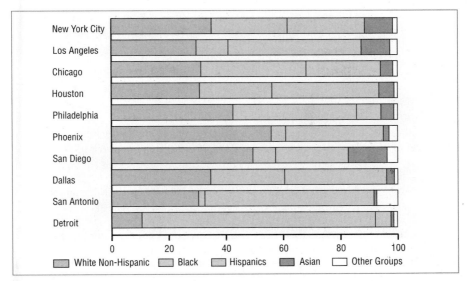

**Figure 1.7** Race and Ethnicity, 10 Largest Cities, 2000
*Source*: Bureau of the Census 2001c.

In the United States, there is a reemergence of ethnic identification by groups that had previously expressed little interest in their heritage. Groups that make up the dominant majority are also reasserting their ethnic heritages. Various nationality groups are rekindling interest in almost forgotten languages, customs, festivals, and traditions. In some instances, this expression of the past has taken the form of a protest against exclusion from the dominant society. For example, Chinese youths chastise their elders for forgetting the old ways and accepting White American influence and control.

The most visible controversy about pluralism is the debate surrounding bilingualism. **Bilingualism** is the use of two or more languages in places of work or education, with each language being treated as equally legitimate. As of 2000, about one of every six people (17 percent) speaks a native language other than English at home. Reflecting this diversity, the demand for interpreters is now unprecedented. One private company, NetworkOmni (2006), provides services to both government and private clients seeking translation services. To meet the need, the business offers interpreters to 911 services, hospitals, and private corporations in 150 languages and dialects ranging from widely spoken languages like Arabic, Spanish, Chinese, and Russian to dozens of lesser-known ones such as Akan, Oromo, and Telagu.

The passionate debate under way in the United States over bilingualism often acknowledges the large number of people who do not speak English at home. In education, bilingualism has seemed to be one way of helping

Diversity brings new challenges but also new opportunities. California-based Network Omni provides translation services in 150 languages to a variety of corporations and government agencies.

millions of people who want to learn English to function more efficiently within the United States.

Bilingualism for almost two decades has been a political issue. A proposed Constitutional amendment has been introduced that designates English as the "official language of the nation." A major force behind the proposed amendment and other efforts to restrict bilingualism is U.S. English, a nationwide organization that views the English language as the "social glue" that keeps the nation together. This organization supports assimilation. By contrast, Hispanic leaders see the U.S. English campaign as a veiled expression of racism.

The reality of learning English offers little reason for concern about language acquisition. Historically, English is the language of choice by the third generation. By 1970, over 90 percent of the grandchildren of immigrants from Germany, Italy, and Poland spoke only English. In 1990, the grandchildren of Asian immigrants were in the same situation. Today, most of the third generation (64 percent of Mexican and 78 percent of Cuban) spoke only English. Given the large Latino enclaves in cities like Miami and the back and forth movement along the Mexico–U.S. border, it is only surprising that English-only is so high today (Massey et al. 2002).

## Who Am I?

When Tiger Woods first appeared on *The Oprah Winfrey Show,* he was asked whether it bothered him, the only child of a Black American father and a Thai mother, to be called an African American. He replied, "It does. Growing up, I came up with this name: I'm a Cabalinasian" (White 1997, 34).

This is a self-crafted acronym to reflect that Tiger Woods is one-eighth Caucasian, one-fourth Black, one-eighth American Indian, one-fourth Thai, and one-fourth Chinese. Soon after he achieved professional stardom, another golfer was strongly criticized for making racist remarks based on seeing Woods only as African American. If Tiger Woods was not so famous, would most people, upon meeting him, see him as anything but an African American? Probably not. Tiger Wood's problem is really the challenge to a diverse society that continues to try to place people in a few socially constructed racial and ethnic boxes.

The diversity of the United States today has made it more difficult for many people to place themselves on the racial and ethnic landscape. It reminds us that racial formation continues to take place. Obviously, the racial and ethnic landscape, as we have seen, is constructed not naturally but socially and therefore is subject to change and different interpretations. Although our focus is on the United States, almost every nation faces the same problems.

The United States tracks people by race and ethnicity for myriad reasons, ranging from attempting to improve the status of oppressed groups to diversifying classrooms. But how can we measure the growing number of people whose ancestry is mixed by anyone's definition? In "Research Focus" we consider how this problem was resolved by the U. S. Census Bureau.

## RESEARCH FOCUS

## Measuring Multiculturalism

Approaching Census 2000, a movement was spawned by people who were frustrated by government questionnaires that forced them to indicate only one race. Take the case of Stacey Davis in New Orleans. The young woman's mother is Thai and her father is Creole, a blend of Black, French, and German. People seeing Stacey confuse her for a Latina, Filipina, or Hawaiian. Officially, she has been "White" all her life because she looked White. Congress was lobbied by groups such as Project RACE (Reclassify All Children Equally) for a category "biracial" or "multiracial" that one could select on census forms instead of a specific race. Race is only one of six questions asked of every person in the United States on census day every ten years. After various trial runs with different wordings on the race question, Census 2000 for the first time gave people the option to check off one or more racial groups. "Biracial" or "multiracial" was not an option because pretests showed very few people would use it. This meant that the government recognized in Census 2000 different social constructions of racial identity—that is, a person could be Asian American and White.

Most people did select one racial category in the Census 2000. Overall, about 7 million people, or 2.4 percent of the total population, selected two or more racial groups. This was a smaller proportion than many had anticipated.

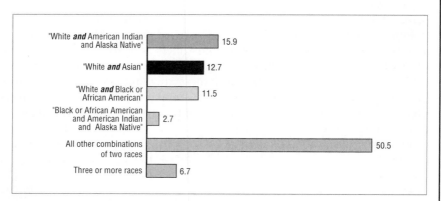

**Figure 1.8** Multiple Race Choices in Census 2000
This figure shows the percentage distribution of the 6.8 million people who chose two or more races out of 281.4 million total population.
*Source*: Grieco and Cassidy 2001.

In fact, not even the majority of mixed-race couples identified their children with more than one racial classification. As shown in Figure 1.8, White and American Indian was the most common multiple identity, with about a million people selecting that response. As a group, American Indians were most likely to select a second category and Whites least likely. Race is socially defined.

Complicating the situation is that people are asked separately whether they are Hispanic or non-Hispanic. So a Hispanic person can be any race. In the 2000 Census 94 percent indicated they were one race but 6 percent indicated two or more races; this proportion was three times higher than among non-Hispanics. Therefore, Latinos are more likely than non-Hispanics to indicate a multiracial ancestry.

The Census Bureau's decision does not necessarily resolve the frustration of hundreds of thousands of people such as Stacey Davis who face on a daily basis people trying to place them in some racial or ethnic category convenient for them. However, it does underscore the complexity of social construction and trying to apply arbitrary definitions to the diversity of the human population.

*Source*: El Nasser 1997; Grieco and Cassidy 2001; Jones and Smith 2001; Tafoya, Johnson, and Hill 2004.

Within little more than a generation, we have witnessed changes in labeling subordinate groups from Negroes to Blacks to African Americans, from American Indians to Native Americans or Native Peoples. However, more Native Americans prefer the use of their tribal name, such as Seminole, instead of a collective label. The old 1950s statistical term of "people with a Spanish surname" has long been discarded, yet there is disagreement over a new term: Latino or Hispanic. Like Native Americans, Hispanic Americans avoid such global terms and prefer their native names, such as Puerto Ricans or Cubans. People of Mexican ancestry indicate preferences for a variety of names, such as Mexican American, Chicano, or simply Mexican.

In the United States and other multiracial, multiethnic societies, panethnicity has emerged. **Panethnicity** is the development of solidarity between ethnic subgroups. The coalition of tribal groups as Native Americans or American Indians to confront outside forces, notably the federal government, is one example of panethnicity. Hispanics or Latinos and Asian Americans are other examples of panethnicity. Although it is rarely recognized by dominant society, the very term Black or African American represents the descendants of many different ethnic or tribal groups, such as Akamba, Fulani, Hausa, Malinke, and Yoruba (Lopez and Espiritu 1990).

Is panethnicity a convenient label for "outsiders" or a term that reflects a mutual identity? Certainly, many people outside the group are unable or unwilling to recognize ethnic differences and prefer umbrella terms such as Asian Americans. For some small groups, combining with others is emerging as a useful way to make themselves heard, but there is always a fear that their own distinctive culture will become submerged. Although many Hispanics share the Spanish language and many are united by Roman Catholicism, only one in four native-born people of Mexican, Puerto Rican, or Cuban descent prefers a panethnic label over nationality or ethnic identity. Yet the growth of a variety of panethnic associations among many groups, including Hispanics, continued through the 1990s (de la Garza et al. 1992; Espiritu 1992).

Add to this cultural mix the many peoples with clear social identities who are not yet generally recognized in the United States. Arabs are a rapidly growing segment whose identity is heavily subject to stereotypes or, at best, is still ambiguous. Haitians and Jamaicans affirm that they are Black but rarely accept the identity of African American. Brazilians, who speak Portuguese, often object to being called Hispanic because of that term's association with Spain. Similarly, there are White Hispanics and non-White Hispanics, some of the latter being Black and others Asian (Bennett 1993; Omi and Winant 1994, 162).

Another challenge to identity is **marginality**, the status of being between two cultures, as in the case of a person whose mother is a Jew and whose father is a Christian. Du Bois (1903) spoke eloquently of the "double consciousness" that Black Americans feel—caught between the conception of being a citizen of the United States but viewed as something quite apart from the dominant social forces of society. Incomplete assimilation by immigrants also results in marginality. Although a Filipino woman migrating to the United States may take on the characteristics of her new host society, she may not be fully accepted and may therefore feel neither Filipino nor American. The marginal person finds himself or herself being perceived differently in different environments, with varying expectations (Billson 1988; Park 1928; Stonequist 1937).

Celebrities such as Mariah Carey are unable to protect their privacy. Much has been made about her racial and ethnic identity. She told *Ebony* magazine that she is very aware of her African American heritage, "and I think sometimes it bothers people that I don't say, 'I'm black' and that's it . . . So when people ask, I say I'm, black, Venezuelan, and Irish, because that's who I am" (Carberry 2005, 5).

As we seek to understand diversity in the United States, we must be mindful that ethnic and racial labels are just that: labels that have been socially constructed. Yet these social constructs can have a powerful impact, whether self-applied or applied by others.

## Resistance and Change

By virtue of wielding power and influence, the dominant group may define the terms by which all members of society operate. This is particularly evident in a slave society, but even in contemporary industrialized nations, the dominant group has a disproportionate role in shaping immigration policy, the curriculum of the schools, and the content of the media.

Subordinate groups do not merely accept the definitions and ideology proposed by the dominant group. A continuing theme in dominant–subordinate relations is the minority group's challenge to its subordination. We will see throughout this book the resistance of subordinate groups as they seek to promote change that will bring them more rights and privileges, if not true equality (Moulder 1996).

Resistance can be seen in efforts by racial and ethnic groups to maintain their identity through newspapers, organizations, and in today's technological age, cable television stations and Internet sites. Resistance manifests itself in social movements such as the civil rights movement, the feminist movement, and gay rights efforts. The passage of such legislation as the Age Discrimination Act or the Americans with Disabilities Act marks the success of oppressed groups in lobbying on their own behalf.

Resistance efforts may begin through small actions. For example, residents of a reservation question a second toxic waste dump being located on their land. Although it may bring in money, they question the wisdom of such a move. Their concerns lead to further investigations of the extent to which American Indian lands are used disproportionately to house dangerous materials. This action in turn leads to a broader investigation of the way in which minority-group people often find themselves "hosting" dumps and incinerators. As we will discuss later, these local efforts eventually led the Environmental Protection Agency to monitor the disproportionate placement of toxic facilities in or near racial and ethnic minority communities. There is little reason to expect that such reforms would have occurred if we had relied on traditional decision-making processes alone.

Change has occurred. At the beginning of the twentieth century lynching was practiced in many parts of the country. At the beginning of the twenty-first century, laws punishing hate crimes were increasingly common and embracing a variety of stigmatized groups. This social progress should not be ignored, but it does allow the nation to focus concern about remaining, significant social inequalities (Best 2001).

An even more basic form of resistance is to question societal values. In this book, we avoid using the term American to describe people of the United States because geographically Brazilians, Canadians, and El Salvadorans are Americans as well. It is very easy to overlook how our understanding of today has been shaped by the way institutions and even the very telling of history have been presented by members of the dominant group. African American studies scholar Molefi Kete Asante (2000) has called for an **Afrocentric perspective** that emphasizes the customs of African cultures and how they have pervaded the history, culture, and behavior of Blacks in the United States and around the world. Afrocentrism counters Eurocentrism and works toward a multiculturalist or pluralist orientation in which no viewpoint is suppressed. The Afrocentric approach could become part of our school curriculum, which has not adequately acknowledged the importance of this heritage.

The Afrocentric perspective has attracted much attention in colleges. Opponents view it as a separatist view of history and culture that distorts both past and present. Its supporters counter that African peoples everywhere can come to full self-determination only when they are able to overthrow White or Eurocentric intellectual interpretations (Early 1994).

In considering the inequalities present today, as we will in the chapters that follow, it is easy to forget how much change has taken place. Much of the resistance to prejudice and discrimination in the past, whether to slavery or to women's prohibition from voting, took the active support of members of the dominant group. The indignities still experienced by subordinate groups continue to be resisted as subordinate groups and their allies among the dominant group seek further change.

## Conclusion

One hundred years ago, sociologist and activist W. E. B. Du Bois took another famed Black activist, Booker T. Washington, to task for saying that the races could best work together apart, like fingers on a hand. Du Bois felt that Black people had to be a part of all social institutions and not create their own. Today among African Americans, Whites, and other groups, the debate persists as to what form society should take. Should we seek to bring everyone together into an integrated whole? Or do we strive to maintain as much of our group identities as possible while working cooperatively as necessary?

In this first chapter, we have attempted to organize our approach to subordinate–dominant relations in the United States. We observed that subordinate groups do not necessarily contain fewer members than the dominant group. Subordinate groups are classified into racial, ethnic, religious, and gender groups. Racial classification has been of interest, but scientific findings do not explain contemporary race relations. Biological differences of race are not supported by scientific data. Yet as the continuing debate over standardized tests demonstrates, attempts to establish a biological meaning of race have not been swept entirely into the dustbin of history. However, the social meaning given to physical differences is very significant. People have defined racial differences in such a way as to encourage or discourage the progress of certain groups.

The oppression of selected racial and ethnic groups may serve some people's vested interests. However, denying opportunities or privileges to an entire group only leads to conflict between dominant and subordinate groups. Societies such as the United States develop ideologies to justify privileges given to some and opportunities denied to others. These ideologies may be subtle, such as assimilation (i.e., "You should be like us"), or overt, such as racist thought and behavior.

Subordinate groups generally emerge in one of three ways: migration, annexation, or colonialism. Once a group is given subordinate status, it does not necessarily keep it indefinitely. Extermination, expulsion, secession, segregation, fusion, and assimilation remove the status of subordination, although inequality still persists.

Subordinate-group members' reactions include the seeking of an alternative avenue to acceptance and success: "Why should we forsake what we are to be accepted by them?" In response to this question, there has been a resurgence of ethnic identification. Pluralism describes a society in which several different groups coexist, with no dominant or subordinate groups. The hope for such a society remains unfulfilled, except perhaps for isolated exceptions.

Subordinate groups have not and do not always accept their second-class status passively. They may protest, organize, revolt, and resist society as defined by the dominant group. Patterns of race and ethnic relations are changing, not stagnant. Furthermore, in many nations, including the United States, the nature of race and ethnicity changes through migration. Indicative of the changing landscape, biracial and multiracial children present us with new definitions of identity emerging through a process of racial formation, reminding us that race is socially constructed.

The two significant forces that are absent in a truly pluralistic society are prejudice and discrimination. In an assimilation society, prejudice disparages out-group differences, and discrimination financially rewards those who shed their past. In the next two chapters, we will explore the nature of prejudice and discrimination in the United States.

# Key Terms

| | | |
|---|---|---|
| Afrocentric perspective   39 | functionalist perspective   18 | minority group   6 |
| amalgamation   30 | fusion   30 | panethnicity   37 |
| assimilation   31 | genocide   26 | pluralism   32 |
| bilingualism   33 | globalization   23 | racial formation   17 |
| biological race   13 | immigration   23 | racial group   8 |
| blaming the victim   20 | intelligence quotient (IQ)   13 | racism   16 |
| class   18 | internal colonialism   25 | segregation   28 |
| colonialism   25 | labeling theory   20 | self-fulfilling prophecy   21 |
| conflict perspective   20 | marginality   37 | sociology   17 |
| dysfunction   19 | melting pot   30 | stereotypes   21 |
| emigration   23 | migration   23 | stratification   17 |
| ethnic cleansing   26 | | world systems theory   25 |
| ethnic group   9 | | |

# Review Questions

1. In what ways have you seen issues of race and ethnicity emerge? Identify groups that have been subordinated for reasons other than race, ethnicity, or gender.
2. How can a significant political or social issue (such as bilingual education) be viewed in assimilationist and pluralistic terms?
3. How does the concept of "double consciousness" popularized by W. E. B. Du Bois relate to the question "Who am I?"

# Critical Thinking

1. How diverse is your city? Can you see evidence that some group is being subordinated? What social construction of categories do you see that may be different in your community as compared to elsewhere?

2. In 1996 Denny Mendéz was crowned Miss Italy, but many people protested her selection because they said she did not reflect the appropriate physical image of the Italian people. Mendéz had moved to Italy from the Dominican Republic when her mother married an Italian and has since become a citizen. What does this controversy around a beauty pageant tell us about the social construction of race? What similar situations have you witnessed in which race and ethnicity can be seen in their social context?

3. Identify some protest and resistance efforts by subordinated groups in your area. Have they been successful? Why are some people who say they favor equality uncomfortable with such efforts? How can people unconnected with such efforts either help or hinder such protests?

# Internet Connections—Research Navigator™

1. To access the full resources of Research Navigator™, please find the access code printed on the inside cover of *OneSearch with Research Navigator™: Sociology*. You may have received this booklet if your instructor recommended this guide be packaged with new textbooks. (If your book did not come with this printed guide, you can purchase one through your college bookstore.) Visit our Research Navigator™ site at *www.ResearchNavigator.com*. Once at this site, click on REGISTER under New Users and enter your access code to create a personal Login Name and Password. (When revisiting the site, use the same Login Name and Password.) Browse the features of the Research Navigator™ Website and search the databases of academic journals, newspapers, magazines, and Web links.

2. For further information relevant to Chapter 1, you may wish to use such keywords as "ethnicity," "IQ," and "biracial," and the search engine will supply relevant and recent scholarly and popular press publications. Use the New York Times Search-by-Subject Archive to find recent news articles related to sociology and the Link Library feature to locate relevant Web links organized by the key terms associated with this chapter.

# 2 Prejudice

## CHAPTER OUTLINE

Reducing Prejudice
■RESEARCH FOCUS
*What's In a Name?*
Ways to Fight Hate
Conclusion
Key Terms/Review Questions/Critical Thinking/
Internet Connections—Research Navigator™

----------------{ H I G H L I G H T S }----------------

P rejudice is a negative attitude that rejects an entire group; discrimination is behavior that deprives a group of certain rights or
opportunities. Prejudice does not necessarily coincide with discrimination, as is made apparent by a typology developed by sociologist
Robert Merton. Several theories have been advanced to explain prejudice: scapegoating, authoritarian personality, exploitation, and normative. These explanations examine prejudice in terms of content
(negative stereotypes) and extent. Prejudice is not limited to the
dominant group; subordinate groups often dislike one another. The
mass media seem to be of limited value in reducing prejudice and may
even intensify ill feeling. Equal-status contact and the shared-coping
approach may reduce hostility between groups. In response to increasing diversity in the workplace, corporations and organizations have
mounted diversity-training programs to increase organizational effectiveness and combat prejudice. There are also ten identifiable steps
that we as individuals can take to stop prejudice and hatred.

On a website available since 1995 to anyone with Internet access, one can find
the latest reports of Black on White crimes and why "Western civilization" won
as well as tips on self-defense. In San Antonio, Texas, a man is sentenced to
prison in 2005 for setting arson fires at three convenience stores run by Muslims.

In the same year, a 13-year-old Pennsylvania boy spray-painted slurs on an Asian American homeowner's fence. So is it a fringe element that engages in negative views of people based only on their racial, ethnic, or religious affiliation?

In a social science laboratory at the University of Colorado, Boulder, subjects in an experiment played video games as researchers recorded their moves. Presented with a rapid-fire series of pictures showing Black and White men holding various objects—cell phones, cameras, wallets, guns—subjects pressed one button if they considered a character harmless and another button to "shoot" characters they believed to be armed. Researchers were studying people's split-second reactions to tests of decision making involving race and the potential for violence. When they analyzed the results, they found that the subjects, most of whom were White, had reacted more quickly to pictures of Black men with guns than to pictures of White men with guns. Subjects were also more likely to mistakenly shoot an unarmed Black character than an unarmed White character. The results were the same for Black subjects as for White subjects.

These results were not unusual. In a similar study at the University of Washington, psychologists asked college students to distinguish virtual citizens and police officers from armed criminals. They found that subjects were more likely to misperceive and shoot images of Black men than of White men in the video game they created. For the last three decades, in fact, research has suggested that people in the United States are more likely to see Black men as being violent than White men, which translated in this study for the Black men to be more likely to be "shot" at.

Are there limits for this hostility? Apparently not. In the commercially successful "Grand Theft Auto: Vice City" video game, players are encouraged to take very violent actions against a variety of images. At one point players are informed that they have come across a "Stinking nest of Haitians. We gonna kill them all. Kill all the Haitians." Why? "Kill all the Haitians, they are all drug dealers." This game, released by Rockstar Video in 2003, bore a parental code declaring that use was inappropriate for children under 17, but aside from the fact that so many youth access such games, we might be left to ponder why such a "game" with this dialogue would be marketed even to young adults (CBS New York 2003; Correll et al. 2002; Greenwald, Oakes, and Hoffman 2003; Kim 2005; Southern Poverty Law Center 2006).

Prejudice is so prevalent that it is tempting to consider it inevitable or, even more broadly, just part of human nature. Such a view ignores its variability from individual to individual and from society to society. People must learn prejudice as children before they exhibit it as adults. Therefore, prejudice is a social phenomenon, an acquired characteristic. A truly pluralistic society would lack unfavorable distinctions made through prejudicial attitudes among racial and ethnic groups.

Ill feeling between groups may result from ethnocentrism. Ethnocentrism is the tendency to assume that one's culture and way of life are superior to all others. The **ethnocentric** person judges other groups and other cultures by the standards of his or her own group. This attitude leads people quite easily

African American artist Jacob Lawrence portrays the separate facilities typical of the treatment received by Blacks in the first half of the twentieth century.

to view other cultures as inferior. We see a woman with a veil and may regard it as strange and backward, yet find it baffling when other societies see U.S. women in short skirts and view the dress as inappropriate. Ethnocentrism and other expressions of prejudice are voiced very often, but unfortunately they also become the motivation for criminal acts.

## Hate Crimes

Although prejudice certainly is not new in the United States, it is receiving increased attention as it manifests itself in neighborhoods, at meetings, and on college campuses. The Hate Crime Statistics Act, which became law in 1990, directs the Department of Justice to gather data on hate or bias crimes. The government defines a

> *An ordinary crime as* **a hate crime** *when offenders choose a victim because of some characteristic—for example, race, ethnicity, or religion—and provide evidence that hatred prompted them to commit the crime." Hate or bias crimes which is another name can also be based on hatred because of national origin or sexual orientation (Harlow 2005:1).*

This law created a national mandate to identify such crimes, whereas previously only twelve states had monitored hate crimes. In 1994, the act was amended to include disabilities, both physical and mental, as factors that could be considered a basis for hate crimes.

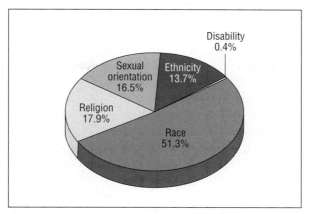

**Figure 2.1** Distribution of Reported Hate Crimes in 2004
*Source:* Department of Justice 2005.

In 2005 law enforcement agencies released hate crime data submitted by police agencies covering 86 percent of the United States. Even though many, many hate crimes are not reported, a staggering number of offenses that come to law agencies' attention were motivated by hate. There were official reports of more than 8,800 hate crimes and bias-motivated incidents. As indicated in Figure 2.1, race was the apparent motivation for the bias in about 51 percent of the reports, and religion, sexual orientation, and ethnicity accounted for 13 to 18 percent each. Vandalism and intimidation were the most common, but 43 percent of the incidents against people involved assault, rape, or murder.

National legislation and publicity have made hate crime a meaningful term, and we are beginning to recognize the victimization associated with such incidents. A current proposal would make a violent crime into a federal crime if it were motivated by racial or religious bias. Although passage is uncertain, the serious consideration of the proposal indicates a willingness to consider a major expansion of federal jurisdiction. Currently, federal law prohibits crimes motivated by race, color, religion, or national origin only if they involve violation of a federally guaranteed right, such as voting.

Most hate crimes are the result of people acting alone or with a few others, but there is a troubling pattern of organized hate groups that dates back more than 130 years in the United States to the founding of the Ku Klux Klan. As shown in Figure 2.2, some people organize into groups with the express purpose of showing their hatred toward other groups of people. Law enforcement agencies attempt to monitor such groups but are limited in their actions by constitutional freedoms of speech and assembly.

Victimized groups are not merely observing these events. Watchdog organizations play an important role in documenting bias-motivated violence; among such groups are the Anti-Defamation League (ADL), the National

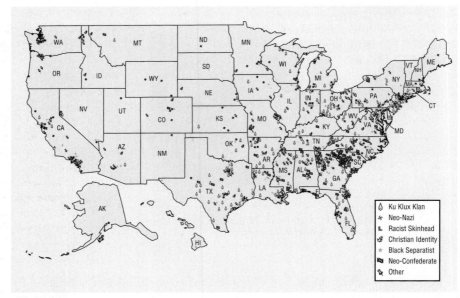

**Figure 2.2** Active Hate Groups
*Source:* Map, "Active Hate Groups in the U.S. in the Year 2004," The Intelligence Project of the Southern Poverty Law Center (2005). Reprinted by permission of Southern Poverty Law Center, Montgomery, AL.

Institute Against Prejudice and Violence, the Southern Poverty Law Center, and the National Gay and Lesbian Task Force.

Established hate groups have even set up propaganda sites on the World Wide Web. This also creates opportunities for previously unknown haters and hate groups to promote themselves. However, hate crime legislation does not affect such outlets because of legal questions involving freedom of speech. An even more recent technique has been to use instant messaging software, which enables Internet users to create a private chat room with another individual. Enterprising bigots use directories to target their attacks through instant messaging, much as harassing telephone calls were placed in the past (Gerstenfeld and Grant 2003; Rivlin 2005).

What causes people to dislike entire groups of other people? Is it possible to change attitudes? This chapter tries to answer these questions about prejudice. Chapter 3 focuses on discrimination.

## Prejudice and Discrimination

Prejudice and discrimination are related concepts but are not the same. **Prejudice** is a negative attitude toward an entire category of people. The two important components in this definition are attitude and entire category.

Prejudice involves attitudes, thoughts, and beliefs, not actions. Prejudice often is expressed through the use of **ethnophaulisms**, or ethnic slurs, which include derisive nicknames such as honky, gook, or wetback. Ethnophaulisms also include speaking about or to members of a particular group in a condescending way ("José does well in school for a Mexican American") or referring to a middle-aged woman as "one of the girls."

A prejudiced belief leads to categorical rejection. Prejudice is not disliking someone you meet because you find his or her behavior objectionable. It is disliking an entire racial or ethnic group, even if you have had little or no contact with that group. A college student who requests a room change after three weeks of enduring his roommate's sleeping all day, playing loud music all night, and piling garbage on his desk is not prejudiced. However, he is displaying prejudice if he requests a change on arriving at school and learning that his new roommate is of a different nationality.

Prejudice is a belief or attitude; discrimination is action. **Discrimination** involves behavior that excludes all members of a group from certain rights, opportunities, or privileges. Like prejudice, it must be categorical. If an employer refuses to hire as a typist an Italian American who is illiterate, it is not discrimination. If she refuses to hire any Italian Americans because she thinks they are incompetent and does not make the effort to see whether an applicant is qualified, it is discrimination.

## Merton's Typology

Prejudice does not necessarily coincide with discriminatory behavior. In exploring the relationship between negative attitudes and negative behavior, sociologist Robert Merton (1949, 1976) identified four major categories (Figure 2.3). The label added to each of Merton's categories may more readily identify the type of person being described. These are

1. The unprejudiced nondiscriminator: all-weather liberal
2. The unprejudiced discriminator: reluctant liberal
3. The prejudiced nondiscriminator: timid bigot
4. The prejudiced discriminator: all-weather bigot

As the term is used in types 1 and 2, liberals are committed to equality among people. The all-weather liberal believes in equality and practices it. Merton was quick to observe that all-weather liberals may be far removed from any real competition with subordinate groups such as African Americans or women. Furthermore, such people may be content with their own behavior and may do little to change themselves. The reluctant liberal is not this committed to equality between groups. Social pressure may cause such a person to discriminate. Fear of losing employees may lead a manager to avoid promoting women to supervisory capacities. Equal-opportunity legislation may be the best way to influence the reluctant liberals.

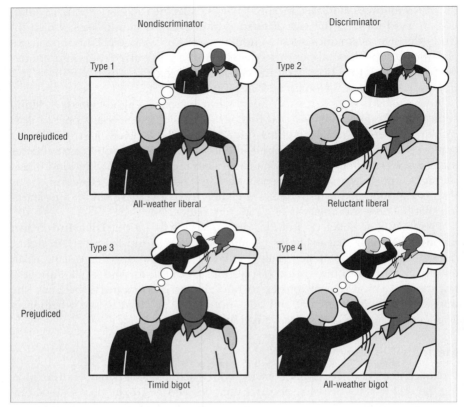

**Figure 2.3** Prejudice and Discrimination
As sociologist Robert Merton's formulation shows, prejudice and discrimination are related to each other but are not the same.

Types 3 and 4 do not believe in equal treatment for racial and ethnic groups, but they vary in their willingness to act. The timid bigot, type 3, will not discriminate if discrimination costs money or reduces profits or if he or she is pressured not to by peers or the government. The all-weather bigot unhesitatingly acts on the prejudiced beliefs he or she holds.

## LaPiere's Study

Merton's typology points out that attitudes should not be confused with behavior. People do not always act as they believe. More than a half century ago, Richard LaPiere (1934, 1969) exposed the relationship between racial attitudes and social conduct. From 1930 to 1932 LaPiere traveled throughout the United States with a Chinese couple. Despite an alleged climate of intolerance of Asians, LaPiere observed that the couple were treated courteously at hotels, motels, and restaurants. He was puzzled by the good reception they received; all the conventional attitude surveys showed extreme prejudice by Whites toward the Chinese.

Was it possible that LaPiere had been fortunate during his travels and consistently stopped at places operated by the tolerant members of the dominant group? To test this possibility, he sent questionnaires asking the very establishments at which they had been served whether the owner would "accept members of the Chinese race as guests in your establishment." More than 90 percent responded no, even though LaPiere's Chinese couple had been treated politely at all the establishments. How can this inconsistency be explained? People who returned questionnaires reflecting prejudice were unwilling to act based on those asserted beliefs; they were timid bigots.

The LaPiere study is not without flaws. First, he had no way of knowing whether the respondent to the questionnaire was the same person who had served him and the Chinese couple. Second, he accompanied the couple, but the questionnaire suggested that the arrival would be unescorted (and, in the minds of some, uncontrolled) and perhaps would consist of many Chinese people. Third, personnel may have changed between the time of the visit and the mailing of the questionnaire (Deutscher, Restello and Restello 1993).

The LaPiere technique has been replicated with similar results. This technique raises the question of whether attitudes are important if they are not completely reflected in behavior. But if attitudes are not important in small matters, they are important in other ways: Lawmakers legislate and courts may reach decisions based on what the public thinks.

This is not just a hypothetical possibility. Legislators in the United States often are persuaded to vote in a certain way by what they perceive as changed attitudes toward immigration, affirmative action, and prayer in public schools. Sociologists have enumerated some of prejudice's functions. For the majority group, it serves to maintain privileged occupations and more power for its members.

The following sections examine the theories of why prejudice exists and discuss the content and extent of prejudice today.

# Theories of Prejudice

Prejudice is learned. Friends, relatives, newspapers, books, movies, television, and the Internet all teach it. Awareness begins at an early age that there are differences between people that society judges to be important. Several theories have been advanced to explain the rejection of certain groups in a society. We will examine four theoretical explanations. The first two (scapegoating and authoritarian personality) tend to be psychological, emphasizing why a particular person harbors ill feelings. The second two are more sociological (exploitation and normative), viewing prejudice in the context of our interaction in a larger society.

Many would regard this statue of colonialist Hannah Dus-
ton in Massachusetts as perpetuating stereotypes about
American Indians. She is honored for killing and scalping
ten Abeenaki Indians in 1697 while defending her family.
Believed to be the first woman ever honored in the United
States with a monument, it portrays her holding a hatchet
in her right hand.

## Scapegoating Theory

**Scapegoating theory** says that prejudiced people believe they are society's
victims. The term scapegoat comes from a biblical injunction telling the
Hebrews to send a goat into the wilderness to symbolically carry away the
people's sins. Similarly, the theory of scapegoating suggests that, rather than
accepting guilt for some failure, a person transfers the responsibility for failure
to some vulnerable group. In the major tragic twentieth-century example, Adolf
Hitler used the Jews as the scapegoat for all German social and economic ills
in the 1930s. This premise led to the passage of laws restricting Jewish life in
pre–World War II Germany and eventually escalated into the mass extermination of Europe's Jews.

Today in the United States, immigrants, whether legal or illegal, often are blamed by "real Americans" for their failure to get jobs or secure desirable housing. The immigrant becomes the scapegoat for one's own lack of skills, planning, or motivation. It is so much easier to blame someone else.

Like exploitation theory, scapegoating theory adds to our understanding of why prejudice exists but does not explain all its facets. For example, scapegoating theory offers little explanation of why a specific group is selected or why frustration is not taken out on the real culprit when possible. Also, both the exploitation and the scapegoating theories suggest that every person sharing the same general experiences in society would be equally prejudiced, but that is not the case. Prejudice varies between individuals who seem to benefit equally from the exploitation of a subordinate group or who have experienced equal frustration. In an effort to explain these personality differences, social scientists developed the concept of the authoritarian personality.

## Authoritarian Personality Theory

A number of social scientists do not see prejudice as an isolated trait that anyone can have. Several efforts have been made to detail the prejudiced personality, but the most comprehensive effort culminated in a volume titled *The Authoritarian Personality* (Adorno et al. 1950). Using a variety of tests and relying on more than 2,000 respondents, ranging from middle-class Whites to inmates of San Quentin (California) State Prison, the authors claimed they had isolated the characteristics of the authoritarian personality.

In these authors' view, the basic characteristics of the **authoritarian personality** are adherence to conventional values, uncritical acceptance of authority, and concern with power and toughness. With obvious relevance to the development of intolerance, the authoritarian personality was also characterized by aggressiveness toward people who did not conform to conventional norms or obey authority. According to the researchers, this personality type developed from an early childhood of harsh discipline. A child with an authoritarian upbringing obeyed and then later treated others as he or she had been raised.

This study has been widely criticized, but the very existence of such wide criticism indicates the influence of the study. Critics have attacked the study's equation of authoritarianism with right-wing politics (although liberals can also be rigid); its failure to see that prejudice is more closely related to other individual traits, such as social class, than to authoritarianism as it was defined; and the research methods used. Graham Kinloch (1974), discussing personality research, added a fourth criticism: The authors concentrated on factors behind extreme racial prejudice rather than on more common expressions of hostility.

## Exploitation Theory

Racial prejudice often is used to justify keeping a group in a subordinate position, such as a lower social class. Conflict theorists, in particular, stress the role of racial and ethnic hostility as a way for the dominant group to keep its position of status and power intact. Indeed, this approach maintains that even the less affluent White working class uses prejudice to minimize competition from upwardly mobile minorities.

This exploitation theory is clearly part of the Marxist tradition in sociological thought. Karl Marx emphasized exploitation of the lower class as an integral part of capitalism. Similarly, the exploitation or conflict approach explains how racism can stigmatize a group as inferior so that the exploitation of that group can be justified. As developed by Oliver Cox (1942), exploitation theory saw prejudice against Blacks as an extension of the inequality faced by the entire lower class.

The **exploitation theory** of prejudice is persuasive. Japanese Americans were the object of little prejudice until they began to enter occupations that brought them into competition with Whites. The movement to keep Chinese out of the country became strongest during the late nineteenth century, when Chinese immigrants and Whites fought over dwindling numbers of jobs. Both the enslavement of African Americans and the removal westward of Native Americans were to a significant degree economically motivated.

Although many cases support the exploitation theory, it is too limited to explain prejudice in all its forms. First, not all minority groups are exploited economically to the same extent. Second, many groups that have been the victims of prejudice have not been persecuted for economic reasons, such as the Quakers or gays and lesbians. Nevertheless, as Gordon Allport (1979)

Preserving culture or expressing pride can sometimes cross the line and intimidate others. In Laurens, South Carolina, one can find the "World's Famous Redneck Shop and Klan Museum" where one can pick up souvenirs that often carry symbolism that is regarded racist by many.

concludes, the exploitation theory correctly points a finger at one of the factors in prejudice, that is, the rationalized self-interest of the privileged.

## Normative Approach

Although personality factors are important contributors to prejudice, normative or situational factors must also be given serious consideration. The **normative approach** takes the view that prejudice is influenced by societal norms and situations that encourage or discourage the tolerance of minorities.

Analysis reveals how societal influences shape a climate for tolerance or intolerance. Societies develop social norms that dictate not only what foods are desirable (or forbidden) but also what racial and ethnic groups are to be favored (or despised). Social forces operate in a society to encourage or discourage tolerance. The force may be widespread, such as the pressure on White Southerners to oppose racial equality while there was slavery or segregation. The influence of social norms may be limited, as when one man finds himself becoming more sexist as he competes with three women for a position in a prestigious law firm.

We should not view the four approaches to prejudice summarized in Table 2.1 as mutually exclusive. Social circumstances provide cues for a person's attitudes; personality determines the extent to which people follow social cues and the likelihood that they will encourage others to do the same. Societal norms may promote or deter tolerance; personality traits suggest the

## Table 2.1 Theories of Prejudice

There is no one explanation of why prejudice exists, but several approaches taken together offer insight.

| Theory | Proponent | Explanation | Example |
| --- | --- | --- | --- |
| Scapegoating | Bruno Bettelheim Morris Janowitz | People blame others for their own failures. | An unsuccessful applicant assumes that a minority member or a woman got "his" job. |
| Authoritarian personality | Adorno and associates | Child rearing leads one to develop intolerance as an adult. | The rigid personality type dislikes people who are different. |
| Exploitation | Oliver C. Cox Marxist theory | People use others unfairly for economic advantage. | A minority member is hired at a lower wage level. |
| Normative | Thomas Pettigrew | Peer and social influences encourage tolerance or intolerance. | A person from an intolerant household is more likely to be openly prejudiced. |

degree to which a person will conform to norms of intolerance. To understand prejudice, we need to use all four approaches together.

## The Content of Prejudice: Stereotypes

On Christmas Day 2001, Arab American Walied Shater boarded an American Airlines flight from Baltimore to Dallas carrying a gun. Immediately, the cockpit crew refused to let him fly, fearing that Shater would take over the plane and use it as a weapon of mass destruction. Yet Walied Shater carried documentation that he was a Secret Service agent, and calls to Washington, DC, confirmed that he was flying to join a presidential protection force at President George W. Bush's ranch in Texas. Nevertheless, the crew could not get past the stereotype of Arab American men posing a lethal threat (Leavitt 2002).

### What Are Stereotypes?

In Chapter 1, we saw that stereotypes play a powerful role in how people come to view dominant and subordinate groups. **Stereotypes** are unreliable generalizations about all members of a group that do not take individual differences into account. Numerous scientific studies have been made of these exaggerated images. This research has shown the willingness of people to assign positive and negative traits to entire groups of people, which are then applied to particular individuals. Stereotyping causes people to view Blacks

as superstitious, Whites as uncaring, and Jews as shrewd. Over the last seventy years of such research, social scientists have found that people have become less willing to express such views openly, but as we will see later, prejudice persists (MacRae, Stangor, and Hewstore 1996).

If stereotypes are exaggerated generalizations, why are they so widely held, and why are some traits more often assigned than others? Evidence for traits may arise out of real conditions. For example, more Puerto Ricans live in poverty than Whites, and so the prejudiced mind associates Puerto Ricans with laziness. According to the New Testament, some Jews were responsible for the crucifixion of Jesus, and so, to the prejudiced mind, all Jews are Christ killers. Some activists in the women's movement are lesbians, and so all feminists are seen as lesbians. From a kernel of fact, faulty generalization creates a stereotype.

Labels take on such strong significance that people often ignore facts that contradict their previously held beliefs. People who believe many Italian Americans to be members of the Mafia disregard law-abiding Italian Americans. Muslims are regularly portrayed in a violent, offensive manner that contributes to their being misunderstood and distrusted. We will consider later in the chapter how this stereotype about Muslims has become widespread since the mid-1970s but intensified after the attack on the World Trade Center on September 11, 2001.

In "Listen to Our Voices," opinion pollster and founder of the Arab American Institute, James Zogby, raised his concerns about how government actives have encouraged the stigmatization of "being Arab" in the United States. He remains optimistic that these policies will change.

## LISTEN TO OUR VOICES

### Pendulum Swings on Civil Rights

*James Zogby*

There is growing concern that the Department of Justice (DOJ) has overreached in the post 9/11 period, implementing several programs that have caused harm to Arab and Muslim immigrants and visitors to the United States.

Of particular concern have been: the large number of detentions and deportations that took place right after the 2001 terrorist attacks; the so-called "voluntary call-in" of 8,000 young Arab and Muslim immigrants; and the special registration program that has targeted visitors from twenty-five Arab and Muslim countries. . . .

These programs created suspicion as well. Some Americans came to feel that if the DOJ was targeting tens of thousands of Arabs and Muslims, based on their religion and ethnicity, then maybe there was reason to suspect these individuals. So even while President Bush was urging Americans not to discriminate against Arabs and Muslims, a different message was being sent by those DOJ initiatives. . . .

As a frequent traveler to the Arab world, I am aware of yet another negative impact of these DOJ initiatives. They have damaged the U.S. image and harmed our credibility and our relationship with the people of the region.

Because the effect of these DOJ programs have been well publicized in the Arab world there is a growing perception that Arab immigrants and visitors are not welcome in the United States. As a result many fewer Arabs are coming to the United States for medical treatment, tourism, study or business.

The good news is that there is a growing political coalition committed to challenging these practices, and they are having an impact. Broad coalitions of immigrant rights advocates have formed to demand an end to profiling, the registration program, and other violations of civil liberties. Similarly, affected institutions like universities, hospitals and major businesses have mobilized to pressure for changes in the restrictive visa procedures that have made the United States appear to be less open to visitors and immigrants. And major studies have been done both by reputable independent institutions and official government oversight bodies that have called into question the legality of some of these practices and their effectiveness.

Last year, for example, the Justice Department's own Inspector General issued a report that vindicated our concerns. The IG found that the Justice Department classified 762 of the detainees as "September 11 detainees." The IG concluded that none of these detainees were charged with terrorist-related offenses, and that the decision to detain them was "extremely attenuated" from the 9/11 investigation. The IG concluded that the Justice Department's designation of detainees of interest to the 9/11 investigation was "indiscriminate and haphazard" and did not adequately distinguish between terrorism suspects and other immigration detainees. . . .

Last week I testified before a Senate Judiciary Committee hearing on "America after 9/11: Freedom Preserved or Freedom Lost?"

There was strong support for change. Many Senators expressed their concern with the behavior of the DOJ and there are now a number of bills in the House and Senate that seek to correct the post 9/11 abuses. In fact, the American public wants civil liberties to be protected, wants the United States to remain open and welcoming to Arab visitors, students, and immigrants. . . .

Two years after the United States was traumatized by terror, the pendulum now appears to be swinging back.

*Source:* "Pendulum Swings on Civil Rights" by James Zogby as posted on www.aaiusa. org/wwatch/112303.htm (November 23, 2003).

## Trends in Stereotypes

In the last thirty years, we have become more and more aware of the power of the mass media to introduce stereotypes into everyday life. Television is a prime example. Almost all television roles showing leadership feature Whites. Even urban-based programs such as *Seinfeld* and *Friends* prospered without any major Black, Hispanic, or Asian American characters. A 1998 national survey of boys and girls aged 10 to 17 asked a very simple question and came up with some disturbing findings. The children were asked, "How often do you see your race on television?" The results showed that 71 percent of White children said "very often," compared with only 42 percent of African Americans, 22 percent of Latinos, and 16 percent of Asian Americans. Even more troubling is that generally the children view the White characters as affluent and well educated, whereas they see the minority characters as "breaking the law or rules," "being lazy," and "acting goofy." Later in this chapter we will consider the degree to which the media have changed in presenting stereotyped images (Children Now 1998).

The labeling of individuals has strong implications for the self-fulfilling prophecy. Studies show that people are all too aware of the negative images other people have of them. When asked to estimate the prevalence of hard-core racism among Whites, one in four Blacks agrees that more than half "personally share the attitudes of groups like the Ku Klux Klan toward Blacks"; only one Black in ten says "only a few" share such views. Stereotypes not only influence how people feel about themselves but, perhaps equally important, also affect how people interact with others. If people feel that others hold incorrect, disparaging attitudes toward them, it undoubtedly will make it difficult to have harmonious relations (Sigelman and Tuch 1997).

Are stereotypes held only by dominant groups about subordinate groups? The answer is clearly no. White Americans even believe generalizations about themselves, although admittedly these are usually positive. Subordinate groups also hold exaggerated images of themselves. Studies before World War II showed a tendency for Blacks to assign to themselves many of the same negative traits assigned by Whites. Today, stereotypes of themselves are largely rejected by African Americans, Jews, Asians, and other minority groups.

## Stereotyping in Action: Racial Profiling

A Black dentist, Elmo Randolph, testified before a state commission that he was stopped dozens of times in the 1980s and 1990s while traveling the New Jersey Turnpike to work. Invariably state troopers asked, "Do you have guns or drugs?" "My parents always told me, be careful when you're driving on the turnpike" said Dr. Randolph, 44. "White people don't have that conversation" (Purdy 2001:37).

Little wonder that Dr. Randolph was pulled over. African Americans accounted for 17 percent of the motorists on that turnpike but 80 percent of the motorists pulled over. Such occurrences gave rise to the charge that we had added a new traffic offense to the books: DWB, or Driving While Black (Bowles 2000).

Actor Danny Glover, with his daughter, holds a press briefing after filing a discrimination complaint with a New York taxi company in 1999. A driver refused to let him sit in the front of the car while his daughter and a friend sat in the back.

In recent years government attention has been given to a social phenomenon with a long history: racial profiling. According to the Department of Justice, **racial profiling** is any police-initiated action based on race, ethnicity, or national origin rather than the person's behavior. Generally, profiling occurs when law enforcement officers, including customs officials, airport security, and police, assume that people fitting certain descriptions are likely to be engaged in something illegal. Beginning in the 1980s with the emergence of the crack cocaine market, skin color became a key characteristic. This profiling can be a very explicit use of stereotypes. For example, the federal antidrug initiative, Operation Pipeline, specifically encouraged officers to look for people with dreadlocks or for Latino men traveling together.

The reliance on racial profiling persists despite overwhelming evidence that it is misleading. Whites are more likely to be found with drugs in the areas in which minority group members are disproportionately targeted. A federal study made public in 2005 found little difference nationwide in the likelihood of being stopped by officers, but African Americans were twice as likely to have their vehicles searched and Latinos were five time more likely. A similar pattern emerged in the likelihood of force being used against drivers with it three times more likely among Latinos and Blacks than White drivers (Lichtblau 2005).

In the 1990s increased attention to racial profiling led not only to special reports and commissions but also to talk of legislating against it. This proved difficult. The U.S. Supreme Court in *Whren v. United States* (1996) upheld the constitutionality of using a minor traffic infraction as an excuse to stop and search a vehicle and its passengers. Nonetheless, states and other government units are discussing policies and training that would discourage racial profiling. At the same time, most law enforcement agencies reject the idea of compiling racial data on traffic stops, arguing that it would be a waste of money and staff time.

The effort to stop racial profiling came to an abrupt end after the September 11, 2001, terrorist attacks on the United States. Suspicions about Muslims and Arabs in the United States became widespread. Foreign students from Arab countries were summoned for special questioning. Legal immigrants identified as Arab or Muslim were scrutinized for any illegal activity and were prosecuted for routine immigration violations that were ignored for people of other ethnic backgrounds and religious faiths. In 2003, President George W. Bush issued guidelines that barred federal agents from using race and ethnicity in investigations but specifically exempted cases involving terrorism and national security matters (Withrow 2006).

National surveys showed that those groups most likely to be stigmatized were not as supportive of using profiling. In a national 2004 survey, people were asked if racial profiling was ever justified when passengers are stopped at airport security checkpoints. Less than a third of all African Americans and 40 percent of Latinos supported such profiling compared to 46 percent of non-Hispanic Whites. Nonetheless, racial profiling moved from a questionable local police action to a reaffirmed matter of national policy (Carlson 2004; Coates 2004; Lichtblau 2003).

## The Extent of Prejudice

Interest in developing theories of prejudice or studying the concept has been exceeded only by interest in measuring it. From the outset, efforts to measure prejudice have suffered from disagreement over exactly what constitutes intolerance and whether there is such a phenomenon as no prejudice at all. Add to these uncertainties the methodological problems of attitude measurement, and the empirical study of prejudice becomes fraught with difficulty.

The extent of prejudice can be measured only in relative differences. For example, we cannot accurately say that prejudice toward Puerto Ricans is four times greater than that toward Portuguese Americans. We can conclude that prejudice is greater toward one group than toward the other; we just cannot quantify how much greater. The social distance scale is especially appropriate to assess differences in prejudice.

## The Social Distance Scale

Robert Park and Ernest Burgess first defined **social distance** as the tendency to approach or withdraw from a racial group (1921, 440). Emory Bogardus (1968) conceptualized a scale that could measure social distance empirically. His social distance scale is so widely used that it is often called the **Bogardus scale**.

The scale asks people how willing they would be to interact with various racial and ethnic groups in specified social situations. The situations describe different degrees of social contact or social distance. The items used, with their corresponding distance scores, follow. People are asked whether they would be willing to work alongside, be a neighbor, and, showing the least amount of social distance, be related through marriage. Over the seventy-year period the tests were administered, certain patterns emerge. In the top third of the hierarchy are White Americans and northern Europeans. Held at greater social distance are eastern and southern Europeans, and generally near the bottom are racial minorities (Bogardus 1968; Song 1991).

More recently the concept of social distance has been applied to how people actually function—who do they hang out with, for example. Sociologists Grace Kao and Kara Joyner released a study in 2004 that considered the responses of more then 90,000 adolescents nationwide in an in-school survey. Among many questions they were asked to identify their best friends and later to identify that person's race and ethnicity. As we can see in Figure 2.4, most people as their primary friendships someone of the same race or ethnicity. While Whites are the numerical majority nationwide, we can see that over 81 percent of White youths had as their best friend someone who was also White. Other racial and ethnic groups are more likely to venture outside their group's boundaries.

Generally, the researchers also found that among the respondents who had friends of different racial and ethnic origin, they were more likely to show greater social distance—that is, they were less likely to have been in each other's homes, share in fewer activities, and were less likely to talk about their problems with each other.

## Trends in Prejudice

We hold certain images or stereotypes of each other, and we also may be more prejudiced toward some groups of people than others. However, is prejudice less than it used to be? The evidence we will see is mixed, with some indications of willingness to give up some old prejudices while new negative attitudes emerge.

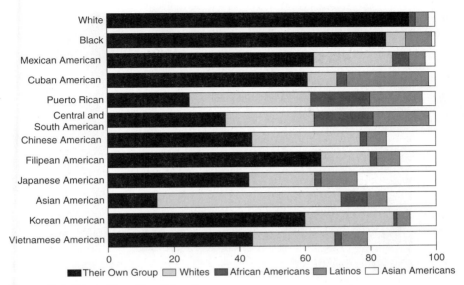

**Figure 2.4** Who's Your Best Friend?
*Source:* Permission adapted from Table I in Grace Kao and Kara Joyner "Do Race and Ethnicity Matter Among Friends?" p. 564 in *The Sociological Quarterly* Vol. 45 Issue 3.

Over the years, nationwide surveys have consistently shown growing support by Whites for integration, even during the Southern resistance and Northern turmoil of the 1960s. National opinion surveys conducted from the 1950s through the 1990s, with few exceptions, show an increase in the number of Whites responding positively to hypothetical situations of increased contact with African Americans. For example, 30 percent of the Whites sampled in 1942 felt that Blacks should not attend separate schools, but by 1970, 74 percent supported integrated schools, and fully 93 percent responded in that manner in 1991 (Davis and Smith 2001).

Attitudes are still important, however. A change of attitude may create a context in which legislative or behavioral change can occur. Such attitude changes leading to behavior changes did occur in some areas in the 1960s. Changes in intergroup behavior mandated by law in housing, schools, public places of accommodation, and the workplace appear to be responsible for making some new kinds of interracial contact a social reality. Attitudes translate into votes, peer pressure, and political clout, each of which can facilitate efforts to undo racial inequality. However, attitudes can work in the opposite direction. In the mid-1990s, surveys showed resistance to affirmative action and immigration. Policymakers quickly developed new measures to respond to these concerns, voiced largely by Whites.

When we survey White attitudes toward African Americans, two conclusions are inescapable. First, attitudes are subject to change, and in periods of

This anti-Semitic graffiti was painted on the outside walls of Pacaducah, Kentucky's Temple Israel in 2004.

dramatic social upheaval, dramatic shifts can occur within one generation. Second, less progress was made in the late twentieth century than was made in the 1950s and 1960s. Researchers have variously called these subtle forms of prejudice symbolic racism, modern racism, or laissez-faire racism. People today may not be as openly racist or prejudiced as in the past in expressing the notion that they are inherently superior to others. Yet much of the opposition to policies related to eradicating poverty or immigration is a smokescreen for those who dislike entire groups of racial and ethnic minorities (Bobo, Kluegel, and Smith 1997; Sniderman and Carmines 1997).

In the 1990s, White attitudes hardened still further as issues such as affirmative action, immigration, and crime provoked strong emotions among members of this dominant group as well as members of subordinate groups. Economically less-successful groups such as African Americans and Latinos have been associated with negative traits to the point where issues such as welfare and crime are now viewed as race issues. Besides making the resolution of very difficult social issues even harder, this is another instance of blaming the victim. These perceptions come at a time when the willingness of government to address domestic ills is limited by increasing opposition to new taxes. Although there is some evidence that fewer Whites are consistently prejudiced on all issues from interracial marriage to school integration, it is also apparent that many Whites continue to endorse some anti-Black statements and that negative

How do children come to develop an image from themselves? Toys and playthings play an important role, and for many children it is unusual to find a toy that looks like themselves. In 2005, a new doll was released called Fulla—an Arab girl who reflects modesty, piety, and respect, yet underneath she wears more chic clothes as might be typically worn by Muslim women in private.

images are widespread as they relate to the major domestic issues of the twenty-first century (Gilens 1996; Hughes 1998; Schaefer 1996).

## The Mood of the Oppressed

Sociologist W. E. B. DuBois relates an experience from his youth in a largely White community in Massachusetts. He tells how, on one occasion, the boys and girls were exchanging cards, and everyone was having a lot of fun. One girl, a newcomer, refused his card as soon as she saw that DuBois was Black. He wrote,

> *Then it dawned upon me with a certain suddenness that I was different from others . . . shut out from their world by a vast veil. I had therefore no desire to tear down that veil, to creep through; I held all beyond it in common contempt and lived above it in a region of blue sky and great wandering shadows. (DuBois 1903:2)*

In using the image of a veil, DuBois describes how members of subordinate groups learn that they are being treated differently. In his case and that of many others, this leads to feelings of contempt toward all Whites that continue for a lifetime.

Opinion pollsters have been interested in White attitudes on racial issues longer than they have measured the views of subordinate groups. This neglect of minority attitudes reflects, in part, the bias of the White researchers. It also stems from the contention that the dominant group is more important to study because it is in a better position to act on its beliefs. The results of nationwide surveys conducted in the United States in 2003 offer insight into sharply different views on the state of race relations today (Figure 2.5). African Americans are much less satisfied with the current situation than are White Americans and Hispanics.

We have focused so far on what usually comes to mind when we think about prejudice: one group hating another group. But there is another form of prejudice: A group may come to hate itself. Members of groups held in low esteem by society may, as a result, have low self-esteem themselves. Many social scientists once believed that members of subordinate groups hated themselves or at least had low self-esteem. Similarly, they argued that Whites had high self-esteem. High self-esteem means that an individual has fundamental respect for himself or herself, appreciates his or her own merits, and is aware of personal faults and will strive to overcome them.

The research literature of the 1940s through the 1960s emphasized the low self-esteem of minorities. Usually, the subject was African Americans, but the argument has also been generalized to include any subordinate racial, ethnic, or nationality group. This view is no longer accepted. We should not assume that minority status influences personality traits in either a good or a bad way. First, such assumptions may create a stereotype. We cannot describe a Black personality any more accurately than we can a White personality. Second, characteristics of minority-group members are not entirely the result of subordinate racial status; they are also influenced by low incomes, poor neighborhoods, and so forth. Third, many studies of personality imply that certain values are normal or preferable, but the values chosen are those of dominant groups.

If assessments of a subordinate group's personality are so prone to misjudgments, why has the belief in low self-esteem been so widely held? Much of the research rests on studies with preschool-age Black children asked to express preferences among dolls with different facial colors. Indeed, one such study, by psychologists Kenneth and Mamie Clark (1947), was cited in the arguments before the U.S. Supreme Court in the landmark 1954 case *Brown v. Board of Education*. The Clarks' study showed that Black children preferred White dolls, a finding suggesting that the children had developed a negative self-image. Although subsequent doll studies have sometimes shown Black children's preference for white-faced dolls, other social scientists contend that this shows a realization of what most commercially sold dolls look

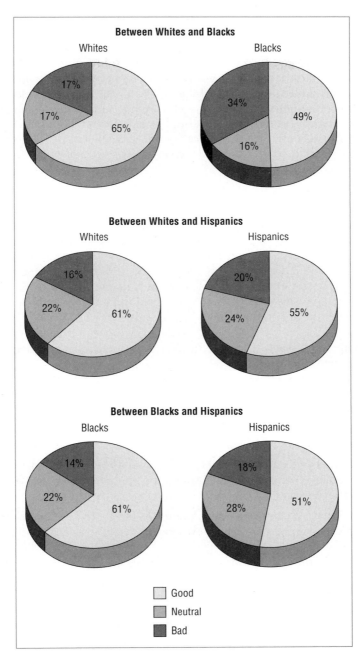

**Figure 2.5** What Is the State of Race Relations?
*Source:* AARP 2004, 36, 41, 44.

like rather than documenting low self-esteem (Bloom 1971; Powell-Hopson and Hopson 1988).

Because African American children, as well as other subordinate groups' children, can realistically see that Whites have more power and resources and therefore rate them higher does not mean that they personally feel inferior. Indeed, studies, even with children, show that when the self-images of middle-class or affluent African Americans are measured, their feelings of self-esteem are more positive than those of comparable Whites (Gray-Little and Hafdahl 2000).

## Intergroup Hostility

Prejudice is as diverse as the nation's population. It exists not only between dominant and subordinate peoples but also between specific subordinate groups. Unfortunately, until recently little research existed on this subject except for a few social distance scales administered to racial and ethnic minorities.

A national survey revealed that, like Whites, many African Americans, Hispanic Americans, and Asian Americans held prejudiced and stereotypical views of other racial and ethnic minority groups:

- Majorities of Black, Hispanic, and Asian American respondents agreed that Whites are "bigoted, bossy, and unwilling to share power." Majorities of these non-White groups also believed that they had less opportunity than Whites to obtain a good education, a skilled job, or decent housing.
- Forty-six percent of Hispanic Americans and 42 percent of African Americans agreed that Asian Americans are "unscrupulous, crafty, and devious in business."
- Sixty-eight percent of Asian Americans and 49 percent of African Americans believed that Hispanic Americans "tend to have bigger families than they are able to support."
- Thirty-one percent of Asian Americans and 26 percent of Hispanic Americans agreed that African Americans "want to live on welfare."

Members of oppressed groups obviously have adopted the widely held beliefs of the dominant culture concerning oppressed groups. At the same time, the survey also revealed positive views of major racial and ethnic minorities:

- More than 80 percent of respondents admired Asian Americans for "placing a high value on intellectual and professional achievement" and "having strong family ties."
- A majority of all groups surveyed agreed that Hispanic Americans "take deep pride in their culture and work hard to achieve a better life."

- Large majorities from all groups stated that African Americans "have made a valuable contribution to American society and will work hard when given a chance." (National Conference of Christians and Jews 1994)

Do we get along? Although this question often is framed in terms of the relationships between White Americans and other racial and ethnic groups, we should recognize the prejudice between groups. In a national survey conducted in 2000, people were asked whether they felt they could generally get along with members of other groups. In Figure 2.6, we can see that Whites felt they had the most difficulty getting along with Blacks. We also see the different views that Blacks, Latinos, Asian Americans, and American Indians hold toward other groups.

Curiously, we find that some groups feel they get along better with Whites than with other minority groups. Why would that be? Often, low-income people are competing on a daily basis with other low-income people and do not readily see the larger societal forces that contribute to their low status. As we can see from the survey results, many Hispanics are more likely to see Asian Americans as getting in their way than the White Americans who are actually the real decision makers in their community.

# Reducing Prejudice

Focusing on how to eliminate prejudice involves an explicit value judgment: Prejudice is wrong and causes problems for those who are prejudiced and for their victims. The obvious way to eliminate prejudice is to eliminate its causes: the desire to exploit, the fear of being threatened, and the need to blame others for one's own failure. These might be eliminated by personal therapy, but therapy, even if it works for every individual, is no solution for an entire society in which prejudice is a part of everyday life.

The answer appears to rest with programs directed at society as a whole. Prejudice is attacked indirectly when discrimination is attacked. Despite prevailing beliefs to the contrary, we can legislate against prejudice: Statutes and decisions do affect attitudes. In the past, people firmly believed that laws could not overcome norms, especially racist ones. Recent history, especially after the civil rights movement began in 1954, has challenged that common wisdom. Laws and court rulings that have equalized the treatment of Blacks and Whites have led people to reevaluate their beliefs about what is right and wrong. The increasing tolerance by Whites during the civil rights era, from 1954 to 1965, seems to support this conclusion.

Much research has been done to determine how to change negative attitudes toward groups of people. The most encouraging findings point to education, mass media, intergroup contact, and workplace training programs.

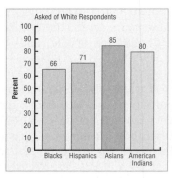

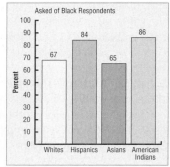

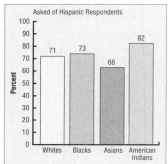

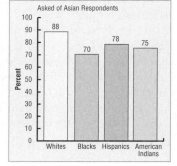

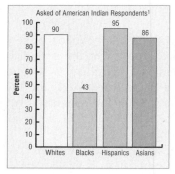

**Figure 2.6** Do We Get Along?

Percentage saying groups get along with each other (Don't Knows excluded).
[1]Sample size for American Indians is very small and subject to large sample variance.
Note: The wording of the question was: "We hear a lot these days about how
various groups in society get along with each other. I'm going to mention several
groups and ask whether you think they generally get along with each other or
generally do not get along with each other." So, in the Asked of White Respondents
graph, Whites are asked how Whites get along with each ethnic group; in the
Asked of Black Respondents graph, Blacks are asked how Blacks get along with
each ethnic group etc.

(*Source:* From Taking America's Pulse II: NCCJ's 2000 Survey of Intergroup
Relations in the United States, by T. Smith 2000:54) National Conference for
Community Justice.

WHATEVER HAPPENED TO THE DAYS OF BLACK & WHITE TV?

IT'S ONLY WHITE TV THESE DAYS!

STAHLER 1999

JEFF STAHLER reprinted by permission of Newspaper Enterprise Association, Inc.

## Education and Mass Media

Research on the mass media and education consists of two types: research performed in artificially (experimentally) created situations and studies examining the influence on attitudes of motion pictures, television, and advertisements.

Leaflets, radio commercials, comic books, billboards, Web pages, and classroom posters bombard people with the message of racial harmony. Television audiences watch a public service message that for 30 seconds shows smiling White and African American infants reaching out toward each other. Law enforcement and military personnel attend in-service training sessions that preach the value of a pluralistic society. Does this publicity do any good? Do these programs make any difference?

Most research studies show that well-constructed programs do have some positive effect in reducing prejudice, at least temporarily. The reduction is rarely as much as one might wish, however. The difficulty is that a single program is insufficient to change lifelong habits, especially if little is done to reinforce the program's message once it ends. Persuasion to respect other groups does not operate in a clear field because, in their ordinary environments, people are still subjected to situations that promote prejudicial feelings. Children and adults are encouraged to laugh at Polish jokes and cheer for a team named "Redskins." Black adolescents may be discouraged by peers from befriending a White youth. All this undermines the effectiveness of prejudice reduction programs (Allport 1979).

Studies consistently document that increased formal education, regardless of content, is associated with racial tolerance. Research data show that more highly educated people are more likely to indicate respect and liking for groups different from themselves. Why should more years of schooling have this effect? It could be that more education gives a broader outlook and makes a person less likely to endorse myths that sustain racial prejudice. Formal education teaches the importance of qualifying statements and the need to question rigid categorizations, if not reject them altogether. Colleges are increasingly including as a graduation requirement a course that explores diversity or multiculturalism. Another explanation is that education does not actually reduce intolerance but simply makes people more careful about revealing it. Formal education may simply instruct people in the appropriate responses, which in some settings could even be prejudiced views. Despite the lack of a clear-cut explanation, either theory suggests that the continued trend toward a better-educated population will contribute to a reduction in overt prejudice.

However, college education may not reduce prejudice uniformly. For example, some White students will come to believe that minority students did not earn their admission into college. Students may feel threatened to see large groups of people of different racial and cultural backgrounds congregating together and forming their own groups. Racist confrontations do occur outside the classroom and, even if they do involve only a few, the events themselves will be followed by hundreds. Therefore, some aspects of the college experience may only foster "we" and "they" attitudes (Schaefer 1986, 1996).

The mass media, like schools, may reduce prejudice without the need for specially designed programs. Television, radio, motion pictures, newspapers, magazines, and the Internet present only a portion of real life, but what effect do they have on prejudice if the content is racist or antiracist, sexist or antisexist? As with measuring the influence of programs designed to reduce prejudice, coming to strong conclusions on the mass media's effect is hazardous, but the evidence points to a measurable effect.

In late spring 1999, as the television networks prepared their schedules for the 1999–2000 season, an article in the *Los Angeles Times* hit the broadcasting industry like a bombshell. In every new prime time series—26 of them—set to debut in the coming season, the *Times* reported, all the leading characters and most of the supporting casts would be White. The public response was immediate. The NAACP, alarmed by the "virtual whitewash in programming," threatened a lawsuit, and a national coalition of Latino groups urged viewers to boycott network TV.

By 2004, reports showed improvement in the representation on Blacks on television but little improvement in Hispanic representation (especially if the *George Lopez Show* is excluded). Asian Americans, Arab Americans, and Native Americans continue to be virtually nonexistent. *West Wing* was praised in 2006 when it depicted a Latino, played by Puerto Rican American Jimmy Smits, elected President. Ironically, the long-running show's President Jed Bartlett is played by Martin Sheen. Yet Sheen was born Ramon Estevez and rarely makes mention of his Hispanic roots.

Why the underrepresentation? Incredibly, network executives seemed surprised by the research demonstrating an all-White season. Producers, writers, executives, and advertisers blamed each other for the alleged oversight. In recent years, the rise of both cable TV and the Internet has fragmented the broadcast entertainment market, siphoning viewers away from the general-audience sitcoms and dramas of the past. With the proliferation of cable channels such as Black Entertainment Television (BET) and the Spanish-language Univision and websites that cater to every imaginable taste, there no longer seems to be a need for broadly popular series such as *The Cosby Show,* whose tone and content appealed to Whites as well as Blacks in a way that the newer series do not. The UPN and WB networks produce situation comedies and even full nights geared toward African American audiences. The result of these sweeping technological changes has been a sharp divergence in viewer preferences.

While BET and Univision were grabbing minority audiences and offering new outlets for minority talent, network executives and writers remained overwhelmingly White. It is not surprising that these mainstream writers and producers, most of whom live far from ethnically and racially diverse inner-city neighborhoods, tend to write and prefer stories about people like themselves. Even urban-based programs such as the successful *Seinfeld* and *Frazier* lasted years on television with almost no people of color crossing the screen. Television series are only part of the picture. Newscasting is overwhelmingly done by Whites: eighty-nine percent in 2000. Among the top 30 correspondents on the major network evening news shows, one was a Latino, one was an African American, and 28 were White. Ironically, this means that if television were to report the research on television and race, the news correspondent probably would be White (Braxton 1999; Bunche Center 2003; Carter 2001; Children Now 2004; Johnson 2001).

Because we acquire prejudice from our social environment, it follows that the mass media and educational programs, as major elements of that environment, influence the level of prejudice. The movement to eliminate the stereotyping of minorities and the sexes in textbooks and on television recognizes this influence. Most of the effort has been to avoid contributing to racial hostility; less effort has been made to attack prejudice actively, primarily because no one knows how to do that effectively. In looking for a way to attack prejudice directly, many people advocate intergroup contact.

## Equal-Status Contact

An impressive number of research studies have confirmed the **contact hypothesis**, which states that intergroup contact between people of equal status in harmonious circumstances will cause them to become less prejudiced and to abandon previously held stereotypes. Most studies indicate that such contact also improves the attitude of subordinate-group members. The importance of equal status in the interaction cannot be stressed enough. If a Puerto Rican is abused by his employer, little interracial harmony is promoted. Similarly, the

situation in which contact occurs must be pleasant, making a positive evalua-
tion likely for both individuals. Contact between two nurses, one Black and
the other White, who are competing for one vacancy as a supervisor may lead
to greater racial hostility (Schaefer 1976).

The key factor in reducing hostility, in addition to equal-status contact, is
the presence of a common goal. If people are in competition, as already
noted, contact may heighten tension. However, bringing people together
to share a common task has been shown to reduce ill feeling when these
people belong to different racial, ethnic, or religious groups. A study released
in 2004 traced the transformations that occurred over the generations in the
composition of the Social Service Employees Union in New York City. Always a mixed membership, the union was founded by Jews and Italian
Americans, only to experience an influx of Black Americans. More recently,
it is comprised of Latin Americans, Africans, West Indians, and South Asians.
At each point, the common goals of representing the workers effectively
overcame the very real cultural differences among the rank-and-file of Mexican and El Salvadoran immigrants in Houston. The researchers found when
the new arrivals had contact with African Americans, intergroup relations
generally improved relations, and the absence of contact tended to foster
ambivalent, even negative attitudes (Fine 2004; Foerster 2004; Sherif and
Sherif 1969).

Researchers in a housing study examined the harassment, threats, and
fears that Blacks face in White schools in which low-income Black students
are in the minority. Did these African American youths experience acceptance, friendships, and positive interactions with their White classmates? The
researchers interviewed youth who had moved to the suburbs and those
who had relocated within the city of Chicago under the auspices of a federally funded program. In this program, low-income Black families received
housing subsidies that allowed them to move from inner-city housing projects into apartment buildings occupied largely by middle-income Whites
and located in middle-income, mostly White suburbs. The study found that
these low-income Black youth did experience some harassment and some
difficulty in gaining acceptance in the suburban schools, but the findings
also suggested that they eventually experienced great success in social integration and felt that they fit into their new environments (Rosenbaum and
Meaden 1992).

As African Americans and other subordinate groups slowly gain access to
better-paying and more responsible jobs, the contact hypothesis takes on
greater significance. Usually, the availability of equal-status interaction is taken
for granted, yet in everyday life intergroup contact does not conform to the
equal-status idea of the contact hypothesis as often as we are assured by researchers, who hope to see a lessening of tension. Furthermore, in a highly
segregated society such as the United States, contact, especially between
Whites and minorities, tends to be brief and superficial (Miller 2002).

Efforts are beginning in the workplace to reduce hostility among workers based on prejudice.

## Corporate Response: Diversity Training

Prejudice carries a cost. This cost is not only to the victim but also to any organization that allows prejudice to interfere with its functioning. Workplace hostility can lead to lost productivity and even attrition. Furthermore, if left unchecked, an organization, whether a corporation, government agency, or nonprofit enterprise, can develop a reputation for having a "chilly climate." This reputation as a business unfriendly to people of color or to women discourages both qualified people from applying for jobs and potential clients from seeking products or services.

In an effort to improve workplace relations, most organizations have initiated some form of diversity training. These programs are aimed at eliminating circumstances and relationships that cause groups to receive fewer rewards, resources, or opportunities. Typically, programs aim to reduce ill treatment based on race, gender, and ethnicity. In addition, diversity training may deal with (in descending order of frequency) age, disability, religion, and language, as well as other aspects, including citizenship status, marital status, and parental status (Society for Human Resource Management 2002).

It is difficult to make any broad generalization about the effectiveness of diversity training programs because they vary so much in structure between organizations. At one extreme are short presentations that seem to have little support from management. People file into the room feeling that this is something they need to get through quickly. Such training is unlikely to be effective and may actually be counterproductive by heightening social tensions. At the other end of the continuum is a diversity training program that

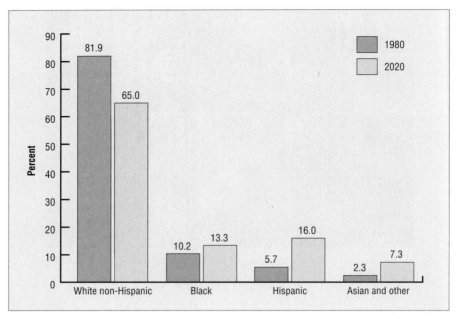

**Figure 2.7** The Changing Workplace
Racial and ethnic composition of the labor force in 1984 and projected to 2014.
*Source:* Toossi 2005, 26.

is integrated into initial job training, reinforced periodically, and presented as part of the overall mission of the organization, with full support from all levels of management. In these businesses, diversity is a core value, and management demands a high degree of commitment from all employees (ADL 2001; Lindsley 1998).

As shown in Figure 2.7, the workforce is becoming more diverse, and management is taking notice. It is not in an organization's best interests if employees start to create barriers based on, for example, racial lines. We saw in the previous section that equal-status contact can reduce hostility. However, in the workplace, people compete for promotions, desirable work assignments, and better office space, to name a few sources of friction. When done well, an organization undertakes diversity training to remove ill feelings among workers, often reflected in the prejudices present in larger society.

The content of diversity training also varies. Generally, it includes sharing information about the diverse composition of the service region, the company, and potential clientele, today and in the future. Videotapes are sometimes used that usually compare proper and awkward ways to handle a situation. Training sessions may break up into smaller group interactions where problem solving and team building are also encouraged.

If it is to have lasting impact on an organization, diversity training should not be separated from other aspects of the organization. For example, even the most inspired program will have little effect on prejudice if the organization promotes a sexist or ethnically offensive image in its advertising. The University of North Dakota launched an initiative in 2001 to become one of the top institutions for Native Americans in the nation. Yet at almost the same time, the administration reaffirmed its commitment, despite tribal objections, to having as its mascot for athletic teams the "Fighting Sioux." It does little to do diversity training if overt actions by an organization propel it in the opposite direction. In 2005, the National Collegiate Athletic Association began a review of logos and mascots that could be considered insulting to Native Americans. Some colleges have resisted suggestions to change or alter their publicity images while others have abandoned the practice (Brownstein 2001; NCAA 2005).

A central function that businesses can perform is to monitor prejudice that may deny opportunities to people largely because of their race, ethnicity, or nationality. In "Research Focus," we consider a recent and innovative experiment to measure prejudice in the workplace.

## RESEARCH FOCUS

## What's in a Name?

As a job applicant, you revise and rework that résumé. Do you include that summer job three years ago? Who should you list as a reference? Do you state specific career objectives? But one thing you never ponder—your name.

**Table 2.2  Names and Interview Success**

| Name on Resume | Callback (%) |
| --- | --- |
| Brad | 15.0 |
| Kristen | 13.6 |
| Meredith | 10.6 |
| Mathew | 9.0 |
| Emily | 8.3 |
| Tanisha | 6.3 |
| Darnell | 4.8 |
| Keisha | 3.8 |
| Rasheed | 3.0 |
| Aisha | 2.2 |

Yet recent research shows your name may be a big factor if the potential interviewer is able to use it as a means to determine your race or nationality. Would a Mohammad be as likely to get a chance to work as a Michael in the United States? Most likely not, in what could be seen as yet another form of profiling, only this one occurs in the job market. Two economists, Marianne Bertrand and Sendhil Mullainathan, sent out 5,000 job applications for 1,300 job openings advertised in the *Boston Globe* and *Chicago Tribune.* The vacancies covered the gamut of the classified advertisements from cashier jobs to sales management positions. Among this massive undertaking, the researchers decided to see if the name of the job applicant made a difference. Carefully, they tracked responses to two different sets of applicants—one with first names most likely to be African American and the other set being more typical of Whites. Names were selected by examining a random sample of Boston birth certificates that identified a person's race as well as his or her name.

The results of this job-seeking experiment were even startling to the researchers. Applicants with White-sounding names were 50 percent more likely to be called for an interview than those with Black-sounding names. Put another way, typical White applicants were contacted for an interview for every ten résumés they sent out, while the "African American" applicant had to send out fifteen applications. Where employers responded positively to more than one résumé, rarely did they contact a "Black" applicant and not also contact a "White" applicant. Because these were hypothetical applicants, we have no way of knowing to what degree these disturbing job results would have continued during the interview, job offer, and salary offered. Yet, clearly, the biggest constraining factor in any person's attempt to get a job is to get that interview.

The researchers took their study one step further. They made conscious efforts to make a portion of the applicants better qualified or to list addresses in more affluent neighborhoods. In both instances, resumes with White-sounding names were given even further advantages, but this had much less positive impact on callbacks to the résumés bearing Black-sounding names. They did find that the apparent pro-White bias was less when employers were located in minority neighborhoods.

This study showed—using a clever, if simple, methodology—that people's prejudices seem to surface even when they scan that top line of a résumé. Many business people apparently read no further if they detect that the applicant is from the wrong group.

*Source:* Bertand and Mullainathan 2003 and Krueger 2002.

Although diversity training is increasingly common in the workplace, it may be undertaken primarily in response to major evidence of wrongdoing. In recent years, companies as diverse as Avis Rent-a-Car, Circuit City, Coca-Cola, Mitsubishi, Denny's Restaurants, Morgan Stanley, and Texaco have become synonymous with racism or sexual harassment. Generally, as a part of multimillion-dollar settlements, organizations agree to conduct comprehensive diversity training programs. So common is this pattern that a human resources textbook even cautions that a company should "avoid beginning such training too soon" after a complaint of workplace prejudice or discrimination (Carrell, Elbert, and Hatfield 2000, 266).

Despite the problems inherent in confronting prejudice, an organization with a comprehensive, management-supported program of diversity training can go a long way toward reducing prejudice in the workplace. The one major qualifier is that the rest of the organization must also support mutual respect.

## Ways to Fight Hate

What can schools do? Television and movie producers? Corporate big shots? It is easy to shift the responsibility for confronting prejudice to the movers and shakers, and certainly they do play a critical role. Yet there are definitely actions one can take in the course of everyday day life to challenge intergroup hostility.

The Southern Poverty Law Center (SPLC), founded in 1971 and based in Montgomery, Alabama, organized committed activists all over the country to mount legal cases and challenges against hate groups such as the Ku Klux Klan. The center's courtroom challenges led to the end of many discriminatory practices. Their cases have now gone beyond conventional race-based cases since they have won equal benefits for women in the armed forces, ended involuntary sterilization of women on welfare, and reformed prison and mental health conditions.

Recognizing that social change can also begin at the individual level, the SPLC has identified ten ways to fight hate based on their experience working at the community level (Carrier 2000).

1. **Act.**   Do something. In the face of hatred, apathy will be taken as acceptance even by the victims of prejudice themselves. The SPLC tells of a time when a cross was burned in the yard of a single mother of Portuguese descent in Missouri; one person acted and set in motion a community uprising against hatred.

2. **Unite.**   Call a friend or co-worker. Organize a group of like-thinking friends from school or your place of worship or club. Create a coalition that is a diverse coalition and includes the young, the old, law enforcement representatives, and the media. Frustrated when a neo-Nazi group got permission to march in Springfield, Illinois, in 1994, a Jewish couple formed Project Lemonade. Money raised helps to create education projects or monuments in communities that witness such decisive events.

3. **Support the Victims.**   Victims of hate crimes are especially vulnerable. Let them know you care by words, by email. If you or your friend

is a victim, report it. In the wake of an outbreak of anti-Native American and anti-Jewish activity in Billings, Montana, a manager of a local sports shop replaced all his usual outdoor advertising and print ads with "Not in Our Town," which soon became a community rallying point for a support network of hate victims.

4. **Do Your Homework.**   If you suspect a hate crime has been committed, do your research to document it. An Indiana father spotted his son receiving a "pastor's license," did some research, and found that the source was a White supremacist group disguised as a church. It helped explain the boy's recent fascination with Nazi symbols. The father wrote the "church," demanded that the contacts be stopped, and threatened suit.

5. **Create an Alternative.**   Never attend a rally where hate is a part of the agenda. Find another outlet for your frustration, whatever the cause. When the Ku Klux Klan held a rally in Madison, Wisconsin, a coalition of ministers organized citizens to spend the day in minority neighborhoods.

6. **Speak Up.**   You too have First Amendment rights. Denounce the hatred, the cruel jokes. If you see a news organization misrepresenting a group, speak up. When a newspaper exposed the 20-year-old national leader of the Aryan Nation in Canada, he resigned and closed his website.

Speak Up! Filipino American World War II veterans protest in 1997 for full veteran's benefits for Filipinos who served in World War II for the United States.

7. **Lobby Leaders.**   Persuade policymakers, business heads, community leaders, and executives of media outlets to take a stand against hate. Levi Strauss contributed $5 million to an antiprejudice project and a program that helps people of color get loans in communities where it has plants: Knoxville, Albuquerque, El Paso, and Valdosta, Georgia.

8. **Look Long Range.**   Participate or organize events such as annual parades or cultural fairs to celebrate diversity and harmony. Supplement it with a website that can be a 24/7 resource. In Selma, Alabama, a major weekend street fair is held on the anniversary of Bloody Sunday, when voting-rights activists attempting to walk across a bridge to Montgomery were beaten back by police.

9. **Teach Tolerance.**   Prejudice is learned and parents and teachers can influence the content of curriculum. In Brooklyn, New York, an interracial basketball program called Flames was founded in the mid-1970s. Since then, it has brought together more than 10,000 youths of diverse backgrounds.

10. **Dig Deeper.**   Look into the issues that divide us—social inequality, immigration, and sexual orientation. Work against prejudice. Dig deep inside yourself for prejudices and stereotypes you may embrace. Find out what is happening and act! As former White supremacist Floyd Cochran declared, "It is not enough to hold hands and sing Kumbaya" (Carrier 2000, 22).

Expressing prejudice and expressing tolerance are fundamentally personal decisions. These steps recognize that we have the ability to change our attitudes and resist ethnocentrism and prejudice and avoid the use of ethnophaulisms and stereotypes.

## Conclusion

This chapter has examined theories of prejudice and measurements of its extent. Prejudice should not be confused with discrimination. The two concepts are not the same: Prejudice consists of negative attitudes, and discrimination consists of negative behavior toward a group.

Several theories try to explain why prejudice exists. Some emphasize economic concerns (the exploitation and scapegoating theories), whereas other approaches stress personality or normative factors. No one explanation is sufficient. Surveys conducted in the United States over the past sixty years point to a reduction of prejudice as measured by the willingness to express stereotypes or maintain social distance. Survey data also show that African Americans, Latinos, Asian Americans, and American Indians do not necessarily feel comfortable with each other. They have adopted attitudes toward other oppressed groups similar to those held by many White Americans. Prejudice aimed at Hispanics, Asian Americans, and large recent immigrant groups such as Arab Americans and Muslim Americans is well documented. Issues such as immigration and affirmative action re-emerge and cause bitter resentment. Furthermore, ill feelings exist between subordinate groups in schools, in the streets, and in the workplace.

Equal-status contact may reduce hostility between groups. However, in a highly segregated society defined by inequality, such opportunities are not typical. The mass media can be of value in reducing discrimination but have not done enough and may even intensify ill feeling by promoting stereotypical images. Although strides are being made in increasing the appearance of minorities in positive roles in television and films, one would not realize how diverse our society is by sampling advertisements, TV programs, or movies.

Even though we can be encouraged by the techniques available to reduce intergroup hostility, there are still sizable segments of the population that do not want to live in integrated neighborhoods,

that do not want to work for or be led by someone of a different race, and that certainly object to the idea of their relatives marrying outside their own group. People still harbor stereotypes toward one another, and this tendency includes racial and ethnic minorities having stereotypes about one another.

Reducing prejudice is important because it can lead to support for policy change. There are steps we can take as individuals to confront prejudice and overcome hatred. Another real challenge and the ultimate objective is to improve the social condition of oppressed groups in the United States. To consider this challenge, we turn to discrimination in Chapter 3. Discrimination's costs are high to both dominant and subordinate groups. With that fact in mind, we will examine some techniquesfor reducing discrimination.

## Key Terms

| | | |
|---|---|---|
| authoritarian personality 53 | ethnocentrism 45 | prejudice 48 |
| Bogardus scale 62 | ethnophaulism 49 | racial profiling 60 |
| contact hypothesis 73 | exploitation theory 54 | scapegoating theory 52 |
| discrimination 49 | hate crimes 46 | social distance 62 |
| | normative approach 55 | stereotype 56 |

## Review Questions

1. How are prejudice and discrimination both related and unrelated to each other?
2. How do theories of prejudice relate to different expressions of prejudice?
3. Why does prejudice develop even toward groups with whom people have little contact?
4. Are there steps that you can identify that have been taken against prejudice in your community?

## Critical Thinking

1. Identify stereotypes associated with a group of people, such as older adults or people with physical handicaps.
2. What social issues do you think are most likely to engender hostility along racial and ethnic lines?

**3.** Consider the television programs you have watched the most. In terms of race and ethnicity, how well do the programs you watch tend to reflect the diversity of the population in the United States?

# Internet Connections—Research Navigator™

Follow the instructions found on page 42 of this text to access the features of Research Navigator™. Once at the Website, enter your Login Name and Password. Then, to use the ContentSelect database, enter keywords such as "racism," "racial profiling," and "diversity training," and the research engine will supply relevant and recent scholarly and popular press publications. Use the *New York Times* Search-by-Subject Archive to find recent news articles related to sociology and the Link Library feature to locate relevant Web links organized by the key terms associated with this chapter.

# 3 Discrimination

## CHAPTER OUTLINE

———————————————{ HIGHLIGHTS }———————————————

Just as social scientists have advanced theories to explain why prejudice exists, they have also presented explanations of why discrimination occurs. Social scientists look more and more at the manner in
which institutions, not individuals, discriminate. Institutional discrimination is a pattern in social institutions that produces or perpetuates
inequalities, even if individuals in the society do not intend to be racist
or sexist. Income data document that gaps exist between racial and
ethnic groups. Historically, attempts have been made to reduce discrimination, usually as a result of strong lobbying efforts by minorities
themselves. Patterns of total discrimination make solutions particularly difficult for people in the informal economy or the underclass.
Affirmative action was designed to equalize opportunity but has encountered significant resentment by those who charge that it constitutes
reverse discrimination. Despite many efforts to end discrimination, glass
ceilings and glass walls remain in the workplace.

Discrimination can take many forms. As the next two incidents indicate, discrimination can be either direct or the result of a complex combination of factors.
It can lead to indignities or death.

Lawrence Otis Graham (1995) had "arrived" by the standards of most
people in the United States. He was a graduate of Harvard Law School, married, and had become a well-regarded member of a Manhattan law firm. But he
was also Black. Despite his success in securing clients for himself and his firm,
Graham had noticed that White attorneys seemed to get a jump on him because of their associations with corporate leaders at private clubs. By tradition,

the clubs were exclusively White. Graham decided to take time out from his law firm and learn more about the workings of these private clubs, which allowed some Whites to mingle in an informal atmosphere and so contributed to their establishing networks. These networks, in turn, allowed people to establish contacts that advanced their success in the business world. Rather than present himself as a successful Ivy League college graduate to become a member, he presented himself as a working-class African American seeking a job as a waiter. From the vantage point of a server, Graham figured he could observe the network of these predominantly White country club members. This was not to be the case. He was not given a job at club after club. Despite all sorts of encouragement when he talked to employers over the phone, he was denied a job when he presented himself, and they saw that this articulate, well-mannered young man was Black. Eventually, he obtained a job as a busboy, clearing tables in a club where the White servers commented that he could do their job better than they could.

Cynthia Wiggins was also African American, but she lived in a different world from Lawrence Otis Graham. She was a 17-year-old single mother struggling to make a living. She had sought jobs near her home but had

Harvard-educated lawyer Lawrence Otis Graham sought a position as a waiter in exclusive clubs to learn more about contemporary discrimination.

found no employment opportunities. Eventually, she found employment as a cashier, but it was far from her home, and she could not afford a car. Still, she was optimistic and looked forward to marrying the man to whom she was engaged. In 1995, she made the 50-minute bus ride from her predominantly Black neighborhood in Buffalo, New York, to her job at the Galleria, a fancy suburban shopping mall. Every day, charter buses unloaded shoppers from as far away as Canada, but city buses were not allowed on mall property. The bus Wiggins rode was forced to stop across the lot and across a seven-lane highway without sidewalks. On a December day, with the roadway lined with mounds of snow, she tried to cross the highway, only to be struck by a dump truck. She died three weeks later. Later investigation showed that the bus company had been trying to arrange for the bus to stop in the mall parking lot, but the shopping center authorities had blocked the move. Before the incident, the mall said it would consider allowing in suburban buses but not public buses from the city. As one mall store owner put it, "You'll never see an inner-city bus on the mall premises" (Barnes 1996:33; Gladwell 1996).

Discrimination has a long history, right up to the present, of taking its toll on people. For some, such as Lawrence Otis Graham, discrimination is being reminded that even when you do try to seek employment, you may be

In this often-reproduced photograph, civil rights hero Rosa Parks is shown defying *de jure* segregation by sitting in the White section of the bus that launched the Montgomery, Alabama, bus boycott in 1955. Actually, while the event was very real, there were no journalists present at the time and this iconic photography was a re-creation with an Associated Press reporter seated behind Rosa Parks.

treated like a second-class citizen. For others, such as Cynthia Wiggins, discrimination meant suffering for the unjust decisions made in a society that quietly discriminated. Williams lost her life not because anyone actually intended to kill her but because decisions made it more likely that an inner-city resident would be an accident victim. Despite legislative and court efforts to eliminate discrimination, members of dominant and subordinate groups pay a price for continued intolerance.

# Understanding Discrimination

**Discrimination** is the denial of opportunities and equal rights to individuals and groups because of prejudice or for other arbitrary reasons. Some people in the United States find it difficult to see discrimination as a widespread phenomenon. "After all," it is often said, "these minorities drive cars, hold jobs, own their homes, and even go to college." This does not mean that discrimination is rare. An understanding of discrimination in modern industrialized societies such as the United States must begin by distinguishing between relative and absolute deprivation.

## Relative versus Absolute Deprivation

Conflict theorists have said correctly that it is not absolute, unchanging standards that determine deprivation and oppression. Although minority groups may be viewed as having adequate or even good incomes, housing, health care, and educational opportunities, it is their position relative to some other group that offers evidence of discrimination.

**Relative deprivation** is defined as the conscious experience of a negative discrepancy between legitimate expectations and present actualities. After settling in the United States, immigrants often enjoy better material comforts and more political freedom than were possible in their old country. If they compare themselves with most other people in the United States, however, they will feel deprived because, although their standard has improved, the immigrants still perceive relative deprivation.

**Absolute deprivation**, on the other hand, implies a fixed standard based on a minimum level of subsistence below which families should not be expected to exist. Discrimination does not necessarily mean absolute deprivation. A Japanese American who is promoted to a management position may still be a victim of discrimination if he or she had been passed over for years because of corporate reluctance to place an Asian American in a highly visible position.

Dissatisfaction is also likely to arise from feelings of relative deprivation. The members of a society who feel most frustrated and disgruntled by the social and economic conditions of their lives are not necessarily worse off in an objective sense. Social scientists have long recognized that what is most significant is how people perceive their situations. Karl Marx pointed out that, although the misery of the workers was important in reflecting their oppressed state, so was their position relative to the ruling class. In 1847, Marx wrote,

> *Although the enjoyment of the workers has risen, the social satisfaction that they have has fallen in comparison with the increased enjoyment of the capitalist.* (Marx and Engels 1955:94)

This statement explains why the groups or individuals who are most vocal and best organized against discrimination are not necessarily in the worst economic and social situation. However, they are likely to be those who most strongly perceive that, relative to others, they are not receiving their fair share. Resistance to perceived discrimination, rather than the actual amount of absolute discrimination, is the key.

## Total Discrimination

Social scientists—and increasingly policymakers—have begun to use the concept of total discrimination. **Total discrimination**, as shown in Figure 3.1, refers to current discrimination operating in the labor market and past discrimination. Past discrimination experienced by an individual includes the poorer education and job experiences of racial and ethnic minorities compared with those of many White Americans. When considering discrimination, therefore, it is not enough to focus only on what is being done to people now. Sometimes a person may be dealt with fairly but may still be at a disadvantage because he or she suffered from poorer health care, inferior counseling in the school system, less access to books and other educational materials, or a poor job record resulting from absences to take care of brothers and sisters.

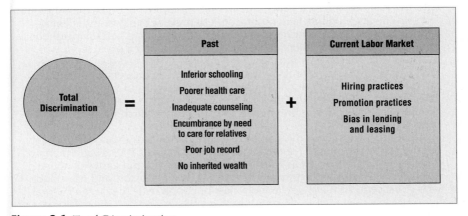

**Figure 3.1** Total Discrimination

Discrimination casts a wide net. While the poor and less educated are most vulnerable and unable to access resources that might help them, it also is faced by the affluent with professional degrees. In "Listen to Our Voices," respected law professor Patricia J. Williams, an African American, describes her inability to secure a mortgage despite initial approval after an analysis of her financial status but before the bank realized she was Black. Her recent experience is not unusual and helps to explain the persistence of discrimination.

We find another variation of this past-in-present discrimination when apparently nondiscriminatory present practices have negative effects because of prior intentionally biased practices. Although unions that purposely discriminated against minority members in the past may no longer do so, some people are still prevented from achieving higher levels of seniority because of

---

## LISTEN TO OUR VOICES

### Of Race and Risk

*Patricia J. Williams*

Several years ago, at a moment when I was particularly tired of the unstable lifestyle that academic careers sometimes require, I surprised myself and bought a real house. Because the house was in a state other than the one where I was living at the time, I obtained my mortgage by telephone. I am a prudent little squirrel when it comes to things financial, always tucking away stores of nuts for the winter, and so I meet the criteria of a quite good credit risk. My loan was approved almost immediately.

A little while later, the contract came in the mail. Among the papers the bank forwarded were forms documenting compliance with the Fair Housing Act, which outlaws racial discrimination in the housing market. The act monitors lending practices to prevent banks from redlining— redlining being the phenomenon whereby banks circle certain neighborhoods on the map and refuse to lend in those areas. It is a practice for which the bank with which I was dealing, unbeknownst to me, had been cited previously—as well as since. In any event, the act tracks the race of all banking customers to prevent such discrimination. Unfortunately, and with the creative variability of all illegality, some banks also use the racial information disclosed on the fair housing forms to engage in precisely the discrimination the law seeks to prevent.

I should repeat that to this point my entire mortgage transaction had been conducted by telephone. I should also note that I speak a Received Standard English, regionally marked as Northeastern perhaps, but not easily identifiable as black. With my credit history, my job as a law professor, and, no doubt, with my accent, I am not only middle class but apparently match the cultural stereotype of a good white person. It is thus, perhaps, that the loan officer of the bank, whom I had never met, had checked off the box on the fair housing form indicating that I was white.

Race shouldn't matter, I suppose, but it seemed to in this case, so I took a deep breath, crossed out "white" and sent the contract back. That will teach them to presume too much, I thought. A done deal, I assumed. But suddenly the transaction came to a screeching halt. The bank wanted more money, more points, and a higher rate of interest. Suddenly I found myself facing great resistance and much more debt. To make a long story short, I threatened to sue under the act in question, the bank quickly backed down, and I procured the loan on the original terms. What was interesting about all this was that the reason the bank gave for its newfound recalcitrance was not race, heaven forbid. No, it was all about economics and increased risk: The reason they gave was that property values in that neighborhood were suddenly falling. They wanted more money to buffer themselves against the snappy winds of projected misfortune.

Initially, I was surprised, confused. The house was in a neighborhood that was extremely stable. I am an extremely careful shopper; I had uncovered absolutely nothing to indicate that prices were falling. It took my realtor to make me see the light. "Don't you get it," he sighed. "This is what always happens." And even though I suppose it was a little thick of me, I really hadn't gotten it: For, of course, I was the reason the prices were in peril. . . .

In retrospect, what has remained so fascinating to me about this experience was the way it so exemplified the problems of the new rhetoric of racism. For starters, the new rhetoric of race never mentions race. It wasn't race but risk with which the bank was so concerned. . . .

By this measure of mortgage-worthiness, the ingredient of blackness is cast not just as a social toll but as an actual tax. A fee, an extra contribution at the door, an admission charge for the high costs of handling my dangerous propensities, my inherently unsavory properties. I was not judged based on my independent attributes or financial worth; not even was I judged by statistical profiles of what my group actually does. (For, in fact, anxiety-stricken, middle-class black people make good cake-baking neighbors when not made to feel defensive by the unfortunate historical strategies of bombs, burnings, or abandonment.) Rather, I was being evaluated based on what an abstraction of White Society writ large thinks we—or I—do, and that imagined "doing" was treated and thus established as a self-fulfilling prophecy. It is a dispiriting message: that some in society apparently not only devalue black people but devalue themselves and their homes just for having us as part of their landscape.

"I bet you'll keep your mouth shut the next time they plug you into the computer as white," laughed a friend when he heard my story. It took me aback, this postmodern pressure to "pass," even as it highlighted the intolerable logic of it all. For by these "rational" economic measures, an investment in my property suggests the selling of myself.

*Source:* P. Williams (1997). "Of Race and Risk" by Patricia J. Williams. Reprinted with permission from the December, 29 issue of *The Nation*. For subscription information, call 1-800-333-8536. Portions of each week's Nation magazine can be accessed at http://www.thenation.com.

those past practices. Personnel records include a cumulative record that is vital in promotion and selection for desirable assignments. Blatantly discriminatory judgments and recommendations in the past remain part of a person's record.

## Institutional Discrimination

Individuals practice discrimination in one-to-one encounters, and institutions practice discrimination through their daily operations. Indeed, a consensus is growing today that this institutional discrimination is more significant than that committed by prejudiced individuals.

Social scientists are particularly concerned with the ways in which patterns of employment, education, criminal justice, housing, health care, and government operations maintain the social significance of race and ethnicity. **Institutional discrimination** is the denial of opportunities and equal rights to individuals and groups that results from the normal operations of a society.

Civil rights activist Stokely Carmichael and political scientist Charles Hamilton are credited with introducing the concept of institutional racism. Individual discrimination refers to overt acts of individual Whites against individual Blacks; Carmichael and Hamilton reserved the term institutional racism for covert acts committed collectively against an entire group. From this perspective, discrimination can take place without an individual's intending to deprive others of privileges and even without the individual's being aware that others are being deprived (Ture and Hamilton 1992).

How can discrimination be widespread and unconscious at the same time? The following are a few documented examples of institutional discrimination.

1. Standards for assessing credit risks work against African Americans and Hispanics seeking to establish businesses because many lack conventional credit references. Businesses in low-income areas where these groups often reside also have much higher insurance costs.
2. IQ testing favors middle-class children, especially the White middle class, because of the types of questions included.
3. The entire criminal justice system, from the patrol officer to the judge and jury, is dominated by Whites who find it difficult to understand life in poverty areas.
4. Hiring practices often require several years' experience at jobs only recently opened to members of subordinate groups.
5. Many jobs automatically eliminate people with felony records or past drug offenses, which disproportionately reduces employment opportunities for people of color.

In some cases, even apparently neutral institutional standards can turn out to have discriminatory effects. African American students at a Midwestern state university protested a policy under which fraternities and sororities that wanted to use campus facilities for a dance were required to post a $150 security deposit to cover possible damage. The Black students complained that this policy had a discriminatory impact on minority student organizations. Campus police countered that the university's policy applied to all student groups interested in using these facilities. However, because, overwhelmingly, White fraternities and sororities at the school had their own houses, which they used for dances, the policy affected only African American and other subordinate groups' organizations.

Ten years later, the entire nation scrambled to make aviation safer in the wake of the 9/11 terrorist attacks. The government saw airport security as a weak link and federalized airport screeners under the newly formed Transport Security Administration. Wages improved and training strengthened. The new screeners also had to be U.S. citizens. This latter provision eliminated the many legal immigrants from Asia, Africa, and Latin America who had previously worked as screeners. Airport screening went from overwhelmingly minority to 61 percent White. Clearly, this measure had the unintended consequences of discriminating against people of color (Alonso-Zaldivar and Oldham 2002).

The U.S. population is becoming more diversified, and examples of institutional discrimination are confronting more and different groups. Many Asian peoples have distinctive customs honoring their deceased family members. Among these traditions is the burning of incense at the gravesite, placing food on the grave markers, and leaving fake money. These practices stem from ancestor worship but often are followed by Christian Chinese Americans who try to hold onto some of the "old ways." Cemetery proprietors maintain standards of what they regard as proper grave decoration to maintain a tidy appearance. Consequently, people of Asian descent find they are unable to bury their loved ones in the cemeteries most convenient to them and must travel to cemeteries that are more open to different ways of memorializing the dead. Cemeteries do not consciously seek to keep people out because they are Asian, but they develop policies, often with little thought, that fail to recognize the pluralistic nature of society (Eng 1998).

The 2000 presidential election created headlines because it took weeks to resolve who won—Bush or Gore. Yet for 1.4 million African Americans who were denied the right to vote, this seemed like a national issue that had left them on the sidelines. The prohibition was not because they were Black, which would have been clearly racist and legally discriminatory, but because they were convicted felons. Seven states prohibit felons from voting for life even after their prison sentence. Because many of these states are in the South and have large Black populations, disproportionately, the voting prohibition covers African American men. Currently 13 percent of the nation's Black male population is precluded from voting by such laws. Florida was the deciding state in the close 2000 elections, and more than 200,000 potential Black voters were excluded. This case of institutional

Institutional discrimination takes many forms. The 2000 presidential election highlighted the restriction in many states that ex-convicts can never vote. In these same states the excluded are most likely to be African American. Here Leroy Jones demonstrates for restoration of voting rights for himself and his fellow ex-felons outside a federal court in Miami in April 2003.

discrimination may have changed the outcome of a presidential election (Cooper 2004).

Institutional discrimination continuously imposes more hindrances on and awards fewer benefits to certain racial and ethnic groups than it does to others. This is the underlying and painful context of American intergroup relations.

## Low-Wage Labor

A disproportionate share of racial and ethnic minority members are either unemployed or employed in low-wage labor. Much of this low-wage labor is in a part of the labor market that provides little opportunities of improvement during one's time working and virtually no protection in terms of health insurance or retirement benefits.

The secondary labor market affecting many members of racial and ethnic minorities has come to be called the **informal economy**. The informal economy (also called the **irregular or underground economy**) consists of transfers of money, goods, or services that are not reported to the government. This label describes much of the work in inner-city neighborhoods and poverty-stricken rural areas, in sharp contrast to the rest of the marketplace. Workers are employed in the informal economy seasonally or infrequently. The work they do may resemble the work of traditional occupations, such as mechanic, cook, or electrician, but these workers lack the formal credentials to enter such employment. Indeed, workers in the informal economy may work sporadically or may moonlight in the regular economy. The informal economy also includes unregulated child-care services, garage sales, and the unreported income of craftspeople and street vendors.

The informal economy exists worldwide and networks nations through globalization. Recently, wide publicity was given to the presence of sweatshops throughout the world and in urban America that supplied clothing for major retailers such as Wal-Mart. Concern has targeted the apparel industry and working conditions of employees. Students have formed a nationwide coalition called United Students Against Sweatshops that brings attention to exploited workers here and abroad. Research also documents that Latinos and African Americans are much more likely than Whites to work "nonstandard shifts" (nights and weekends) without receiving premium wages (Appelbaum and Dreier 1999; Bonacich and Appelbaum 2000; Presser 2003).

Many people work in the informal economy with little prospect of moving into the primary, better-paying economy. Pictured is a street vendor in New York City.

According to the **dual labor market** model, minorities have been relegated to the informal economy. Although the informal economy may offer employment to the jobless, it provides few safeguards against fraud or malpractice that victimizes the workers. There are also few of the fringe benefits of health insurance and pensions that are much more likely to be present in the conventional marketplace. Therefore, informal economies are criticized for promoting highly unfair and dangerous working conditions. To be consigned to the informal economy is yet another example of social inequality.

Sociologist Edna Bonacich (1972, 1976) outlined the dual or split labor market that divides the economy into two realms of employment, the secondary one being populated primarily by minorities working at menial jobs. Even when not manual, labor is still rewarded less when performed by minorities. In keeping with the conflict model, this dual market model emphasizes that minorities fare unfavorably in the competition between dominant and subordinate groups.

The workers in the informal economy are ill prepared to enter the regular economy permanently or to take its better-paying jobs. Frequent changes in employment or lack of a specific supervisor leaves them without the kind of résumé that employers in the regular economy expect before they hire. Some of the sources of employment in the informal economy are illegal, such as fencing stolen goods, narcotics peddling, pimping, and prostitution. More likely, the work is legal but not transferable to a more traditional job. An example is an "information broker," who receives cash in exchange for such information as where to find good buys or how to receive maximum benefits from public assistance programs (Pedder 1991).

Workers in the informal economy have not necessarily experienced direct discrimination. Because of past discrimination, they are unable to secure traditional employment. Working in the informal economy provides income but does not lead them into the primary labor market. A self-fulfilling cycle continues that allows past discrimination to create a separate work environment.

Efforts to end discrimination continue to run up against discrimination of all sorts. As described in "Research Focus," while we can document discrimination in research studies, it is often very difficult to prove even if one had the time and money to bring the incident to the attention of the legal system.

Not all low-wage laborers are a part of the informal economy, but many workers are driven into such jobs as better-paying jobs either move far away from where African Americans and Latinos live or even move abroad as globalization creates more and more of an international labor market.

The absence of jobs casts a wider shadow in poor neighborhoods beyond the lousy employment opportunities. People in poor urban neighborhoods often live in what has been termed "commercial deserts" where they have little access to major grocers, pharmacies, or other retailers but have plenty of

## RESEARCH FOCUS

# Discrimination in Job Seeking

A dramatic confirmation of discrimination came with research begun by sociologist Devah Pager in 2003. She sent four men out as trained "testers" to look for entry-level jobs in Milwaukee, Wisconsin, requiring no experience or special training. Each was a 23-year-old college student but each one presented himself as having a high school diploma with similar job histories.

The job-seeking experiences with 350 different employers were vastly different among the four men. Why was that? Two of the testers where Black and two were White. Furthermore, one tester of each pair indicated in the job application that he had served 18 months of jail time for a felony conviction (possession of cocaine with intent to distribute). As you can see in Figure 3.2, applicants with a prison record received significantly fewer callbacks. But as dramatic a difference as a criminal record made, race was clearly more important.

The differences were to the point that a White job applicant with a jail record actually received more callbacks for further consideration than a Black man with no criminal record. Whiteness has a privilege even when it comes to jail time; race, it seems, was more of a concern to potential employers than a criminal background.

"I expected there to be an affect of race, but I did not expect it to swamp the results as it did," Pager told an interviewer. Her finding was especially significant because the majority of convicts who are released from prison each year (52 percent) are, in fact, Black men. Pager's research, which was widely publicized, eventually contributed to a change in public policy. In his 2004 State of the Union address, President George W. Bush specifically referring to Pager's work announced a $300 million monitoring program for ex-convicts who are attempting to reintegrate into society.

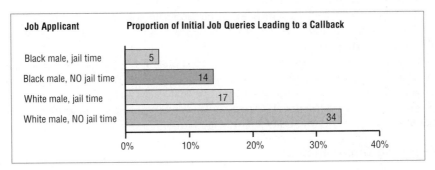

**Figure 3.2** Discrimination in Job Seeking
*Source:* Pager 2003, 958.

*Sources:* Bordt 2005; Bureau of Justice Statistics 2004; Krueger 2005, Pager 2003; Pager and Quillian 2005.

liquor stores and fast-food restaurants nearby. Not only does this affect the quality of life but it exacerbates the exodus of good job opportunities (Kelly 2005; Gallagher 2005).

It is commonly believed that there are jobs available for the inner-city poor, but they just do not seek them. A study looked at jobs that were advertised in a help-wanted section of the *Washington Post*. The analysis showed that most of the jobs were beyond the reach of the underclass; perhaps 5 percent of all openings could even remotely be considered reasonable job prospects for people without skills or experience. During interviews with the employers, researchers found that an average of 21 people applied for each position, which typically was filled within three days of when the advertisement appeared. The mean hourly wage was $6.12, 42 percent offered no fringe benefits, and the remaining positions offered meager fringe benefits after six months or one year of employment. This study, like others before it, counters the folk wisdom that there are plenty of jobs around for the underclass (Pease and Martin 1997).

# Discrimination Today

In 2003, the Legal Assistance Foundation of Metropolitan Chicago sent matched pairs of a White woman and a Black woman to seek jobs in suburban Chicago. They applied for a variety of jobs that were advertised or that posted "Help Wanted" signs in the window. Many of the jobs were retail positions in shopping centers or malls. Employers were 16 percent more likely to offer jobs to Whites than to Blacks, even though the Black applicant always applied first and presented stronger job-related qualifications. Black applicants were four times as likely to be asked about their absenteeism record and nearly twice as likely to be specifically asked why they left their previous job. This was in 2003, not 1953. It was also where jobs in urban America tend to be available—the suburbs (Lodder, McFarland, and White 2003).

Discrimination is widespread in the United States. It sometimes results from prejudices held by individuals. More significantly, it is found in institutional discrimination and the presence of the informal economy. The presence of an underclass is symptomatic of many social forces, and total discrimination—past and present discrimination taken together—is one of them.

## Measuring Discrimination

How much discrimination is there? As in measuring prejudice, problems arise in quantifying discrimination. Measuring prejudice is hampered by the difficulties in assessing attitudes and by the need to take many factors into account. It is further limited by the initial challenge of identifying different treatment. A second difficulty of measuring discrimination is assigning a cost to the discrimination.

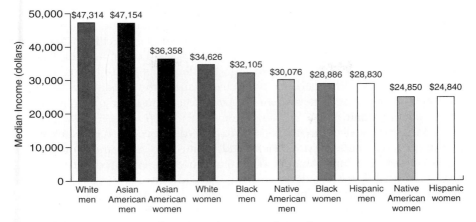

**Figure 3.3** Median Income by Race, Ethnicity, and Gender
Even at the very highest levels of schooling, the income gap remains between Whites and
Blacks. Education also has little apparent effect on the income gap between male and female
workers. Even a brief analysis reveals striking differences in earning power between White men
and other groups in the United States. Furthermore, the double jeopardy is apparent for African
American and Hispanic women.
Note: Median income is from all sources and is limited to year-round, full-time workers over
25 years old. Data for White men and women are for non-Hispanics.
Note: Data released in 2005 for income earned in 2004
*Source:* DeNavas-Walt, Proctor, and Mills 2005; for Native Americans, author's estimate based
on Bureau of the Census 2003b.

Some tentative conclusions about discrimination can be made, however.
Figure 3.3 uses income data to show vividly the disparity in income between
African Americans and Whites, and also between men and women. This encompasses all full-time workers. White men, with a median income of
$47,314, earn one-third more than Black men and nearly twice what Hispanic
women earn in wages.

Clearly, White men earn most, followed by Black men, White women, Hispanic men, and Hispanic women. The sharpest drop is between White and
Black men. Even worse, relatively speaking, is the plight of women. **Double
jeopardy** refers to the combination of two subordinate statuses, defined as
experienced by women of color. This disparity between the incomes of Black
women and White men has remained unchanged over the more than fifty years
during which such data have been tabulated. It illustrates yet another instance
of the double jeopardy experienced by minority women. Also, Figure 3.3 includes only data for full-time, year-round workers; it excludes homemakers and
the unemployed. Even in this comparison, the deprivation of Blacks, Hispanics,
and women is confirmed again.

Are these differences entirely the result of discrimination in employment?
No, individuals within the four groups are not equally prepared to compete

for high-paying jobs. Past discrimination is a significant factor in a person's present social position. As discussed previously and illustrated in Figure 3.1, past discrimination continues to take its toll on modern victims. Taxpayers, predominantly White, were unwilling to subsidize the public education of African Americans and Hispanics at the same levels as White pupils. Even as these actions have changed, today's schools show the continuing results of this uneven spending pattern from the past. Education clearly is an appropriate variable to control.

In Table 3.1, median income is compared, holding education constant, which means that we can compare Blacks and Whites and men and women with approximately the same amount of formal schooling. More education means more money, but the disparity remains. The gap between races does narrow somewhat as education increases. However, both African Americans and women lag behind their more affluent counterparts. The contrast remains dramatic: Women with a master's degree typically receive $51,316, which means they earn almost $6,000 less than men who complete only a bachelor's degree.

What do these individual differences look like if we consider them on a national level? Economist Andrew Brimmer (1995), citing numerous government

### Table 3.1  Median Income by Race and Sex, Holding Education Constant

Even at the very highest levels of schooling, the income gap remains between Whites and Blacks. Education also has little apparent effect on the income gap between male and female workers.

| | Race | | | Sex | |
|---|---|---|---|---|---|
| | *White Families* | *Black Families* | *Hispanic Families* | *Male* | *Female* |
| Total | $62,093 | $36,868 | $36,745 | $55,469 | $31,990 |
| HIGH SCHOOL | | | | | |
| Nongraduate | 31,052 | 21,473 | 27,831 | 26,277 | 19,162 |
| Graduate | 50,094 | 32,811 | 38.352 | 35,725 | 26,629 |
| COLLEGE | | | | | |
| Some college | 67,370 | 40,367 | 50,884 | 41,895 | 30,816 |
| Bachelor's degree | 84,832 | 63,711 | 63,958 | 57,220 | 41,681 |
| Master's degree | 100,000+ | 81,342 | 767,515 | 71,530 | 51,316 |
| Doctorate degree | 100,000++ | Data available | Data available | 82,401 | 68,875 |

Notes: Data released in 2005 for income earned in 2004.

Figures are median income from all sources except capital gains. Included are public assistance payments, dividends, pensions, unemployment compensation, and so on. Incomes are for all workers over 25 years of age. High school graduates include those with GEDs. Data for Whites are for White non-Hispanics. "Some college" excludes associate degree holders. Black data for doctorate is author's estimate.

*Source:* DeNavas-Walt et al. 2005.

studies, estimates that about 3 or 4 percent of the gross domestic product (GDP, or the value of goods and services) is lost annually by the failure to use African Americans' existing education. There had been little change in this economic cost from the mid-1960s to the mid-1990s. This estimate would be even higher if we took into account economic losses caused by the under-use of the academic talents of women and other minorities.

Now that education has been held constant, is the remaining gap caused by discrimination? No, not necessarily. Table 3.1 uses only the amount of school-ing, not its quality. Racial minorities are more likely to attend inadequately financed schools. Some efforts have been made to eliminate disparities between school districts in the amount of wealth available to tax for school support, but with little success. The inequality of educational opportunity may seem less important in explaining sex discrimination. Although women usually are not segregated from men, educational institutions encourage talented women to enter fields that pay less (nursing or elementary education) than other occupa-tions requiring similar amounts of training.

## Eliminating Discrimination

Two main agents of social change work to reduce discrimination: voluntary associations organized to solve racial and ethnic problems and the federal government, including the courts. The two are closely related: Most efforts ini-tiated by the government were urged by associations or organizations repre-senting minority groups, following vigorous protests against racism by African Americans. Resistance to social inequality by subordinate groups has been the key to change. Rarely has any government of its own initiative sought to end discrimination based on such criteria as race, ethnicity, and gender.

All racial and ethnic groups of any size are represented by private organi-zations that are to some degree trying to end discrimination. Some groups originated in the first half of the twentieth century, but most have been founded since World War II or have become significant forces in bringing about change only since then. These include church organizations, fraternal social groups, minor political parties, and legal defense funds, as well as more militant organizations operating under the scrutiny of law enforcement agencies. The purposes, membership, successes, and failures of these resis-tance organizations dedicated to eliminating discrimination are discussed throughout this book.

Government action toward eliminating discrimination is also recent. An-tidiscrimination actions have been taken by each branch of the government: the executive, the judicial, and the legislative.

The first antidiscrimination action at the executive level was President Franklin D. Roosevelt's 1943 creation of the Fair Employment Practices Com-mission (FEPC), which handled thousands of complaints of discrimination, mostly from African Americans, despite strong opposition by powerful eco-nomic and political leaders and many southern Whites. The FEPC had little

Relatively few workers are hired due to affirmative action pressure, yet many minority workers are viewed by their colleagues at work as taking the place of someone "more qualified."

actual power. It had no authority to compel employers to stop discriminating but could only ask for voluntary compliance. Its jurisdiction was limited to federal government employees, federal contractors, and labor unions. State and local governments and any business without a federal contract were not covered. Furthermore, the FEPC never enjoyed vigorous support from the White House, was denied adequate funds, and was part of larger agencies that were hostile to the commission's existence. This weak antidiscrimination agency was finally dropped in 1946, to be succeeded by an even weaker one in 1948.

The judiciary, charged with interpreting laws and the U.S. Constitution, has a much longer history of involvement in the rights of racial, ethnic, and religious minorities. However, its early decisions protected the rights of the dominant group, as in the 1857 U.S. Supreme Court's *Dred Scott* decision, which ruled that slaves remained slaves even when living or traveling in states where slavery was illegal. Not until the 1940s did the Supreme Court revise earlier decisions and begin to grant African Americans the same rights as those held by Whites. The 1954 *Brown v. Board of Education* decision, which stated that "separate but equal" facilities, including education, were unconstitutional, heralded a new series of rulings, arguing that distinguishing between races in order to segregate was inherently unconstitutional.

It was assumed incorrectly by many that *Brown* and other judicial actions would lead quickly to sweeping change. In fact, little change occurred initially, and resistance to racism continued. The immediate effect of many court rulings was minimal because the executive branch and the Congress did not want to violate the principle of **states' rights**, which holds that each state is sovereign in most of its affairs and has the right to order them without interference from the federal government. In other words, supporters of states' rights felt that the federal government had to allow state governments to determine how soon the rights of African Americans would be protected. Gradually, U.S. society became more committed to the rights of individuals. Legislation in the 1960s committed the federal government to protecting civil rights actively rather than merely leaving action up to state and local officials.

The most important legislative effort to eradicate discrimination was the Civil Rights Act of 1964. This act led to the establishment of the Equal Employment Opportunity Commission (EEOC), which had the power to investigate complaints against employers and to recommend action to the Department of Justice. If the Justice Department sued and discrimination was found, the court could order appropriate compensation. The act covered employment practices of all businesses with more than 25 employees and nearly all employment agencies and labor unions. A 1972 amendment broadened the coverage to employers with as few as 15 employees.

The act also prohibited different voting registration standards for White and Black voting applicants. It also prohibited discrimination in public accommodations—that is, hotels, motels, restaurants, gasoline stations, and amusement parks. Publicly owned facilities, such as parks, stadiums, and swimming pools, were also prohibited from discriminating. Another important provision forbade discrimination in all federally supported programs and institutions, such as hospitals, colleges, and road construction projects.

The Civil Rights Act of 1964 covered discrimination based on race, color, creed, national origin, and sex. Although the inclusion of gender in employment criteria had been prohibited in the federal civil service since 1949, most laws and most groups pushing for change showed little concern about sex discrimination. There was little precedent for attention to sex discrimination even at the state level. Only Hawaii and Wisconsin had enacted laws against sex discrimination before 1964. As first proposed, the Civil Rights Act did not include mention of gender. One day before the final vote, opponents of the measure offered an amendment on gender bias in an effort to defeat the entire act. The act did pass with prohibition against sex bias included, an event that can only be regarded as a milestone for women seeking equal employment rights with men.

The Civil Rights Act of 1964 was not perfect. Since 1964, several acts and amendments to the original act have been added to cover the many areas of discrimination it left untouched, such as criminal justice and housing. Even in areas singled out for enforcement in the Civil Rights Act of 1964, discrimination still occurs. Federal agencies charged with its enforcement complain that they are underfunded or are denied wholehearted support by the White House. Also, regardless of how much the EEOC may want to act in a particular case, the person who alleges discrimination has to pursue the complaint over a long time, marked by long periods of inaction. Despite these efforts, devastating forms of discrimination persist. African Americans, Latinos, and others fall victim to redlining. **Redlining** is the pattern of discrimination against people trying to buy homes in minority and racially changing neighborhoods. Research finds that in 25 metropolitan areas, housing agents showed fewer housing units to Blacks and Latinos, steered them to minority neighborhoods, and gave them far less assistance in finding housing that met their needs. The concept of redlining is now being applied to areas other than homebuying. People living in predominantly minority neighborhoods have found that service deliverers refuse to go to their area. In one case that attracted national attention, in 1997, Kansas City's Pizza Hut refused to deliver 40 pizzas to an honor program at a high school in an all-Black neighborhood. A Pizza Hut spokesperson called the neighborhood unsafe and said that almost every city has "restricted areas" to which the company will not deliver. This admission was particularly embarrassing because the high school already had a $170,000-a-year contract with Pizza Hut to deliver pizzas as a part of their school lunch program.

Service redlining covers everything from parcel deliveries to repair people as well as food deliveries. The red pencil appears not be have been set aside in cities throughout the United (Fuller 1998; Rusk 2001; Schwartz 2001; Turner et al. 2002; Yinger 1995).

Although civil rights laws often have established rights for other minorities, the Supreme Court made them explicit in two 1987 decisions involving groups other than African Americans. In the first of the two cases, an Iraqi American professor asserted that he had been denied tenure because of his Arab origins; in the second, a Jewish congregation brought suit for damages in response to the defacing of its synagogue with derogatory symbols. The Supreme Court ruled unanimously that, in effect, any member of an ethnic minority may sue under federal prohibitions against discrimination. These decisions paved the way for almost all racial and ethnic groups to invoke the Civil Rights Act of 1964 (Taylor 1987).

A particularly insulting form of discrimination seemed finally to be on its way out in the late 1980s. Many social clubs had limitations forbidding membership to minorities, Jews, and women. For years, exclusive clubs argued that they were merely selecting friends, but, in fact, a principal function of these clubs is as a forum to transact business. Denial of membership meant more than the inability to attend a luncheon; it also seemed to exclude one from part of the marketplace, as Lawrence Otis Graham observed at the beginning of this chapter. The Supreme Court ruled unanimously in the 1988 case, *New York State Clubs Association v. City of New York,* that states and cities may ban sex discrimination by large private clubs where business lunches and similar activities take place. Although the ruling does not apply to all clubs and leaves the issue of racial and ethnic barriers unresolved, it did chip away at the arbitrary exclusiveness of private groups (Taylor 1988).

A remaining area of discrimination is the legal provision allowing private clubs to set exclusionary standards. Professional atheletes such as Tiger Woods and Venus and Serena Williams have brought attention to a practice that still continues today.

Memberships and restrictive organizations remain perfectly legal. The rise to national attention of professional golfer Tiger Woods, of mixed Native American, African, and Asian ancestry, made the public aware that there were at least twenty-three golf courses he would be prohibited from playing by virtue of race. In 2002, women's groups tried unsuccessfully to have the golf champion speak out as the Master's and British Open played on courses closed to women as members (Scott 2003).

The inability of the Civil Rights Act, similar legislation, and court decisions to end discrimination does not result entirely from poor financial and political support, although they played a role. The number of federal employees assigned to investigate and prosecute bias cases is insufficient. Many discriminatory practices, such as those described as institutional discrimination, are seldom subject to legal action.

## Environmental Justice

Discrimination takes many forms and is not necessarily apparent, even when its impact can be far reaching. Take the example of Kennedy Heights, a well-kept working-class neighborhood nestled in southeastern Houston. This community faces a real threat, and it is not from crime or drugs. The threat they

The location of health hazards near minority and low-income neighborhoods is regarded as a concern of environmental justice. Pictured here is a youth basketball court next to an oil refinery in Norco, Louisiana, that has been dubbed "cancer alley."

fear is under their feet, in the form of three oil pits abandoned by Gulf Oil in 1927. The residents, most of whom are African American, argue that they have suffered high rates of cancer, lupus, and other illnesses because the chemicals from the oil fields poison their water supply. The residents first sued Chevron USA in 1985, and the case is still making its way through the courtrooms of no less than six states and the federal judiciary.

Lawyers and other representatives for the residents say that the oil company is guilty of environmental racism because it knowingly allowed a predominantly Black housing development to be built on the contaminated land. They are able to support this charge with documents, including a 1954 memorandum from an appraiser who suggested that the oil pits be drained of any toxic substances and the land filled for "low-cost houses for White occupancy." When the land did not sell right away, an oil company official in a 1967 memorandum suggested a tax-free land exchange with a developer who intended to use the land for "Negro residents and commercial development." For this latter intended use by African Americans, there was no mention of environmental cleanup of the land. The oil company counters that it just assumed the developer would do the necessary cleanup of the pits (Maning 1997; Verhovek 1997).

The conflict perspective sees the case of the Houston suburb as one in which pollution harms minority groups disproportionately. **Environmental justice** refers to the efforts to ensure that hazardous substances are controlled so that all communities receive protection regardless of race or socioeconomic circumstance. After the Environmental Protection Agency (EPA) and other organizations documented discrimination in the locating of hazardous waste sites, an Executive Order was issued in 1994 that requires all federal agencies to ensure that low-income and minority communities have access to better information about their environment and have an opportunity to participate in shaping government policies that affect their community's health. Initial efforts to implement the policy have met widespread opposition, including criticism from some proponents of economic development who argue that the guidelines unnecessarily delay or block altogether locating new industrial sites.

Sociologist Robert Bullard (1990) has shown that low-income communities and areas with significant minority populations are more likely to be adjacent to waste sites than are affluent White communities. Undergraduate student researchers at Occidental College in California found in 1995 that the poor, African Americans, Latinos, Asian Americans, and Native Americans were especially likely to be living near Los Angeles County's 82 potential environmental hazards. Another study in 2001 also showed the higher probability that people of color live closer to sources of air pollution. Yet a third study, released in 2003, found that grade schools in Florida nearer environmental hazards are disproportionately Black or Latino. People of color jeopardized by environmental problems also lack the resources and political muscle to do something about it (Institutes of Medicine 1999; Moffat 1995; Polakovic 2001; Streteksy and Lynch 2002).

Issues of environmental justice are not limited to metropolitan areas. Another continuing problem is abuse of Native American reservation land. Many American Indian leaders are concerned that tribal lands are too often regarded as dumping grounds for toxic waste that go to the highest bidder. On

So desperate are the economic conditions of isolated Indian tribes that they often seek out questionable forms of economic development. The Skull Valley Goshute Indian Reservation in Utah is trying to attract a nuclear waste dump but local and state officials are trying to block this possibility.

the other hand, the economic devastation faced by some tribes in isolated areas has led one tribe in Utah to actually seek out becoming a depot for discarded nuclear waste (*New York Times* 2005a; Skull Valley Goshutes 2006).

As with other aspects of discrimination, experts disagree. There is controversy within the scientific community over the potential hazards of some of the problems, and there is even some opposition within the subordinate communities being affected. This complexity of the issues in terms of social class and race is apparent, as some observers question the wisdom of an executive order that slows economic development coming to areas in dire need of employment opportunities. On the other hand, some counter that such businesses typically employ few less-skilled workers and only make the environment less livable for those left behind. Despite such varying viewpoints, environmental justice is an excellent example of resistance and change in the 1990s that could not have been foreseen by the civil rights workers of the 1950s.

# Affirmative Action

**Affirmative action** is the positive effort to recruit subordinate-group members, including women, for jobs, promotions, and educational opportunities. The phrase affirmative action first appeared in an executive order issued by President Kennedy in 1961. The order called for contractors to "take affirmative action to ensure that applicants are employed, and that employees are treated during employment, without regard to their race, creed, color, or national origin." However, at this early time, no enforcement procedures were specified. Six years later, the order was amended to prohibit discrimination on the basis of sex, but affirmative action was still defined vaguely.

Today, affirmative action has become a catch-all term for racial preference programs and goals. It has also become a lightning rod for opposition to any programs that suggest special consideration of women or racial minorities.

## Affirmative Action Explained

Affirmative action has been viewed as an important tool for reducing institutional discrimination. Whereas previous efforts were aimed at eliminating individual acts of discrimination, federal measures under the heading of affirmative action have been aimed at procedures that deny equal opportunities, even if they are not intended to be overtly discriminatory. This policy has been implemented to deal with both the current discrimination and the past discrimination outlined earlier in this chapter.

Affirmative action has been aimed at institutional discrimination in such areas as:

- Height and weight requirements that are unnecessarily geared to the physical proportions of White men without regard to the actual characteristics needed to perform the job and therefore exclude women and some minorities.

- Seniority rules, when applied to jobs historically held only by White men, that make more recently hired minorities and females more subject to layoff—the "last hired, first fired" employee—and less eligible for advancement.

- Nepotism-based membership policies of some unions that exclude those who are not relatives of members, who, because of past employment practices, are usually White.

- Restrictive employment leave policies, coupled with prohibitions on part-time work or denials of fringe benefits to part-time workers, that make it difficult for the heads of single-parent families, most of whom are women, to get and keep jobs and also meet the needs of their families.

- Rules requiring that only English be spoken at the workplace, even when not a business necessity, which result in discriminatory employment practices toward people whose primary language is not English.

- Standardized academic tests or criteria geared to the cultural and educational norms of middle-class or White men when these are not relevant predictors of successful job performance.

- Preferences shown by law and medical schools in admitting children of wealthy and influential alumni, nearly all of whom are White.

- Credit policies of banks and lending institutions that prevent the granting of mortgages and loans in minority neighborhoods or prevent the granting of credit to married women and others who have previously been denied the opportunity to build good credit histories in their own names.

Employers have also been cautioned against asking leading questions in interviews, such as "Did you know you would be the first Black to supervise all Whites in that factory?" or "Does your husband mind your working on weekends?" Furthermore, the lack of minority-group (Blacks, Asians, Native Americans, and Hispanics) or female employees may in itself represent evidence for a case of unlawful exclusion (Commission on Civil Rights 1981).

## The Legal Debate

How far can an employer go in encouraging women and minorities to apply for a job before it becomes unlawful discrimination against White men? Since the late 1970s, a number of bitterly debated cases on this difficult aspect of affirmative action have reached the U.S. Supreme Court. The most significant cases are summarized in Table 3.2. Furthermore, as we will see, the debate has moved into party politics.

In the 1978 *Bakke* case (*Regents of the University of California v. Bakke*), by a narrow 5–4 vote, the Court ordered the medical school of the University of California at Davis to admit Allan Bakke, a qualified White engineer who

## Table 3.2  Key Decisions on Affirmative Action

In a series of split and often very close decisions, the Supreme Court has expressed a variety of reservations in specific situations.

| Year | Favorable/ Unfavorable to Policy | Case | Vote | Ruling |
|------|--------------------------------|------|------|--------|
| 1971 | + | *Griggs v. Duke Power Co.* | 9–0 | Private employers must provide a remedy where minorities were denied opportunities, even if unintentional. |
| 1978 | − | *Regents of the University of California v. Bakke* | 5–4 | Prohibited specific number of places for minorities in college admissions. |
| 1979 | + | *United Steelworkers of America v. Weber* | 5–2 | Okay for union to favor minorities in special training programs. |
| 1984 | − | *Firefighters Local Union No 1784 (Memphis, TN) v. Stotts* | 6–1 | Seniority means recently hired minorities may be laid off first in staff reductions. |
| 1986 | + | *International Association of Firefighters v. City of Cleveland* | 6–3 | May promote minorities over more senior Whites. |
| 1986 | + | *New York City v. Sheet Metal* | 5–4 | Approved specific quota of minority workers for union. |
| 1987 | + | *United States v. Paradise* | 5–4 | Endorsed quotas for promotions of state troopers. |
| 1987 | + | *Johnson v. Transportation Agency, Santa Clara, CA* | 6–3 | Approved preference in hiring for minorities and women over better-qualified men and Whites. |
| 1989 | − | *Richmond v. Croson Company* | 6–3 | Ruled a 30 percent set-aside program for minority contractors unconstitutional. |
| 1989 | − | *Martin v. Wilks* | 5–4 | Ruled Whites may bring reverse discrimination claims against court-approved affirmative action plans. |
| 1990 | + | *Metro Broadcasting v. FCC* | 5–4 | Supported federal programs aimed at increasing minority ownership of broadcast licenses. |

*(continued)*

**Table 3.2   (continued)**

| Year | Favorable/ Unfavorable to Policy | Case | Vote | Ruling |
|---|---|---|---|---|
| 1995 | − | *Adarand Constructors Inc. v. Peña* | 5–4 | Benefits based on race are constitutional only if narrowly defined to accomplish a compelling interest. |
| 1996 | − | *Texas v. Hopwood* | * | Let stand a lower court decision covering Louisiana, Mississippi, and Texas that race could not be used in college admissions. |
| 2003 | + | *Grutter v. Bollinger* | 5–4 | Race can be a factor in admissions at the University of Michigan Law School. |
| 2003 | − | *Gratz v. Bollinger* | 6–3 | Cannot use a strict formula awarding advantage based on race for admissions to the University of Michigan. |

*5th U.S. Circuit Court of Appeals decision.

had originally been denied admission solely on the basis of his race. The justices ruled that the school had violated Bakke's constitutional rights by establishing a fixed quota system for minority students. However, the Court added that it was constitutional for universities to adopt flexible admission programs that use race as one factor in making decisions.

Colleges and universities responded with new policies designed to meet the *Bakke* ruling while broadening opportunities for traditionally underrepresented minority students. However, in 1996 the Supreme Court allowed a lower court decision to stand that affirmative action programs for African American and Mexican American students at the University of Texas law school were unconstitutional. The ruling effectively prohibited schools in the lower court's jurisdiction of Louisiana, Mississippi, and Texas from taking race into account in admissions. In 2003, the Supreme Court made two rulings concerning the admissions policies at the University of Michigan. In one case involving the law school, the Court upheld the right of the school to use applicants' race as criteria for admission decisions but found against a strict admissions formula awarding points to minority applicants who applied to

SIGNE
*PHILADELPHIA DAILY NEWS*
Philadelphia
USA

the university's undergraduate school. Given the various legal actions, further challenges to affirmative action can be expected (Greenhouse 2003).

Has affirmative action actually helped alleviate employment inequality on the basis of race and gender? This is a difficult question to answer, given the complexity of the labor market and the fact that there are other antidiscrimination measures, but it does appear that affirmative action has had significant impact in the sectors where it has been applied. Sociologist Barbara Reskin (1998) reviewed available studies looking at workforce composition in terms of race and gender in light of affirmative action policies. She found that gains in minority employment can be attributed to affirmative action policies. This includes both firms mandated to follow affirmative action guidelines and those that took them on voluntarily. There is also evidence that some earnings gains can be attributed to affirmative action. Economists M. V. Lee Badgett and Heidi Hartmann (1995), reviewing twenty-six other research studies, came to similar conclusions: Affirmative action and other federal compliance programs have had a modest impact, but it is difficult to assess, given larger economic changes such as recessions or the rapid increase in women in the paid labor force.

## Reverse Discrimination

While researchers debated the merit of affirmative action, the general public—particularly Whites but also some affluent African Americans and Hispanics—questioned the wisdom of the program. Particularly strident were the charges of reverse discrimination: that government actions cause better-qualified White men to be bypassed in favor of women and minority men. **Reverse discrimination** is an emotional term because it conjures up the notion that somehow women and minorities will subject White men in the United States to the same treatment received by minorities during the last three centuries. Increasingly, critics of affirmative action call for color-blind policies that would end affirmative action and, they argue, allow all people to be judged fairly. Of major significance, often overlooked in public debates, is that a color-blind policy implies a very limited role for the state in addressing social inequality between racial and ethnic groups (Kahng 1978; Skrentny 1996; Winant 1994).

Is it possible to have color-blind policies in the United States as we move into the twenty-first century? Supporters of affirmative action contend that as long as businesses rely on informal social networks, personal recommendations, and family ties, White men will have a distinct advantage built on generations of being in positions of power. Furthermore, an end to affirmative action should also mean an end to the many programs that give advantages to certain businesses, homeowners, veterans, farmers, and others. Most of these preference holders are White (Kilson 1995; Mack 1996).

Consequently, by the 1990s, affirmative action had emerged as an increasingly important issue in state and national political campaigns. Generally, discussion focused on the use of quotas in hiring practices. Supporters of affirmative action argue that hiring goals establish "floors" for minority inclusion but do not exclude truly qualified candidates from any group. Opponents insist that these "targets" are, in fact, quotas that lead to reverse discrimination.

The state of California, in particular, was a battleground for this controversial issue. The California Civil Rights Initiative was placed on the ballot in 1996 as a referendum to amend the state constitution and prohibit any programs that give preference to women and minorities for college admission, employment, promotion, or government contracts. Overall, 54 percent of the voters backed the state proposition, with 61 percent of men in favor compared with only 48 percent of women. Whites, who represented 74 percent of the voters, voted in favor of the measure overwhelmingly, with 63 percent backing Proposition 209. This compares with 26 percent of African Americans, 24 percent of Hispanics, and 39 percent of Asian Americans favoring the end of affirmative action in state-operated institutions. Obviously, the voters—Whites and men—who perceived themselves as least likely to benefit from affirmative action overwhelmingly favored Proposition 209.

Legal challenges continue concerning Proposition 209, which is being implemented unevenly throughout the state. Much of the attention has focused on the impact that reducing racial preference programs will have in law and medical schools, in which competition for admission is very high. The courts have upheld the measures, and in 1998 voters in Washington state passed a similar anti–affirmative action measure (Dolan 2000).

# The Glass Ceiling

We have been talking primarily about racial and ethnic groups as if they have uniformly failed to keep pace with Whites. Although that is accurate, there are tens of thousands of people of color who have matched and even exceeded Whites in terms of income. For example, in 2000, more than 815,000 Black households and more than 556,000 Hispanic households earned more than $100,000. What can we say about affluent members of subordinate groups in the United States (Bureau of the Census 2001e)?

Prejudice does not necessarily end with wealth. Black newspaper columnist De Wayne Wickham (1993) wrote of the subtle racism he had experienced. He heard a White clerk in a supermarket ask a White customer whether she knew the price of an item the computer would not scan; when the problem occurred while the clerk was ringing up Wickham's groceries, she called for a price check. Affluent subordinate-group members routinely report being blocked as they move toward the first-class section aboard airplanes or seek service in upscale stores. Another journalist, Ellis Cose (1993), has called these insults the soul-destroying slights to affluent minorities that lead to the "rage of a privileged class."

Discrimination persists for even the educated and qualified from the best family backgrounds. As subordinate-group members are able to compete successfully, they sometimes encounter attitudinal or organizational bias that prevents them from reaching their full potential. They have confronted what has come to be called the **glass ceiling**. This refers to the barrier that blocks the promotion of a qualified worker because of gender or minority membership (Figure 3.4). Often, people entering nontraditional areas of employment become marginalized and are made to feel uncomfortable, much like the situation of immigrants who feel a part of two cultures, as we discussed in Chapter 1.

The reasons for glass ceilings are as many as the occurrences. It may be that one Black or one woman vice president is regarded as enough, so the second potential candidate faces a block to movement up through management. Decision makers may be concerned that their clientele will not trust them if they have too many people of color or may worry that a talented woman could become overwhelmed with her duties as a mother and wife and thus perform poorly in the workplace.

Concern about women and minorities climbing a broken ladder led to the formation in 1991 of the Glass Ceiling Commission, with the U.S. Secretary of Labor chairing the 21-member group. Initially, it regarded some of the glass ceiling barriers as:

- Lack of management commitment to establishing systems, policies, and practices for achieving workplace diversity and upward mobility.
- Pay inequities for work of equal or comparable value.
- Sex-, race-, and ethnicity-based stereotyping and harassment.

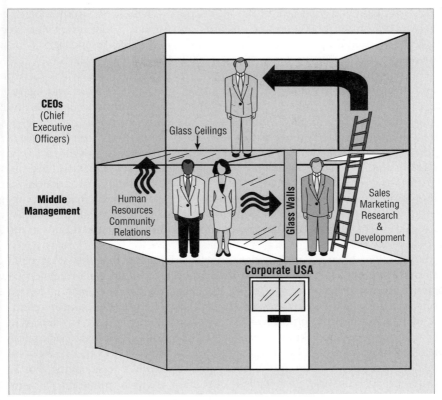

**Figure 3.4** Glass Ceilings and Glass Walls

Women and minority men are moving up in corporations but encounter glass ceilings that block entry to top positions. In addition, they face glass walls that block lateral moves to areas from which executives are promoted.

- Unfair recruitment practices.
- Lack of family-friendly workplace policies.
- "Parent-track" policies that discourage parental leave policies.
- Limited opportunities for advancement to decision-making positions.

These barriers contribute to women not moving into the ultimate decision-making positions in the nation's corporate giants.

This significant underrepresentation of women and minority males in managerial positions results in large part from the presence of glass ceilings. Sociologist Max Weber wrote over a hundred years ago that the privileged class monopolizes the purchase of high-priced consumer goods and wields the power to grant or withhold opportunity from others. To grasp just how White and male the membership of this elite group is, consider the following: Eighty-two percent of the 11,500 people who serve on the boards of directors of Fortune 1,000 corporations are non-Hispanic White males. For every 82 White men on these boards, there are 2 Latinos, 2 Asian Americans, 3 African Americans, and 11 White women (Strauss 2002; Weber [1913–1922] 1947).

Glass ceilings are not the only barrier. There are also glass walls. Catalyst, a nonprofit research organization, conducted interviews in 1992 and again in 2001 with senior and middle managers from larger corporations. The study found that even before glass ceilings are encountered, women and racial and ethnic minorities face **glass walls** that keep them from moving laterally. Specifically, the study found that women tend to be placed in staff or support positions in areas such as public relations and human resources and are often directed away from jobs in core areas such as marketing, production, and sales. Women are assigned to, and therefore trapped in, jobs that reflect their stereotypical helping nature and encounter glass walls that cut off access to jobs that might lead to broader experience and advancement (Catalyst 2001; Lopez 1992).

Researchers have documented a differential impact that the glass ceiling has on White males. It appears that men who enter traditionally female occupations are more likely to rise to the top. Male elementary teachers become principals and male nurses become supervisors. The **glass escalator** refers to the male advantage experienced in occupations dominated by women. While females may become tokens when they enter traditionally male occupations, men are more likely to be advantaged when they move out of sex-typical jobs. In summary, women and minority men confront a glass ceiling that limits upward mobility and glass walls reduce their ability to move into fast-track jobs that lead to the highest reaches of the corporate executive suite. Meanwhile, men who do choose to enter female-dominated occupations are often rewarded with promotions and positions of responsibility coveted by their fellow female workers (Budig 2002; Cognard-Black 2004).

## Conclusion

Discrimination takes its toll, whether a person who is discriminated against is part of the informal economy or not. Even members of minority groups who are not today being overtly discriminated against continue to fall victim to past discrimination. We have also identified the costs of discrimination to members of the privileged group. The attitudes of Whites and even members of minority groups themselves are influenced by the images they have of racial and ethnic groups. These images come from what has been called statistical discrimination,

which causes people to act based on stereotypes they hold and the actions of a few subordinate-group members.

From the conflict perspective, it is not surprising to find the widespread presence of the informal economy proposed by the dual labor market model and even an underclass. Derrick Bell (1994), an African American law professor, has made the sobering assertion that "racism is permanent." He contends that the attitudes of dominant Whites prevail, and society is willing to advance programs on behalf of subordinate groups only when they coincide with needs as perceived by those Whites.

The surveys presented in Chapter 2 show gradual acceptance of the earliest efforts to eliminate discrimination, but that support is failing, especially as it relates to affirmative action. Indeed, concerns about doing something about alleged reverse discrimination are as likely to be voiced as concerns about racial or gender discrimination or glass ceilings and glass walls.

Institutional discrimination remains a formidable challenge in the United States. Attempts to reduce discrimination by attacking institutional discrimination have met with staunch resistance. Partly as a result of this outcry from some of the public, especially White Americans, the federal government gradually deemphasized its affirmative action efforts in the 1980s and 1990s. As we turn to examine the various groups that make up the American people, through generations of immigration and religious diversity, look for the types of programs designed to reduce prejudice and discrimination that were discussed here. Most of the material in this chapter has been about racial groups, especially Black and White Americans. It would be easy to see intergroup hostility as a racial phenomenon, but that would be incorrect. Throughout the history of the United States, relations between some White groups have been characterized by resentment and violence. The next two chapters examine the ongoing legacy of immigration and the nature and relations of White ethnic groups.

## Key Terms

| | | |
|---|---|---|
| absolute deprivation  88 | glass escalator  116 | redlining  104 |
| affirmative action  108 | glass wall  116 | relative deprivation  88 |
| discrimination  88 | informal economy  95 | reverse discrimination  113 |
| double jeopardy  99 | institutional discrimination | states' rights  103 |
| dual labor market  96 | 92 | total discrimination  89 |
| environmental justice  106 | irregular or underground | |
| glass ceiling  114 | economy  95 | |

## Review Questions

1. Why might people still feel disadvantaged, even though their incomes are rising and their housing circumstances have improved?
2. Why does institutional discrimination sometimes seem less objectionable than individual discrimination?
3. In what way does an industrial society operate on several economic levels?
4. Why are questions raised about affirmative action while inequality persists?
5. Distinguish between glass ceilings and glass walls. How do they differ from more obvious forms of discrimination in employment?

## Critical Thinking

1. Discrimination can take many forms. Consider the college you attend. Select a case of discrimination that you think just about everyone would agree is wrong. Then

describe another incident in which the alleged discrimination was of a more subtle form. Who is likely to condemn and who is likely to overlook such situations?

2. Resistance is a continuing theme of intergroup race relations. Discrimination implies the oppression of a group, but how can discrimination also unify the oppressed group to resist such unequal treatment? How can acceptance, or integration, for example, weaken the sense of solidarity within a group?

3. Voluntary associations such as the NAACP and government units such as the courts have been important vehicles for bringing about a measure of social justice. In what ways can the private sector—corporations and businesses—also work to bring about an end to discrimination?

## Internet Connections—Research Navigator™

Follow the instructions found on page 42 of this text to access the features of Research Navigator™. Once at the website, enter your Login Name and Password. Then, to use the ContentSelect database, enter keywords such as "informal economy," "affirmative action," and "glass ceiling," and the research engine will supply relevant and recent scholarly and popular press publications. Use the New York Times Search-by-Subject Archive to find recent news articles related to sociology, and the Link Library feature to locate relevant Web links organized by the key terms associated with this chapter.

# 4

# Immigration and the United States

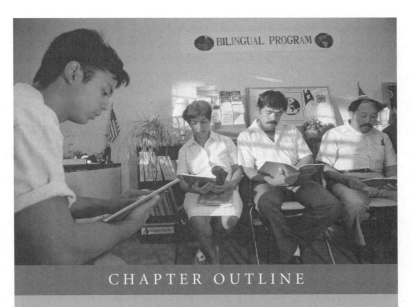

BILINGUAL PROGRAM

## CHAPTER OUTLINE

---------------------------------{ HIGHLIGHTS }--------------------------------

The diversity of the American people is unmistakable evidence of the variety of places from which immigrants have come. Yet each succeeding generation of immigrants found itself being reluctantly accepted, at best, by the descendants of earlier arrivals. The Chinese were the first immigrant group to be singled out for restriction, with the passage of the 1882 Exclusion Act. The initial Chinese immigrants became scapegoats for the sagging U.S. economy in the last half of the nineteenth century. Growing fears that too many non-American types were immigrating motivated the creation of the national origin system and the quota acts of the 1920s. These acts gave preference to certain nationalities, until the passage of the Immigration and Naturalization Act in 1965 ended that practice. Many immigrants are transnationals who still maintain close ties to their country of origin, sending money back, keeping current with political events, and making frequent return trips. Concern about both illegal and legal immigration has continued through today with increased attention in the aftermath of the September 11, 2001, terrorist attacks. Restrictionist sentiment has grown, and debates rage over whether immigrants, even legal ones, should receive services such as education, government-subsidized health care, and welfare. Controversy also continues to surround the policy of the United States toward refugees.

Two very different experiences of coming of age in the United States point to the different lives of immigrants in the United States.

Growing up in Pennington, New Jersey, Pareha Ahmed watched Bollywood videos and enthusiastically attended with her parents the annual Pakistan Independence Day Parade in New York City. By middle school, such outward expressions of her Pakistani heritage had become uncool. She tried to fit in by dying her hair blond, wearing hazel contact lenses, and even avoiding home-cooked foods that might give her a distinctive odor. In college she began to embrace her heritage and the diversity of cultures of her fellow students. Now 23, she gets excited about not only celebrating her Pakistani heritage's special days but those of her non-Asian friends such as the Islamic holiday Id-al-Fitr and Christmas—occasions never celebrated in her family's home.

Fernando Fernandez, Jr., of Gila Bend, Arizona, speaks with pride how his father gained legal entry to the United States more then fifty years ago. Three years old at the time, Fernandez became a citizen and is now married with two children. While holding down two jobs—one as a purchasing agent at a nearby Air Force base and the other as a janitor—he has sought to sponsor his aunt and her son to come to the United States legally. Several years and after submitting lots of documents, they are here now. He's financially responsible for them, and therefore they cannot seek public assistance or government medical assistance. Pondering the presence around him of many illegal immigrants, he sees some unfairness but does not regret the trouble he and his father went to give them security in a new country (Bartlett and Steele 2004; Chu and Mustafa 2006).

These dramas being played out in Arizona and Pennsylvania illustrate the themes in immigration today. Immigrant labor is needed, but transition can be difficult, even if for immigrants individually it ultimately means a better life economically. For the next generation it gets a little easier and, for some, perhaps too easy as they begin to forget their family's heritage. Many come legally, applying for immigrant visas, but others enter illegally. In the United States we may not like lawbreakers, but often we seek services and low-priced products made by people who come here illegally. How do we control this immigration without violating the principle of free movement within the nation? How do we decide who enters? And how do we treat those who come here either legally or illegally?

The diversity of ethnic and racial backgrounds of Americans today is the living legacy of immigration. Except for descendants of Native Americans or of Africans brought here enslaved, today's population is entirely the product of people who chose to leave familiar places to come to a new country.

The social forces that cause people to emigrate are complex. The most important have been economic: financial failure in the old country and expectations of higher incomes and standards of living in the new land. Other factors include dislike of new regimes in their native lands, racial or religious bigotry, and a desire to reunite families. All these factors push people from their homelands and pull them to other nations such as the United States. Immigration into the United States, in particular, has been facilitated by cheap ocean transportation and by other countries' removal of restrictions on emigration.

## Patterns of Immigration

There have been three unmistakable patterns of immigration to the United States: The number of immigrants has fluctuated dramatically over time, largely due to government policy changes; settlement has not been uniform across the country but centered in certain regions and cities; and the source of immigrants has changed over time. We will first look at the historical picture of immigrant numbers.

Vast numbers of immigrants have come to the United States. Figure 4.1 in-dicates the high but fluctuating number of immigrants who have arrived during

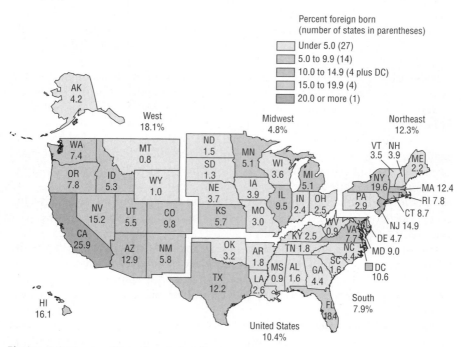

**Figure 4.1** Foreign-Born Population for States, 2000
*Source*: Census Bureau data in Bureau of the Census 2001a, 12.

every decade from the 1820s through the 1990s. The United States received the largest number of legal immigrants during the 1990s, but in the period from 1900 through 1910, the country was much smaller, so the numerical impact was even greater.

The reception given to these immigrants in this country has not always been friendly. Open bloodshed, restrictive laws, and the eventual return of almost one-third of immigrants and their children to their home countries attest to the uneasy feeling toward strangers who want to settle here.

Opinion polls in the United States generally show only about 10 percent of the population favoring increasing the number of legal immigrants and around 40 percent favoring a decrease, but the more emotional issue lately has been the policy toward illegal immigrants. While generally thinking it is a serious problem about which not enough is being done, people differ on whether the United States is better off for their presence and what should be done about those already here illegally. We will consider the thorny issue of illegal immigration and economic impact of immigration in general later (Davis et al. 2005; Tumulty 2006).

## Today's Foreign-Born Population

Before considering the sweep of past immigration policies, let's consider today's immigrant population. About 12 percent of the nation's people are foreign born; this proportion is between the high figure of 15 percent in 1890 and a low of 5 percent in 1970. By global comparisons, the foreign-born population in the United States is large but not unusual. While most industrial countries have a foreign population of around 5 percent, Canada's foreign population is 19 percent and Australia's is 25 percent.

As noted earlier, immigrants have not settled evenly across the nation. As shown in the map (Figure 4.2) six states—California, New York, Florida, Texas, New Jersey, and Illinois—account for 70 percent of the nation's total foreign-born population but less than 40 percent of the nation's total population.

Cities in these states are the focus of the foreign-born population. Almost half (43.3 percent) live in the central city of a metropolitan area, compared with about one-quarter (27.0 percent) of the nation's population. More than a third of residents in the cities of Miami, Los Angeles, San Francisco, San Jose, and New York City are now foreign born (Singer 2004).

The third pattern of immigration is that the source of immigrants has changed. As shown in Figure 4.3, the majority of today's 32.5 million foreign-born people are from Latin America. Primarily they came from Central America—more specifically, Mexico. By contrast, Europeans, who dominated the early settlement of the United States, now account for less than one in six of the foreign born today.

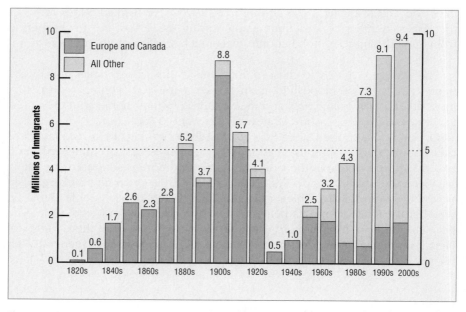

**Figure 4.2** Legal Migration in the United States, 1820 through 2010
*Sources*: Bureau of the Census 2005a, 11; Immigration and Naturalization Services 2002; and estimates by the author for the period 2000–2010.

## Early Immigration

European explorers of North America were soon followed by settlers, the first immigrants to the Western Hemisphere. The Spanish founded St. Augustine, Florida, in 1565, and the English founded Jamestown, Virginia, in 1607. Protestants from England emerged from the colonial period as the dominant force numerically, politically, and socially. The English accounted for 60 percent of the 3 million White Americans in 1790. Although exact statistics are lacking for the early years of the United States, the English were soon outnumbered by other nationalities, as the numbers of Scots-Irish and Germans, in particular, swelled. However, the English colonists maintained their dominant position, as Chapter 5 will examine.

Throughout U.S. history, immigration policy has been politically controversial. The policies of the English king, George III, were criticized in the Declaration of Independence for obstructing immigration to the colonies. Toward the end of the nineteenth century, the U.S. republic itself was criticized for enacting immigration restrictions. In the beginning, however, the country encouraged immigration. At first, legislation fixed the residence requirement for naturalization at five years, although briefly, under the Alien Act of 1798, it

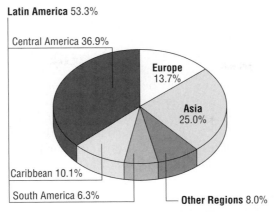

**Latin America** 53.3%

Central America 36.9%

Caribbean 10.1%

South America 6.3%

**Europe**
13.7%

**Asia**
25.0%

**Other Regions** 8.0%

**Figure 4.3** Foreign Born by World Regions of Birth
*Source*: Data for 2003 reported in 2004 in L. Larsen 2004.

was fourteen years, and so-called dangerous people could be expelled. Despite this brief harshness, immigration was unregulated through most of the 1800s, and naturalization was easily available.

Besides holding the mistaken belief that concerns about immigration are something new, we also assume that immigrants to the United States rarely reconsider their decision to come to a new country. Analysis of available records beginning in the early 1900s suggests that about 35 percent of all immigrants to the United States eventually emigrated back to their home country. The proportion varies, with the figures for some countries being much higher, but the overall pattern is clear: About one in three immigrants to this nation eventually chooses to return home (Wyman 1993).

## The Anti-Catholic Crusade

The relative absence of federal legislation from 1790 to 1881 does not mean that all new arrivals were welcomed. **Xenophobia** (the fear or hatred of strangers or foreigners) led naturally to **nativism** (beliefs and policies favoring native-born citizens over immigrants). Roman Catholics in general and the Irish in particular were among the first Europeans to be ill treated. Anti-Catholic feeling originated in Europe and was brought by the early Protestant immigrants. The Catholics of colonial America, although few, were subject to limits of their civil and religious rights.

From independence until around 1820, little evidence appeared of the anti-Catholic sentiment of colonial days, but the cry against Roman Catholicism grew as Irish immigration increased. Prominent citizens encouraged hatred of these new arrivals. Samuel F. B. Morse, inventor of the telegraph and an accomplished painter, wrote a strongly worded anti-Catholic work in 1834 titled *A Foreign Conspiracy Against the Liberties of the United States*. Morse felt that the Irish were "shamefully illiterate and without opinions of their own" (1835, 61). In the mind of the prejudiced people, the Irish were particularly unwelcome because they were Catholic. Many readily believed Morse's warning that the Pope planned to move the Vatican to the Mississippi River Valley (Silverman 2003).

This antagonism was not limited to harsh words. From 1834 to 1854, mob violence against Catholics across the country led to death, the burning of a Boston convent, the destruction of a Catholic church and the homes of Catholics, and the use of Marines and state militia to bring peace to U.S. cities as far west as St. Louis.

A frequent pattern saw minorities striking out against each other rather than at the dominant class. Irish Americans opposed the Emancipation Proclamation and the freeing of the slaves because they feared Blacks would compete for the unskilled work open to them. This fear was confirmed when free Blacks were used to break a longshoremen's strike in New York. Therefore, much of the Irish violence during the 1863 riot was directed against Blacks, not against the Whites, who were most responsible for the conditions in which the immigrants found themselves (Duff 1971; Warner 1968).

In retrospect, the reception given to the Irish is not difficult to understand. Many immigrated after the 1845–1848 potato crop failure and famine in Ireland. They fled not so much to a better life as from almost certain death. The Irish Catholics brought with them a celibate clergy, who struck the New England aristocracy as strange and reawakened old religious hatreds. The Irish were worse than Blacks, according to the dominant Whites, because unlike the slaves and even the freed Blacks, who "knew their place," the Irish did not suffer their maltreatment in silence. Employers balanced minorities by judiciously mixing immigrant groups to prevent unified action by the laborers. For the most part, nativist efforts only led the foreign born to emphasize their ties to Europe.

By the 1850s, nativism became an open political movement pledged to vote only for "native" Americans, to fight Catholicism, and to demand a 21-year naturalization period. Party members were instructed to divulge nothing about their program and to say that they knew nothing about it. As a result, they came to be called the Know-Nothings. Although the Know-Nothings soon vanished, the antialien mentality survived and occasionally became formally organized into such societies as the Ku Klux Klan in the 1860s and the anti-Catholic American Protective Association in the 1890s. Revivals of anti-Catholicism continued well into the twentieth century. However, the most dramatic outbreak of nativism in the nineteenth century was aimed at the Chinese. If there had been any doubt by the mid-1800s that the United States could harmoniously accommodate all, debate on the Chinese Exclusion Act would negatively settle the question once and for all (Gerber 1993; Wernick 1996).

Chinese workers, such as these pictured in 1844, played a major role in building railroads in the West.

## The Anti-Chinese Movement

Before 1851, official records show that only 46 Chinese had immigrated to the United States. Over the next thirty years, more than 200,000 came to this country, lured by the discovery of gold and the opening of job opportunities in the West. Overcrowding, drought, and warfare in China also encouraged them to take a chance in the United States. Another important factor was improved oceanic transportation; it was actually cheaper to travel from Hong Kong to San Francisco than from Chicago to San Francisco. The frontier communities of the West, particularly in California, looked on the Chinese as a valuable resource to fill manual jobs. As early as 1854, so many Chinese wanted to emigrate that ships had difficulty handling the volume.

In the 1860s, railroad work provided the greatest demand for Chinese labor, until the Union Pacific and Central Pacific railroads were joined at Promontory, Utah, in 1869. The Union Pacific relied primarily on Irish laborers, but 90 percent of the Central Pacific labor force was Chinese because Whites generally refused the backbreaking work over the Western terrain. Despite the contribution of the Chinese, White workers physically prevented them from attending the driving of the golden spike to mark the joining of the two railroads.

With the dangerous railroad work largely completed, people began to rethink the wisdom of encouraging Chinese to immigrate to do the work no one else would do. Reflecting their xenophobia, White settlers found the Chinese immigrants and their customs and religion difficult to understand. Indeed, few people actually tried to understand these immigrants from Asia. Although they had had no firsthand contact with Chinese Americans, Easterners and legislators were soon on the anti-Chinese bandwagon as they read sensationalized accounts of the lifestyle of the new arrivals.

Even before the Chinese immigrated, stereotypes of them and their customs were prevalent. American traders returning from China, European diplomats, and Protestant missionaries consistently emphasized the exotic and sinister aspects of life in China. The **sinophobes,** people with a fear of anything associated with China, appealed to the racist theory developed during the slavery controversy that non-Europeans were subhuman. Similarly, Americans were beginning to be more conscious of biological inheritance and disease, so it was not hard to conjure up fears of alien genes and germs. The only real challenge the anti-Chinese movement had was to convince people that the negative consequences of unrestricted Chinese immigration outweighed any possible economic gain. Perhaps briefly, racial prejudice had earlier been subordinated to industrial dependence on Chinese labor for the work that Whites shunned, but acceptance of Chinese was short-lived. The fear of the "yellow peril" overwhelmed any desire to know more about Asian people and their customs (Takaki 1989).

Another nativist fear of Chinese immigrants was based on the threat they posed as laborers. Californians, whose labor force felt the effects of the Chinese immigration first, found support throughout the nation as organized labor feared that the Chinese would be used as strikebreakers. By 1870, Chinese workers had been used for that purpose as far east as Massachusetts. When Chinese workers did unionize, they were not recognized by major labor organizations. Samuel Gompers, founder of the American Federation of Labor (AFL), consistently opposed any effort to assist Chinese workers and refused to consider having a union of Chinese restaurant employees admitted into the AFL. Gompers worked effectively to see future Chinese immigration ended and produced a pamphlet titled "Chinese Exclusion: Meat vs. Rice: American Manhood Against Asiatic Coolieism—Which Shall Survive?" (Gompers and Gustadt 1908; Hill 1967).

Employers were glad to pay the Chinese low wages, but laborers came to direct their resentment against the Chinese rather than against their compatriots' willingness to exploit the Chinese. Only a generation earlier, the same concerns had been felt about the Irish, but with the Chinese, the hostility reached new heights because of another factor.

Although many arguments were voiced, racial fears motivated the anti-Chinese movement. Race was the critical issue. The labor market fears were largely unfounded, and most advocates of restrictions at the time knew that. There was no possibility that Chinese would immigrate in numbers that would match those of Europeans at the time, so it is difficult to find an explanation other than racism for their fears (Winant 1994).

From the sociological perspective of conflict theory, we can explain how the Chinese immigrants were welcomed only when their labor was necessary to fuel growth in the United States. When that labor was no longer necessary, the welcome mat for the immigrants was withdrawn. Furthermore, as conflict theorists would point out, restrictions were not applied evenly: Americans focused on a specific nationality (the Chinese) to reduce the overall number of foreign workers in the nation. Because decision making at that time rested in the hands of the descendants of European immigrants, the steps to be taken were most likely to be directed against the least powerful: immigrants from China who, unlike Europeans seeking entry, had few allies among legislators and other policymakers.

In 1882 Congress enacted the Chinese Exclusion Act, which outlawed Chinese immigration for ten years. It also explicitly denied naturalization rights to the Chinese in the United States; that is, they were not allowed to become citizens. There was little debate in Congress, and discussion concentrated on how suspension of Chinese immigration could best be handled. No allowance was made for spouses and children to be reunited with their husbands and fathers in the United States. Only brief visits of Chinese government officials, teachers, tourists, and merchants were exempted.

The rest of the nineteenth century saw the remaining loopholes allowing Chinese immigration closed. Beginning in 1884, Chinese laborers were not allowed to legally enter the United States from any foreign place, a ban that lasted ten years. Two years later, the Statue of Liberty was dedicated, with a poem by Emma Lazarus inscribed on its base. To the Chinese, the poem welcoming the tired, the poor, and the huddled masses must have seemed a hollow mockery (Ryo 2006).

In 1892 Congress extended the Exclusion Act for another ten years and added that Chinese laborers had to obtain certificates of residence within a year or face deportation. After the turn of the century, the Exclusion Act was extended again. Two decades later, the Chinese were not alone; the list of people restricted by immigration policy expanded many times.

## Restrictionist Sentiment Increases

As Congress closed the door to Chinese immigration, the debate on restricting immigration turned in new directions. Prodded by growing anti-Japanese feelings, the United States entered into the so-called Gentlemen's Agreement, completed in 1908. Japan agreed to halt further immigration to the United States, and the United States agreed to end discrimination against the Japanese who had already arrived. The immigration ended, but anti-Japanese feelings continued. Americans were growing uneasy that the "new immigrants" would overwhelm the culture established by the "old immigrants." The earlier immigrants, if not Anglo-Saxon, were from similar groups such as the Scandinavians, the Swiss, and the French Huguenots. These people were more experienced in democratic political practices and had a greater affinity with the dominant Anglo-Saxon culture. By the end of the nineteenth century, however, more and more immigrants were neither English speaking nor Protestant and came from dramatically different cultures.

In 1917 Congress finally overrode President Wilson's veto and enacted an immigration bill that included the controversial literacy test. Critics of the bill, including Wilson, argued that illiteracy does not signify inherent incompetence but reflects lack of opportunity for instruction. Such arguments were not heeded, however. The act seemed innocent at first glance—it merely required immigrants to read 30 words in any language—but it was the first attempt to restrict immigration from Western Europe. The act also prohibited immigration from the South Sea islands and other parts of Asia not already excluded. Curiously, this law that closed the door on non-Anglo-Saxons permitted a waiver of the test if the immigrants came because of their home government's discrimination against their race (*New York Times* 1917a, 1917b).

## The National Origin System

Beginning in 1921, a series of measures was enacted that marked a new era in U.S. immigration policy. Whatever the legal language, the measures were drawn up to block the growing immigration from southern Europe, such as from Italy and Greece.

Anti-immigration sentiment, combined with the isolationism that followed World War I, caused Congress to severely restrict entry privileges not only of the Chinese and Japanese but of Europeans as well. The national origin system

Italian Americans aboard a ship arrive at Ellis Island.

was begun in 1921 and remained the basis of immigration policy until 1965. This system used the country of birth to determine whether a person could enter as a legal alien, and the number of previous immigrants and their descendants was used to set the group's annual immigration cap.

To understand the effect of the national origin system on immigration, it is necessary to clarify the quota system. The quotas were deliberately weighted in favor of immigration from northern Europe. Because of the ethnic composition of the country in 1920, the quotas placed severe restrictions on immigration from the rest of Europe and from other parts of the world. Immigration from the Western Hemisphere (i.e., Canada, Mexico, Central and South America, and the Caribbean) continued unrestricted. The quota for each nation was set at 3 percent of the number of people descended from each nationality recorded in the 1920 census. Once the statistical manipulations were completed, almost 70 percent of the quota for the Eastern Hemisphere went to just three countries: Great Britain, Ireland, and Germany.

The absurdities of the system soon became obvious, but it was nevertheless continued. British immigration had fallen sharply, so most of its quota of 65,000 went unfilled. However, the openings could not be transferred, even though countries such as Italy, with a quota of only 6,000, had 200,000 people who wanted to enter. However one rationalizes the purpose behind the act, the result was obvious: Any English person, regardless of skill and whether related to anyone already here, could enter the country more easily than, say, a Greek doctor whose children were U.S. citizens. The quota for Greece was 305, with the backlog of people wanting to come reaching 100,000.

By the end of the 1920s, annual immigration had dropped to one-fourth of its pre–World War I level. The worldwide economic depression of the 1930s decreased immigration still further. A brief upsurge in immigration just before World War II reflected the flight of Europeans from the oppression of expanding Nazi Germany. The war virtually ended transatlantic immigration. The era of the great European migration to the United States had been legislated out of existence.

## The 1965 Immigration and Naturalization Act

The national origin system was abandoned with the passage of the 1965 Immigration and Naturalization Act, signed into law by President Lyndon B. Johnson at the foot of the Statue of Liberty. The primary goals of the act were to reunite families and protect the U.S. labor market. The act also initiated restrictions on immigration from Latin America. After the act, immigration increased by one-third, but the act's influence was primarily on the composition rather than the size of immigration. The sources of immigrants now included Italy, Greece, Portugal, Mexico, the Philippines, the West Indies, and South America. The effect is apparent when we compare the changing sources of immigration over the last 180 years, as shown in Figure 4.4. The most recent period shows that Asian and Latin American immigrants combined to account for 81 percent of the people who were permitted entry. This contrasts sharply with early immigration, which was dominated by arrivals from Europe.

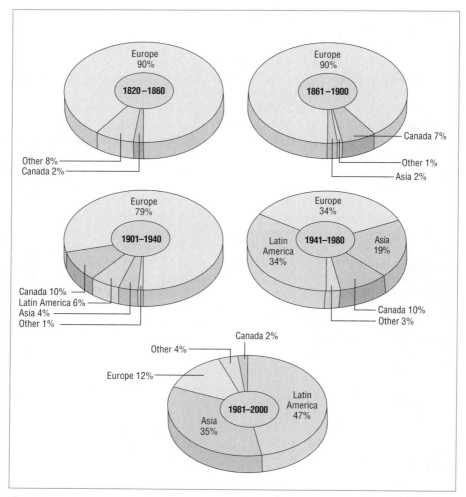

**Figure 4.4** Legal Immigrants Admitted to the United States by Region of Last Residence, 1820–2000
*Source*: Office of Immigration Statistics 2006: 10–13.

As reflected in the title of this act, the law set down the rules for becoming a citizen. **Naturalization** is the conferring of citizenship on a person after birth. The general conditions for becoming naturalized in the United States are:

- 18 years of age
- Continuous residence for at least five years (three years for the spouses of U.S. citizens)
- Good moral character as determined by the absence of conviction of selected criminal offenses

## Table 4.1  So You Want to Be a Citizen?

Try these sample questions from the naturalization test (answers below).

1. What do the stripes on the flag represent?
2. How many changes, or amendments, are there to the Constitution?
3. Who is the chief justice of the Supreme Court?
4. What are some of the requirements to be eligible to become president?
5. In what year was the Constitution written?
6. What is the introduction to the Constitution called?
7. Name one right or freedom guaranteed by the first amendment.
8. What kind of government does the United States have?

Answers:

1. The first 13 states;    2. 27;    3. John Roberts;    4. Candidates for President must be natural-born citizens, be at least 35 years old, and have lived in the United States for at least 14 years;    5. 1787;    6. The Preamble; 7. The rights are freedom of speech, of religion, of assembly, and to petition the government;    8. A republic

Source: Bureau of Citizenship and Immigrant Services 2006.

- Ability to read, write, and speak and understand words of ordinary usage in the English language
- Ability to pass a test in U.S. government and history

In Table 4.1 we offer a sample of the type of questions immigrants face on the citizenship test.

The nature of immigration laws is exceedingly complex and is subjected to frequent, often minor, adjustments. In the period from 2000–2004, between 850,000 and 1,100,000 people were legally admitted annually, for the following reasons:

| | |
|---|---|
| Citizen family unification | |
| Spouses | 27% |
| Children and adoptees | 11 |
| Parents | 8 |
| Other relatives | 10 |
| Spouses of legal residents | 10 |
| Employment-based | 16 |
| Refugees/people seeking political asylum | 7 |
| Diversity (lottery among applications from nations historically sending few immigrants) | 5 |
| Other | 6 |

Overall, two-thirds of legal immigrants come to join their families, one-seventh because of skills needed in the United States, and one-twelfth because of special refugee status (Office of Immigration Statistics 2006).

# Contemporary Concerns

Although our current immigration policies are less restrictive than other nations' restrictions, they are the subject of great debate. In Table 4.2, we summarize the benefits and concerns regarding immigration to the United States. We will consider three continuing criticisms of our immigration policy: the brain drain, population growth, and illegal immigration. All three, but particularly illegal immigration, have provoked heated debates and continuing efforts to resolve them with new policies. We will then consider the economic impact of immigration, followed by the nation's policy toward refugees, a group distinct from immigrants.

## The Brain Drain

How often have you identified your science or mathematics teacher or your physician as someone who was not born in the United States? This nation has clearly benefited from attracting human resources from throughout the world, but this phenomenon has had its price for the nations of origin.

The **brain drain** is the immigration to the United States of skilled workers, professionals, and technicians who are desperately needed by their home countries. In the mid-twentieth century, many scientists and other professionals from industrial nations, principally Germany and Great Britain, came to the United States. More recently, however, the brain drain has pulled emigrants from developing nations, including India, Pakistan, the Philippines, and several African nations. One out of four physicians in the United States in foreign born and plays a critical role in serving areas with too few doctors. Thousands of skilled, educated Indians now seek to enter the United States, pulled by the economic opportunity. The pay differential is so great that, beginning in 2004, when foreign physicians were no longer favored with entry in the United States, physicians in the Philippines were retraining as nurses so that they could immigrate to the United States where, employed as nurses, they would make four times what they would as doctors in the Philippines (Mullan 2005; *New York Times* 2005b).

**Table 4.2  Immigration Benefits and Concerns**

| *Potential Benefits* | *Areas of Concern* |
| --- | --- |
| Provide needed skills | Drain needed resources from home country |
| Contribute to taxes | Send remittances (or migradollars) home |
| May come with substantial capital to start business | Less-skilled immigrants compete with those already disadvantaged |
| Diversify the population (intangible gain) | Population growth |
| Maintain ties with countries throughout | May complicate foreign policy by lobbying the government |

Even during times of strongest sentiment against immigration, provisions exist to allow legal entry to overseas technical workers who are in short supply in the United States.

The brain drain controversy was evident long before the passage of the 1965 Immigration Act. However, the 1965 act seemed to encourage such immigration by placing the professions in one of the categories of preference. Various corporations, including Motorola and Intel, now find that one-third of their high-tech jobs are held by people born abroad, although many received their advanced education in the United States. Furthermore, these immigrants have links to their old countries and are boosting U.S. exports to the fast-growing economic regions of Asia and Latin America (Bloch 1996).

Many foreign students say they plan to return home. Fortunately for the United States, many do not and make their talents available in the United States. One study showed that the majority of foreign students receiving their doctorates in the sciences and engineering are still here four years later. Yet critics note that this supply allows the country to overlook its minority scholars. Presently, for every two minority doctorates, there are five foreign citizens receiving this degree. In the physical sciences, for every doctorate issued to a minority citizen, eleven are received by foreign citizens. More attention needs to be given to encourage African Americans and Latinos to enter high-tech career paths (Hoffer et al. 2001; Wessel 2001).

Conflict theorists see the current brain drain as yet another symptom of the unequal distribution of world resources. In their view, it is ironic that the United States gives foreign aid to improve the technical resources of African and Asian countries while maintaining an immigration policy that encourages professionals in such nations to migrate to our shores. These are the very countries that have unacceptable public health conditions and need native scientists, educators, technicians, and other professionals. In addition, by relying on foreign talent, the United States does not need to take the steps necessary to encourage native members of subordinate groups to enter these desirable fields of employment.

## Population Growth

The United States, like a few other industrial nations, continues to accept large numbers of permanent immigrants and refugees. Although such immigration has increased since the passage of the 1965 Immigration and Naturalization Act, the nation's birthrate has decreased. Consequently, the contribution of immigration to population growth has become more significant.

Legal immigration accounts for about 45 to 60 percent of the nation's growth in the first years in the twenty-first century. To some observers, the United States is already overpopulated. The respected environmentalist group Sierra Club debated for several years about taking an official position favoring restricting immigration, recognizing that more people put greater strain on the nation's natural resources. The majority of the members have indicated thus far a desire to keep a neutral position rather than enter the politically charged immigration debate (Barringer 2004; Bean et al. 2004).

The patterns of uneven settlement in the United States are expected to continue so that future immigrants' impact on population growth will be felt much more in certain areas—say, California and New York, rather than Iowa or Massachusetts. Although immigration and population growth may be viewed as national concerns, their impact is localized in certain areas such as southern California and large urban centers nationwide (Bean et al. 2004).

## Illegal Immigration

The most bitterly debated aspect of U.S. immigration policy has been the control of illegal or undocumented immigrants. These immigrants and their families come to the United States in search of higher-paying jobs than their home countries can provide. Individuals, often accompanied by their families, seek employment in the United States even if they are not able to enter legally.

In "Listen to Our Voices," journalist Dean Murphy ponders what the impact on citizens would be if all illegal immigrants were suddenly to disappear.

Since by definition illegal immigrants are in the country illegally, the exact number of these undocumented or unauthorized workers is subject to estimates and disputes. Based on the best available information there are more than 11 million illegal immigrants in the United States and probably closer to 12 million. This compares to about 4 million in 1992. Today about 7.2 million are employed accounting for about 5 percent of the entire civilian labor force (Broder 2006; Passel 2006).

Illegal immigrants, and even legal immigrants, have become tied by the public to almost every social problem in the nation. They become the scapegoats for unemployment; they are labeled as "drug runners" and, especially

A consistent theme in the United States is the desire to employ people at low-wage jobs that are often in the country illegally but at the same time to organize efforts to stop the influx of foreigners seeking employment. The Minuteman Project is a volunteer effort to patrol borders and identify people in the United States illegally.

since September 11, 2001, "terrorists." Yet their vital economic and cultural contribution to the United States is generally overlooked, as it has been for more than a hundred years.

The cost of the federal government's attempt to police the nation's borders and locate illegal immigrants is sizable. There are significant costs for aliens, that is, foreign-born noncitizens, and for other citizens as well. Civil rights advocates have expressed concern that the procedures used to apprehend and deport people are discriminatory and deprive many aliens of their legal rights. American citizens of Hispanic or Asian origin, some of whom were born in the United States, may be greeted with prejudice and distrust, as if their names automatically imply that they are illegal immigrants. Furthermore, these citizens and legal residents of the United States may be unable to find work because employers wrongly believe that their documents are forged.

In the context of this illegal immigration, Congress approved the Immigration Reform and Control Act of 1986 (IRCA) after debating it for nearly a decade. The act marked a historic change in immigration policy compared with earlier laws, as summarized in Table 4.3. Amnesty was granted to 1.7 million illegal immigrants who could document that they had established long-term residency in the United States. Under the IRCA, hiring illegal aliens became illegal, so that employers are subject to fines and even prison sentences. It appears

## LISTEN TO OUR VOICES

## Imagining Life Without Illegal Immigrants

*Dean E. Murphy*

Imagine America without illegal immigrants, the people who flip the burgers, clean the toilets, watch the kids, and send their children to public schools. Would the grass be greener?

The question got an answer of sorts last month in California, where about a third of the country's estimated 8 million to 10 million illegal immigrants live. Thousands of Latinos stayed home from school and work one Friday, protesting the repeal of a contentious new law that would have allowed illegal immigrants to obtain driver's licenses.

The boycott was not nearly the success its organizers had hoped for. Nonetheless, there were reports of fast-food counters closing and lawns going uncut. A few shops in cities with big immigrant populations, like Fresno, did not bother opening, and in Los Angeles, the second-largest school district in the country, the absentee rate nearly tripled from the Friday before. . . .

The Pew Hispanic Center estimated in 2001 that the unauthorized labor force in the United States totaled 5.3 million workers, including 700,000 restaurant workers, 250,000 household employees, and 620,000 construction workers. In addition, about 1.2 million of the 2.5 million wage-earning farm workers live here illegally, according to a study by Philip L. Martin, a professor at the University of California at Davis who studies immigration and farm labor.

That is a whole lot of cheap labor.

Without it, fruit and vegetables would rot in fields. Toddlers in Manhattan would be without nannies. Towels at hotels in states like Florida, Texas, and California would go unlaundered. Commuters at airports from Miami to Newark would be stranded as taxi cabs sat driverless. Home improvement projects across the Sun Belt would grind to a halt. And bedpans and lunch trays at nursing homes in Chicago, New York, Houston, and Los Angeles would go uncollected. . . .

Immigrant advocacy groups dispute the notion that illegal immigration is a drag on America. Raul Yzaguirre, president of the National Council of La Raza, a Latino civil rights organization, said the economic impact of immigration plays out differently at the local and national levels.

While hospitals and clinics in Los Angeles County, for example, bear huge health care costs associated with uninsured illegal immigrants—one study put the total at $340 million in 2002—the federal government enjoys a "bonanza" from many of the same immigrants who pay federal taxes but receive no benefits in return, Mr. Yzaguirre said.

Mr. Yzaguirre suggested that Social Security would go broke without the payments of undocumented workers, many of whom, contrary to popular perception, do have regular payroll taxes deducted from their paychecks by employers. (In some instances, undocumented workers use false Social Security numbers, while others have valid numbers from when they had worked legitimately.)

Mr. Yzaguirre also rejected suggestions that Americans would maintain their standard of living without the low-wage contributions of those workers. He agreed with Professor Borjas that some Americans would enjoy fatter paychecks, but he said all Americans would be punished by having to pay more for everything from a McDonald's hamburger to a new house.

In a 2002 study conducted with the cooperation of immigrant rights organizations, researchers at the Center for Urban Economic Development at the University of Illinois at Chicago concluded that the 300,000 or so illegal immigrants in Chicago did not use government benefits at a substantial rate. The study also estimated that 70 percent of the undocumented workers paid payroll taxes, like Social Security and unemployment insurance. The researchers calculated other economic benefits, finding that consumer spending by illegal migrants generated more than 31,000 jobs and contributed $5.34 billion annually to the gross regional product in Chicago.

Which side to believe? The problem with gathering data about illegal immigrants, and the idea of an America without them, is that they tend to blend into the vast tapestry of legal immigrants.

Source: The New York Times, January 11, 2004. Copyright © 2004 by The New York Times Co. Reprinted with permission.

that the act has had mixed results in terms of illegal immigration. According to data compiled by the U.S. Border Patrol, arrests along the border declined substantially in the first three years after the law took effect. However, illegal immigration eventually returned to the levels of the early 1980s.

Many illegal immigrants continue to live in fear and hiding, subject to even more severe harassment and discrimination than before. From a conflict perspective, these immigrants, primarily poor and Hispanic or Asian, are being

**Table 4.3 Major Immigration Policies**

| Policy | Target Group | Impact |
|---|---|---|
| Chinese Exclusion Act, 1882 | Chinese | Effectively ended all Chinese immigration for more than sixty years |
| National origin system, 1921 | Southern Europeans | Reduced overall immigration and significantly reduced likely immigration from Greece and Italy |
| Immigration and Naturalization Act, 1965 | Western Hemisphere | Facilitated entry of skilled workers and the less skilled and relatives of U.S. residents |
| Immigration Reform and Control Act of 1986 | Illegal immigration | Modest reduction of illegal immigration |
| Illegal Immigration Reform and Responsibility Act of 1996 | Illegal immigration | Greater border surveillance and increased scrutiny of legal immigrants seeking benefits |

firmly lodged at the bottom of the nation's social and economic hierarchies. However, from a functionalist perspective, employers, by paying low wages, are able to produce goods and services that are profitable for industry and more affordable to consumers. Despite the poor working conditions often experienced by illegal immigrants here, they continue to come because it is still in their best economic interest to work here in disadvantaged positions rather than to seek wage labor unsuccessfully in their home countries.

Little workplace enforcement occurs for the hiring of undocumented workers. While never a priority, prosecution of employers came to the point in 2005 were only wireless 5 employers were fined involving a total of 400 workers (Echaveste 2005).

Amidst heated debate, Congress passed a compromise, called the Illegal Immigration Reform and Immigrant Responsibility Act of 1996, which emphasized more effort to keep immigrants from entering the country illegally. Illegal immigrants will not have access to such benefit programs as Social Security and welfare. For now, legal immigrants will be entitled to such benefits, although social service agencies are required to verify their legal status. Another significant element was to increase border control and surveillance.

The illegal alien or undocumented workers are not necessarily transient—a 2006 estimate indicated 60% had been here for at least 5 years. Many have established homes, families, and networks with relatives and friends into the United States whose legal status might differ. For the most part, their lives are little different from legal residents except when they seek services where citizenship status needs to be documented. (Passel 2006).

Policymakers continue to avoid the only real way to stop illegal immigration, and that is to discourage employment opportunities. The public often thinks in terms of greater surveillance at the border. After the terrorist attacks of September 11, 2001, greater control of border traffic took on a new sense of urgency, even though almost all the men who took over the planes had entered the United States legally. It is very difficult to secure the vast boundaries that mark the United States on land and sea.

Reflecting the emphasis on heightened security, a potentially major shake-up recently took place. Since 1940, the Immigration and Naturalization Service has been in the Department of Justice, but in 2003 it was transferred to the newly formed Department of Homeland Security (see Table 4.4). The various functions of the INS were split into three agencies with a new Bureau of Citizenship and Immigration Services and two other units separately concerned with customs and border protection. For years, immigrant advocates had argued to separate border enforcement from immigration, but the placement of immigrant services in the office responsible for protecting the United States from terrorists sends a chilling message to immigrants.

Numerous civil rights groups and migrant advocacy organizations have expressed alarm over the large number of people now crossing into the United States illegally who perish in their attempt. Death occurs to some in deserts, in isolated canyons, and while concealed in containers or locked in trucks during

**Table 4.4    Transformation of Immigration Management**

Following 9/11, management of immigration in the United States was reorganized, as of March 1, 2003, from INS in the Department of Justice to three new agencies in the new Department of Homeland Security.

| *Before* | *After* |
|---|---|
| Located in Department of Justice | Located in Department of Homeland Security |
| Immigration and Naturalization Services (INS) | INS dissolved |
| Immigration services<br>Naturalization (citizenship)<br>Applications<br>Visas | U.S. Citizen and Immigration Services (USCIS) |
| U.S. Border Patrol<br>Inspections at border<br>Deportations at border | U.S. Customs and Borders Protection (CBP) |
| Immigration enforcement-interior<br>(includes removals and detentions) | U.S. Immigration and Customs Enforcement (ICE) |

smuggling attempts. Several hundred die annually in the Southwest, seeking more and more dangerous crossing points as border control has increased. However, this death toll has received little attention, causing one journalist to liken it to a jumbo jet crashing between Los Angles and Phoenix every year without anyone giving it much notice (del Olmo 2003; Sullivan 2005).

What certainly was noticed was the public debate in 2006 over how to stop further illegal immigration and what to do about those illegal immigrants already inside the United States. Debate over hardening the border by erecting a 700 hundred miles long high double concrete wall brought concerns that desperate immigrants would take even more chances with their lives in order to work in the United States. A Congressional proposal to make assisting an illegal immigrant already here a felony led to strong counterdemonstrations drawing tens of thousands of cities across the United States. Meanwhile the federal government, as it has for a century, struggled between the need to attract workers to do jobs many people here legally would not want to do against the desire to enforce the laws governing legal immigration (Tumulty 2006).

# The Economic Impact of Immigration

There is much public and scholarly debate about the economic effects of immigration, both legal and illegal. Varied, conflicting conclusions have resulted from research ranging from case studies of Korean immigrants' dominance

among New York City greengrocers to mobility studies charting the progress of all immigrants and their children. The confusion results in part from the different methods of analysis. For example, the studies do not always include political refugees, who generally are less prepared than other refugees to become assimilated. Sometimes the research focuses only on economic effects, such as whether people are employed or on welfare; in other cases, it also considers cultural factors such as knowledge of English.

Perhaps the most significant factor is whether a study examines the national impact of immigration or only its effects on a local area. Overall, we can conclude from the research that immigrants adapt well and are an asset to the local economy. In some areas, heavy immigration may drain a community's resources. However, it can also revitalize a local economy. Marginally employed workers, most of whom are either themselves immigrants or African Americans, often experience a negative impact by new arrivals. With or without immigration, competition for low-paying jobs in the United States is high, and those who gain the most from this competition are the employers and the consumers who want to keep prices down (Steinberg 2005).

According to survey data, many people in the United States hold the stereotypical belief that immigrants often end up on welfare and thereby cause increases in taxes. Economist David Card (et al. 1998) studied the 1980 "Mariel" boatlift that brought 125,000 Cubans into Miami and found that even this substantial addition of mainly low-skilled workers had no measurable impact on the wages or unemployment rates of low-skilled White and African American workers in the Miami area.

About 70 percent of illegal immigrant workers pay taxes of one type or another. Many of them do not file to receive entitled refunds or benefits. For example, in 2005, the Social Security Administration identified thousands of unauthorized workers contributing to the fund about $7 billion that could not be credited properly (Porter 2005).

Social science studies generally contradict many of the negative stereotypes about the economic impact of immigration. A variety of recent studies found that immigrants are a net economic gain for the population. But despite national gains, in some areas and for some groups, immigration may be an economic burden or create unwanted competition for jobs (Fix, Zimmerman, and Passel 2001; Moore 1998; Smith and Edmonston 1997).

## RESEARCH FOCUS

## How Well Are Immigrants Doing?

In 2001, the respected Urban Institute released its comprehensive study of the progress immigrants are making in the United States. They acknowledged that there is great diversity in the immigrant experience between nationality groups. Furthermore, even within the most successful immigrating groups, people have to confront the challenge of adapting to a society that rewards assimilation and typically punishes those who want to maintain cultural practices different from those that dominate society.

Considering contemporary immigrants as a group, we can make some conclusions, which show a mix of some success and evidence that adaptation typically is very difficult.

### Less Encouraging

- Although immigrants have lower divorce rates and are less likely to form single-parent households than natives, their rates equal or exceed these rates by the second generation.
- Children in immigrant families tend to be healthier than U.S.-born children, but the advantage declines.
- Immigrants are less likely to have health insurance.
- Immigrant children attend schools that are disproportionately attended by other poor children and students with limited English proficiency, so they are ethnically, economically, and linguistically isolated.

### Positive Signs

- Immigrant families, and, more broadly, noncitizen households, are more likely to be on public assistance, but their time on public assistance is less, and they receive fewer benefits. This is even true when considering special restrictions that may apply to noncitizens.
- Second-generation immigrants (i.e., children of immigrants) are overall doing as well as or better than White non-Hispanic natives in

educational attainment, labor force participation, wages, and household income.
- Immigrants overwhelmingly (65 percent) continue to see learning English as an ethical obligation of all immigrants.

These positive trends diverge between specific immigrant groups, with Asian immigrants doing better than European immigrants, who do better than Latino immigrants.

*Source*: Capps, Leighton, and Fix 2002; Farkas 2003; Fix et al. 2001; Meyers, Pitlain, and Park 2004; Ottaviano and Peri 2005.

In "Research Focus," we consider the most recent research on how immigrants are doing in the United States. One economic aspect of immigration that has received increasing attention is the effort to measure remittances. **Remittances (or migradollars)** are the monies that immigrants return to their country of origin. The amounts are significant and measure in the hundreds of millions of dollars flowing from the United States to a number of countries where they are a very substantial source of support for families and even venture capital for new businesses. Although some observers express concern over this outflow of money, others counter that it probably represents a small price to pay for the human capital that the United States is able to use in the form of the immigrants themselves. Global remittances bring $232 billion according to a World Bank estimate which developing countries surpasses all foreign aid (Hagenbaugh Ozden and Schiff 2006).

States have sought legal redress because the federal government has not seriously considered granting impact aid to heavily burdened states. In 1994, Florida joined California in suing the U.S. government to secure strict enforcement of immigration laws and reimbursement for services rendered to illegal immigrants. As frustration mounted, California voters approved a 1994 referendum (Proposition 187) banning illegal immigrants from public schools, public assistance programs, and all but emergency medical care. Although the proposal was later found not to be constitutional, voters heavily favored the referendum. Subsequently, California and other states have tried to enact measures that would partially reflect this view, such as prohibiting illegal immigrants from getting driver's licenses. Only fourteen states knowingly issue driver's license to illegal immigrants, reasoning that it is better to regulate driving and document that drivers are insured (Katel 2005).

The concern about immigration in the 1990s is both understandable and perplexing. The nation has always been uneasy about new arrivals, especially those who are different from the more affluent and the policymakers. Yet the 1990s were marked by low unemployment, low inflation, and much-diminished anxiety about our economic future. This paradoxical situation—a strong economy and concerns about immigration framed in economic arguments—suggests that other concerns, such as ethnic and racial tension, are more important in explaining current attitudes toward immigration in the United States (Cornelius 1996).

Remittances or migradollars are a significant source of income for many nations whose citizens immigrate to the United States. Pictured are Uruguayan citizens walking past a board showing the exchange rate of the Uruguayan Peso.

# The Global Economy and Immigration

Immigration exists because of political boundaries that bring the movement of peoples to the attention of national authorities. Within the United States, people may move their residence, but they are not emigrating. For residents in the member nations of the European Union, free movement of people within the union is also protected.

Yet, increasingly, people recognize the need to think beyond national borders and national identity. As was noted in Chapter 1, **globalization** is the worldwide integration of government policies, cultures, social movements, and financial markets through trade, movement of people, and the exchange of ideas. In this global framework, even immigrants are less likely to think of themselves as residents of only one country. For generations, immigrants have used foreign-language newspapers to keep in touch with events in their home country. Today, cable channels carry news and variety programs from other countries, and the Internet offers immediate access to homelands and kinfolk thousands of miles away.

While bringing the world together, globalization has also sharpened the focus on the dramatic economic inequalities between nations. Today, people in North America, Europe, and Japan consume 32 times more resources than the billions of people in developing nations. Thanks to tourism, the media, and other aspects of globalization, the people of less-affluent countries know of this affluent lifestyle and, of course, often aspire to it (Diamond 2003).

**Transnationals** are immigrants who sustain multiple social relationships linking their societies of origin and settlement. Immigrants from the Dominican Republic identify with Americans but also maintain very close ties to their Caribbean homeland. They return for visits, send remittances (migradollars), and host extended stays of relatives and friends. Back in the Dominican Republic, villages reflect these close ties, as shown in billboards promoting special long-distance services to the United States and by the presence of household appliances sent by relatives. The volume of remittances—perhaps $80 billion worldwide—is easily the most reliable source of foreign money going to poor countries, far outstripping foreign aid programs (Kapur and McHale 2003).

The growing number of transnationals, as well as immigration in general, directly reflects the world systems analysis we considered in Chapter 1. A global economic system that has such sharp contrasts between the industrial haves and the developing have-not nations only serves to encourage movement across borders. The industrial haves gain benefits from it even when they seem to discourage it. The movement back and forth only serves to increase globalization and the creation of informal social networks between people seeking a better life and those already enjoying increased prosperity.

Seen in this 1989 x-ray photo taken by Mexican authorities at the border are a wide shot, on top, and a close up version of human forms. New technology is used to scan passing trucks to detect human cargo as well as drugs and weapons.

# Refugees

**Refugees** are people living outside their country of citizenship for fear of political or religious persecution. Enough refugees exist to populate an entire nation. There are approximately 12 to 14 million refugees worldwide. That makes the nation of refugees larger than Belgium, Sweden, or Cuba. The United States has touted itself as a haven for political refugees. However, as we shall see, the welcome to political refugees has not always been unqualified.

The United States makes the largest financial contribution of any nation to worldwide assistance programs. The United States resettles about 70,000 refugees annually and served as the host to a cumulative 1 million refugees between 1990 and 2003. The post–9/11 years have seen the procedures become much more cumbersome for foreigners to acquire refugee status and gain entry to the United States. Many other nations much smaller and much poorer than the United States have many more refugees than the United States with Jordan, Iran, and Pakistan hosting over a million refugees each (Immigration and Refugee Services of America 2004; U.S. Committee for Refugees 2003).

The United States, insulated by distance from wars and famines in Europe and Asia, has been able to be selective about which and how many refugees are welcomed. Since the arrival of refugees uprooted by World War II, the United States through the 1980s had allowed three groups of refugees to enter in numbers greater than regulations would ordinarily permit: Hungarians, Cubans, and Southeast Asians. Compared with the other two groups, the nearly 40,000 Hungarians who arrived after the unsuccessful revolt against the Soviet Union of November 1956 were few indeed. At the time, however, theirs was the fastest mass immigration to this country since before 1922. With little delay, the United States amended the laws so that the Hungarian refugees could enter. Because of their small numbers and their dispersion throughout this country, the Hungarians are in little evidence nearly fifty years later. The much larger and longer period of movement of Cuban and Southeast Asian refugees into the United States continues to have a profound social and economic impact.

Despite periodic public opposition, the U.S. government is officially committed to accepting refugees from other nations. According to the United Nations treaty on refugees, which our government ratified in 1968, countries are obliged to refrain from forcibly returning people to territories where their lives or liberty might be endangered. However, it is not always clear whether a person is fleeing for his or her personal safety or to escape poverty. Although people in the latter category may be of humanitarian interest, they do not meet the official definition of refugees and are subject to deportation.

Refugees are people who are granted the right to enter a country while still residing abroad. **Asylees** are foreigners who have already entered the United States and now seek protection because of persecution or a well-founded fear of persecution. This persecution may be based on the individual's race, religion, nationality, membership in a particular social group, or political opinion. Asylees are eligible to adjust to lawful permanent resident status after one year of continuous presence in the United States. The number of asylees is currently limited to 10,000 per year, but there is sharp debate over how asylum is granted.

Because asylees, by definition, are already here, the outcome is either to grant them legal entry or to return them. It is the practice of deporting people fleeing poverty that has been the subject of criticism. There is a long tradition in the United States of facilitating the arrival of people leaving Communist nations, such as the Cubans. Mexicans who are refugees from poverty, Liberians fleeing civil war, and Haitians running from despotic rule are not similarly welcomed. The plight of Haitians has become one of particular concern.

Haitians began fleeing their country, often on small boats, in the 1980s. The U.S. Coast Guard intercepted many Haitians at sea, saving some of these boat people from death in their rickety and overcrowded wooden vessels. The Haitians said they feared detentions, torture, and execution if they remained in Haiti. Yet both Republican and Democratic administrations viewed most of the Haitian exiles as economic migrants rather than political refugees and opposed granting them asylum and permission to enter the United States. Once apprehended, the Haitians are returned. In 1993, the U.S. Supreme Court, by an 8–1 vote, upheld the government's right to intercept Haitian refugees at sea and return them to their homeland without asylum hearings.

African Americans and others denounce the Haitian refugee policy as racist. They contrast it to the "wet foot, dry foot" policy toward Cuban refugees. If the government intercepts Cubans at sea, they are returned; but if they escape detection and make it to the mainland, they may apply for asylum. About 75 percent of Cubans seeking asylum are granted refugee status, compared with only 22 percent of Haitians.

Even with only about a thousand Haitians successfully making it into the United States each year, there is an emerging Haitian American presence, especially in south Florida. An estimated 60,000 immigrants and their descendants live in the Little Haiti portion of Miami, where per capita income is a meager $5,700. Despite continuing obstacles, the community exhibits pride in those who have succeeded, from a Haitian American Florida state legislator to hip-hop musician Wyclef Jean (Dahlburg 2001; U.S. Committee for Refugees 2003).

## Conclusion

For its first hundred years, the United States allowed all immigrants to enter and become permanent residents. However, the federal policy of welcome did not mean that immigrants would not encounter discrimination and prejudice. With the passage of the Chinese Exclusion Act, discrimination against one group of potential immigrants became law. The Chinese were soon joined by the Japanese as peoples forbidden by law to enter and prohibited from becoming naturalized citizens. The development of the national origin system in the 1920s created a hierarchy of nationalities, with people from northern Europe encouraged to enter, whereas other Europeans and Asians encountered long delays. The possibility of a melting pot, which had always been a fiction, was legislated out of existence.

In the 1960s and again in 1990, the policy was liberalized so that the importance of nationality was minimized, and a person's work skills and relationship to an American were emphasized. This liberalization came at a time when most Europeans no longer wanted to immigrate into the United States.

One out of 10 people in the United States is foreign born; many of them are technical, professional, and craft workers. Also, 34 percent are household workers, and 33 percent of our farm laborers are foreign born. The U.S. economy and society are built on immigrant labor from farm fields to science laboratories (Parker 2001).

Throughout the history of the United States, as we have seen, there has been intense debate over the nation's immigration and refugee policies. In a sense, this debate reflects the deep value conflicts in the U.S. culture and parallels the "American dilemma" identified by Swedish social economist Gunnar Myrdal (1944). One strand of our culture, epitomized by the words "Give us your tired, your poor, your huddled masses," has emphasized egalitarian principles and a desire to help people in their time of need. At the same time, however, hostility to potential immigrants and refugees, whether the Chinese in the 1880s, European Jews in the 1930s and 1940s, or Mexicans, Haitians, and Arabs today, reflects not only racial, ethnic, and religious prejudice but also a desire to maintain the dominant culture of the in-group by keeping out those viewed as outsiders. The conflict between these cultural values is central to the American dilemma of the 21st century.

At present the debate about immigration is highly charged and emotional. Some people see it in economic terms, whereas others see the new arrivals as a challenge to the very culture of our society. Clearly, the general perception is that immigration presents a problem rather than a promise for the future.

Today's concern about immigrants follows generations of people coming to settle in the United States. This immigration in the past produced a very diverse country in terms of both nationality and religion, even before the immigration of the last fifty years. Therefore, the majority of Americans today are not descended from the English, and Protestants are just over half of all worshipers. This diversity of religious and ethnic groups is examined in Chapter 5.

## Key Terms

| | | |
|---|---|---|
| asylees   147 | naturalization   132 | sinophobes   128 |
| brain drain   134 | refugees   147 | transnationals   146 |
| globalization   145 | remittances (or migradollars) | xenophobia   125 |
| nativism   125 |    144 | |

## Review Questions

1. What are the functions and dysfunctions of immigration?

2. What were the social and economic issues when public opinion mounted against Chinese immigration into the United States?

3. Ultimately, what do you think is the major concern people have about contemporary immigration to the United States: the numbers of immigrants or their nationalities?

4. What principles appear to guide U.S. refugee policy?

## Critical Thinking

1. What is the immigrant root story of your family? Consider how your ancestors arrived in the United States and also how your family's past has been shaped by other immigrant groups.

2. Can you find evidence of the brain drain in terms of the professionals with whom you come in contact? Do you regard this as a benefit? What groups in the United States may not have been encouraged to fill such positions by the availability of such professionals?

## Internet Connections–Research Navigator™

Follow the instructions found on page 42 of this text to access the features of Research Navigator™. Once at the website, enter your Login Name and Password. Then, to use the ContentSelect database, enter keywords such as "remittances," "asylum," and "refugees," and the research engine will supply relevant and recent scholarly and popular press publications. Use the New York Times Search-by-Subject Archive to find recent news articles related to sociology, and the Link Library feature to locate relevant Web links organized by the key terms associated with this chapter.

# Ethnicity and Religion

## CHAPTER OUTLINE

Ethnicity, Religion, and Social Class
Religion in the United States
Limits of Religious Freedom: The Amish
Conclusion
Key Terms/Review Questions/Critical Thinking/
Internet Connections—Research Navigator™

---------------------------------⟨ H I G H L I G H T S ⟩---------------------------------

The United States includes a multitude of ethnic and religious groups. Do they coexist in harmony or in conflict? How significant are they as sources of identity for their members? White is a race, so how this identity is socially constructed has received significant attention. Many White ethnic groups have transformed their ethnic status into Whiteness. In the 1960s and 1970s, there was a resurgence of interest in White ethnicity, partly in response to the renewed pride in the ethnicity of Blacks, Latinos, and Native Americans. We have an ethnicity paradox in which White ethnics seem to enjoy their heritage while at the same time seeking to assimilate into larger society. White ethnics are the victims of humor (or respectable bigotry) that some still consider socially acceptable, and they find themselves with little power in big business. Religious diversity continues and expands with immigration and the growth in the followings of non-Christian faiths. Religious minorities have experienced intolerance in the present as well as in the past. Constitutional issues such as school prayer, secessionist minorities, creationism, and public religious displays are regularly taken to the Supreme Court. Italian Americans and the Amish are presented as case studies of the experiences of specific ethnic and religious groups in the United States.

Betty O'Keefe is a 60-year-old Californian who is a fifth-generation Irish American, meaning that her grandmother's grandmother came to the United States from Ireland. Sociologist Mary Waters (1990, 97) asked her what it was like growing up in the United States.

> *When I was in high school my maiden name was Tynan. This was 1940. I was dating some boys from school, and two different times when the parents found out I was an Irish Catholic, they told him he couldn't go out with me. The Protestants were like that. . . . One of his brothers later married someone named O'Flannery and I was so thrilled. I said I hope your mother is turning in her grave. So I am happy that my children have the name O'Keefe. So that people know right away what their background is. I think it is better. They would never be put in the position I was in.*
>   *Do you think something like that could happen now?*
>   *I don't think so openly. But I think it is definitely still there. You are not as bad (being an Irish Catholic) as a Black, but you are not Protestant. You are not Jewish either, which would be worse, but still you are not of their church.*

Their names may be Badovich, Hoggarty, Jablonski, Reggio, or Williams. They may follow any one of thousands of faiths and gather at any of the 360,000 churches, mosques, synagogues, and temples. Our nation's motto is *E Pluribus Unum,* and although there may be doubt that we are truly united into one common culture following a single ideology, there is little doubt about our continuing diversity as a nation of peoples.

Indeed, the very complexity of relations between dominant and subordinate groups in the United States today is partly the result of its heterogeneous population. No one ethnic origin or religious faith encompasses all the inhabitants of the United States. Even though our largest period of sustained immigration is three generations past, an American today is surrounded by remnants of cultures and practitioners of religions whose origins are foreign to this country. Religion and ethnicity continue to be significant in defining a person's identity.

## Ethnic Diversity

The ethnic diversity of the United States at the beginning of the twenty-first century is apparent to almost everyone. Passersby in New York City were undoubtedly surprised once when two street festivals met head-to-head. The procession of San Gennaro, the patron saint of Naples, marched through Little Italy, only to run directly into a Chinese festival originating in Chinatown. Teachers in many public schools often face students who speak only one language, and it is not English. Students in Chicago are taught in Spanish, Greek, Italian, Polish, German, Creole, Japanese, Cantonese, or the language of a Native American tribe. In the Detroit metropolitan area, classroom instruction is conveyed in 21 languages, including Arabic, Portuguese, Ukrainian, Latvian, Lithuanian, and Serbian. In many areas of the United States, you can refer to a special Yellow Pages and find a driving instructor who speaks Portuguese or a psychotherapist who will talk to you in Hebrew.

Germans are the largest ancestral group; the 2000 Census showed almost one-sixth of Americans saying they had at least some German ancestry. Although most German Americans are assimilated, it is possible to see the ethnic tradition in some areas, particularly in Milwaukee, whose population has 48 percent German ancestry. There, three Saturday schools teach German, and one can affiliate with 34 German American clubs and visit a German library that operates within the public library system. Just a bit to the south in River Forest, a Chicago suburb, *kinderwerksatt* meets weekly to help parents and children alike to maintain German culture (Carvajal 1996; Freedman 2004; Johnson 1992; Usdansky 1992).

Germany is one of 21 European nations from which at least 1 million people claim to have ancestry. The numbers are striking when one considers the size of some of the sending countries. For example, there are over 33 million Irish Americans, and the Republic of Ireland had a population of 3.7 million in 1998. Similarly, nearly 5 million people claim Swedish ancestry, and there are 8.9 million people living in Sweden today. Of course, many Irish and Swedish Americans are of mixed ancestry, but not everyone in Ireland is Irish, nor is everyone in Sweden Swedish.

## Why Don't We Study Whiteness?

Race is socially constructed, as we learned in Chapter 1. Sometimes we come to define race in a clear-cut manner. A descendant of a Pilgrim is White, for example. But sometimes race is more ambiguous: People who are the children of an African American and Vietnamese American union are biracial or "mixed," or whatever they come to be seen as by others. Our recognition that race is socially constructed has sparked a renewed interest in what it means to be White in the United States. Two aspects of White as a race are useful to consider: the historical creation of whiteness and how contemporary White people reflect on their racial identity.

When the English immigrants established themselves as the political founders of the United States, they also came to define what it meant to be White. Other groups that today are regarded as White, such as Irish, Germans, Norwegians, or Swedes, were not always considered White in the eyes of the English. Differences in language and religious worship, as well as past allegiance to a king in Europe different from the English, all caused these groups to be seen not as Whites in the Western Hemisphere but more as nationals of their home country who happened to be residing in North America.

The old distrust in Europe, where, for example, the Irish were viewed by the English as socially and culturally inferior, continued on this side of the Atlantic Ocean. Karl Marx, writing from England, reported that the average English worker looked down on the Irish the way poor Whites in the U.S. South looked down on Black people (Ignatiev 1994, 1995; Roediger 1994).

In "Listen to Our Voices," Diane Glancy, Macalester College professor of Native American literature and creative writing, draws on both insider and outsider perspectives on being White in the United States. As she describes, she is descended from Native Americans (American Indians) and from English and Germans. As this chapter continues, we will consider in a variety of ways what it means to be White in the United States at the beginning of the twenty-first century.

## LISTEN TO OUR VOICES

## When the Boats Arrived

*Diane Glancy*

Some of my ancestors came from Europe on boats. Others were already here when the boats arrived. I have done a lot of my writing examining the Indian part of my heritage, which came through my father. The white part didn't seem to need definition. It just was. Is. And shall be. But what does it mean to be part white? What does whiteness look like viewed from the other, especially when that other is also within oneself?

I can say whiteness is the dominant culture, for now anyway. Or I can say I was taught that whiteness gives definition instead of receiving it. It is the upright. The unblemished. The milk or new snow. It is the measure by which others are measured. There's nothing off center in it to make it aware of itself as outside or other. It doesn't need examination or explanation, but is the center around which others orbit. It is the plumb line. Other races/cultures/ethnicities are looked at in terms of their distance from whiteness.

Whiteness is a heritage I can almost enter, but I have unwhiteness in me. There is something that is not milk or new snow. I am a person of part color. I can feel my distance from whiteness. There is a dividing line into it I cannot cross. But neither can I cross fully into the Indian, because I am of mixed heritage.

When I look at my white heritage, it is as fragmented and hard to pinpoint as the native side. My mother's family came from England and Germany. They settled in Pennsylvania, then Virginia, and finally on the Missouri–Kansas border. What do I know of them any more than of my father's family? The European part of the family were practical, middle-of-the-road people. They got their work done. They didn't say a lot about it. They were fair-minded and tenacious. They were churchgoers and voters who migrated from the farm to the city in my parents' generation. They educated their children and died without much ceremony.

As for the white culture I saw in my mother's family—every Christmas Eve, they served Canadian bacon, which my father brought from the stockyards where he worked. I received an Easter basket on Easter. I got a sparkler on the Fourth of July. But that hardly defines culture.

I can look at the whiteness in my mother's family and say there was a de-termination, a punctuality, a dependability. There was a sense of Manifest Destiny, which was another tool for dominance. There was a need for mainte-nance and responsibility. A sense of a Judeo-Christian God. A holding to one's own. There was a need to be goal oriented. To make use of resources.

There also was opportunity to do all these things.

Who can say what will happen to whiteness as the people of color become the majority in the new century? Who can say what will happen as the cul-tures of the minorities deepen, as the white is mixed with others and gets harder to define? Can the white culture continue to be defined by its lack of ceremonies, its Elvises and White Castles, its harbor of ideas? Will it continue to invent its inventiveness? Will it continue to thrive?

I guess I would define white American culture as industriousness without overwhelming tradition. It doesn't seem to have anchors, but slides past oth-ers into port. Into the port it created, after all.

*Source*: Diane Glancy. "When the Boats Arrived." First appeared in *The Hungry Mind Review*, Spring 1998.

## Whiteness

As European immigrants and their descendants assimilated to the English and distanced themselves from other oppressed groups such as American In-dians and African Americans, they came to be viewed as White rather than as part of a particular culture. Writer Noel Ignatiev (1994, 84), contrasting being White with being Polish, argues that "Whiteness is nothing but an ex-pression of race privilege." This strong statement argues that being White, as opposed to being Black or Asian, is characterized by being a member of the dominant group.

Whites as people don't think of themselves as a race or have a conscious racial identity. The only occasion when a White racial identity emerges is mo-mentarily when Whites fill out a form asking for self-designation of race or one of those occasions when they are culturally or socially surrounded by people who are not White.

Therefore, contemporary White Americans generally give little thought to "being White." Consequently, there is little interest in studying "Whiteness" or considering "being White" except that it is "not being Black." Unlike non-Whites, who are much more likely to interact with Whites, take orders from Whites, and see Whites as the leading figures in the mass media, Whites enjoy the privilege of not being reminded of their Whiteness.

Unlike racial minorities, Whites downplay the importance of their racial identity while being willing to receive the advantages that come from being White. This means that advocacy of a "color-blind" or "race-neutral" outlook permits the privilege of Whiteness to prevail (Bonilla-Silva 2002; Yancey 2003).

White privilege as described by Peggy McIntosh includes holding a position in a company without co-workers suspecting it came because of one's race.

The new interest seeks to look at Whiteness, but not from the vantage point of a White supremacist. Rather, focusing on White people as a race or on what it means today to be White goes beyond any definition that implies superiority over non-Whites. It is also recognized that "being White" is not the same as experience for all any more than "being Asian American" or "being Black." Historian Noel Ignatiev observes that studying whiteness is a necessary stage to "abolition of whiteness"—just as, in Marxist analysis, class consciousness is a necessary stage to the abolition of class. By confronting Whiteness, society grasps the all-encompassing power that accompanies socially constructed race (Lewis 2004; McKinney 2003).

## White Privilege

Whiteness carries with it a sense of identity of being White as opposed to being, for example, Asian or African. For many people it may not be easy to establish a social identity of Whiteness, as in the case of biracial children. However, one can argue that the social identity of Whiteness exists if one enjoys the privilege of being White.

Scholar Peggy McIntosh of the Wellesley College Center for Research on Women looked at the privilege that comes from being White and the added privilege of being male. The other side of racial oppression is the privilege enjoyed by dominant groups. Being White or being successful in establishing a White identity carries with it distinct advantages. Among those that McIntosh (1988) identified were:

- Being considered financially reliable when using checks, credit cards, or cash.
- Taking a job without having coworkers suspect it came because of one's race.
- Never having to speak for all the people of one's race.
- Watching television or reading a newspaper and seeing people of one's own race widely represented.
- Speaking effectively in a large group without being called a credit to one's race.
- Assuming that if legal or medical help is needed that one's race will not work against oneself.

Whiteness does carry privileges, but most White people do not consciously think of them except on the rare occasions when they are questioned. We will return to the concepts of Whiteness and White privilege, but let us also consider the rich diversity of religion in the United States, which parallels the ethnic diversity of this nation.

## The Rediscovery of Ethnicity

Robert Park (1950, 205), a prominent early sociologist, wrote in 1913 that "a Pole, Lithuanian, or Norwegian cannot be distinguished, in the second generation, from an American, born of native parents." At one time, sociologists saw the end of ethnicity as nearly a foregone conclusion. W. Lloyd Warner and Leo Srole (1945) wrote in their often-cited *Yankee City* series that the future of ethnic groups seemed to be limited in the United States and that they would be quickly absorbed. Oscar Handlin's *Uprooted* (1951) told of the destruction of immigrant values and their replacement by American culture. Although Handlin was among the pioneers in investigating ethnicity, assimilation was the dominant theme in his work.

Many writers have shown almost a fervent hope that ethnicity would vanish. The persistence of ethnicity was for some time treated by sociologists as dysfunctional because it meant a continuation of old values that interfered with the allegedly superior new values. For example, to hold on to one's language delayed entry into the larger labor market and the upward social mobility it afforded. Ethnicity was expected to disappear not only because of assimilation but also because aspirations to higher social class and status demanded that it vanish. Somehow, it was assumed that one could not be ethnic and middle class, much less affluent.

## The Third-Generation Principle

Historian Marcus Hansen's (1952) **principle of third-generation interest** was an early exception to the assimilationist approach to White ethnic groups. Simply stated, Hansen maintained that in the third generation—the grandchildren of the original immigrants—ethnic interest and awareness would actually increase. According to Hansen, "What the son wishes to forget the grandson wishes to remember."

Hansen's principle has been tested several times since it was first put forth. John Goering (1971), in interviewing Irish and Italian Catholics, found that ethnicity was more important to members of the third generation than it was to the immigrants themselves. Similarly, Mary Waters (1990), in her interviews of White ethnics living in suburban San Jose, California, and suburban Philadelphia, Pennsylvania, observed many grandchildren wanting to study their ancestors' language, even though it would be a foreign language to them. They also expressed interest in learning more of their ethnic group's history and a desire to visit the homeland.

Social scientists in the past were quick to minimize the ethnic awareness of blue-collar workers. In fact, ethnicity was viewed as merely another aspect of White ethnics' alleged racist nature, an allegation that will be examined later in this chapter. Curiously, the very same intellectuals and journalists who bent over backward to understand the growing solidarity of Blacks, Hispanics, and Native Americans refused to give White ethnics the academic attention they deserved (Wrong 1972).

The new assertiveness of Blacks and other non-Whites of their rights in the 1960s unquestionably presented White ethnics with the opportunity to reexamine their own position. "If solidarity and unapologetic self-consciousness might hasten Blacks' upward mobility, why not ours?" asked the White ethnics, who were often only a half step above Blacks in social status. The African American movement pushed other groups to reflect on their past. The increased consciousness of Blacks and their positive attitude toward African culture and the contributions worldwide of African Americans are embraced in what we called the Afrocentric perspective (Chapter 1). Therefore, the mood was set in the 1960s for the country to be receptive to ethnicity. By legitimizing Black cultural differences from White culture, along with those of Native Americans and Hispanics, the country's opinion leaders legitimized other types of cultural diversity.

For many Irish American participants in a St. Patrick's Day Parade, this is their most visible expression of symbolic ethnicity during an entire year.

## Symbolic Ethnicity

Observers comment both on the evidence of assimilation and on the signs of ethnic identity that seem to support a pluralistic view of society. How can both be possible?

First, there is the very visible evidence of **symbolic ethnicity,** which may lead us to exaggerate the persistence of ethnic ties among White Americans. According to sociologist Herbert Gans (1979), ethnicity today increasingly involves the symbols of ethnicity, such as eating ethnic food, acknowledging ceremonial holidays such as St. Patrick's Day, and supporting specific political issues or the issues confronting the old country. One example was the push in 1998 by Irish Americans to convince state legislatures to make it compulsory in public schools to teach about the Irish potato famine, which was a significant factor in immigration to the United States. This symbolic ethnicity may be more visible, but this type of ethnic heritage does not interfere with what people do, read, or say, or even whom they befriend or marry.

The ethnicity of the twenty-first century embraced by English-speaking Whites is largely symbolic. It does not include active involvement in ethnic activities or participation in ethnic-related organizations. In fact, sizable proportions of White ethnics have gained large-scale entry into almost all clubs, cliques, and fraternal groups. Such acceptance is a key indicator of assimilation. Ethnicity has become increasingly peripheral to the lives of the members of the ethnic group. Although they may not relinquish their ethnic identity, other identities become more important.

Second, the ethnicity that does exist may be more a result of living in the United States than actual importing of practices from the past or the old country.

Many so-called ethnic foods or celebrations, for example, began in the United States. The persistence of ethnic consciousness, then, may not depend on foreign birth, a distinctive language, and a unique way of life. Instead, it may reflect the experiences in the United States of a unique group that developed a cultural tradition distinct from that of the mainstream. For example, in Poland the *szlachta,* or landed gentry, rarely mixed socially with the peasant class. In the United States, however, even with those associations still fresh, they interacted together in social organizations as they settled in concentrated communities segregated physically and socially from others (Glazer 1971; Glazer and Moynihan 1970; Lopata 1993).

Third, maintaining ethnicity can be a critical step toward successful assimilation. This **ethnicity paradox** facilitates full entry into the dominant culture. The ethnic community may give its members not only a useful financial boost but also the psychological strength and positive self-esteem that will allow them to compete effectively in larger society. Thus, we may witness people participating actively in their ethnic enclave while trying to cross the bridge into the wider community (Lal 1995).

Therefore, ethnicity gives continuity with the past in the form of an affective or emotional tie. The significance of this sense of belonging cannot be emphasized enough. Whether reinforced by distinctive behavior or by what Milton Gordon (1964) called a sense of "peoplehood," ethnicity is an effective, functional source of cohesion. Proximity to fellow ethnics is not necessary for a person to maintain social cohesion and in-group identity. Fraternal organizations or sports-related groups can preserve associations between ethnics who are separated geographically. Members of ethnic groups may even maintain their feelings of in-group solidarity after leaving ethnic communities in the central cities for the suburban fringe.

## The Price Paid by White Ethnics

Many White ethnics shed their past and want only to be Americans, with no ancestral ties to another country. Some ethnics do not want to abandon their heritage, but to retain their past as a part of their present, they must pay a price because of prejudice and discrimination. Although the levels of present and past intolerance toward White ethnics are much less than those we saw in Chapters 2 and 3 toward African Americans, Latinos, Asian Americans, and Native Americans, this intolerance is a part of multicultural America.

### Prejudice Toward White Ethnic Groups

Our examination of immigration to the United States in Chapter 4 pointed out the mixed feelings that have greeted European immigrants. They are apparently still not well received. In 1944, well after most immigration from Poland had ended, the Polish-American Congress, an umbrella organization of 40 Polish fraternities, was founded to defend the image of Polish Americans. Young Polish Americans are made to feel ashamed of their ethnic origin when teachers find their names unpronounceable and when they hear Polish jokes bandied about in a way that anti-Black or anti-Semitic humor is not. One survey found that half of second-generation Polish Americans encounter prejudice.

Curiously, it was socially proper to condemn the White working class as racist but improper to question the negative attitude of middle-class people toward White ethnics. Michael Lerner (1969) called this hostility toward White ethnics **respectable bigotry.** Polish jokes are acceptable, whereas anti-Black humor is considered to be in poor taste.

White ethnics in the early 1970s felt that the mass media unfairly ridiculed them and their culture while celebrating Black Power and African culture. For instance, Italian Americans remain concerned that their image is overwhelmed by stereotypes of organized crime, spaghetti, overweight mothers, and sexy women. Even television's Italian police seem to conform to the old stereotypes. In response to such stereotyping, the Columbian Coalition, founded in 1971, employs lawyers to handle cases of Italian Americans who claim they are victims of bigotry.

Even the broad group of White ethnics who still dominate Roman Catholicism have expressed feelings of being victimized. In 2000, a Roman Catholic was appointed chaplain of the U.S. House of Representatives for the first time. This led to angry sentiments against a Catholic being granted this symbolic position rather than keeping it in the hands of the Protestant clergy. About the same time, candidate George W. Bush appeared at the avowedly anti-Catholic Bob Jones University during the South Carolina primary campaign. The response to this appearance raised questions in some quarters about lingering hostility toward Roman Catholics and the Roman Catholic Church. A national survey taken of Roman Catholics at that time found that the majority (56 percent) did not believe such a bias existed, but one-third did perceive the presence of anti-Catholic bias in the country (Bendyna and Pearl 2000).

## The Prejudice of Ethnics

In the 1960s, as the civil rights movement moved north, White ethnics replaced the southern White as the typical bigot portrayed in the mass media. The chanting of protestors resulted in ugly incidents that made White ethnics and bigots synonymous. This stereotype of the prejudiced White ethnic has rarely been questioned. The danger of this and any stereotype is that it becomes indistinguishable from fact. David Matza (1964, 1) referred to these mental pictures, that "tend to remain beyond the reach of such intellectual correctives as argument, criticism and scrutiny. . . . Left unattended, they return to haunt us by shaping or bending theories that purport to explain major social phenomena." This 1964 picture of ethnics and the degree of truth behind it must be examined.

The first issue to resolve is whether White ethnic groups are more prejudiced than other Whites. Sociologist Andrew Greeley (1974a, 1977; Nie, Curry, and Greeley 1974) examined attitudes toward race, social welfare, and U.S. involvement in Vietnam. The evidence pointed to minimal differences between ethnics and others. Some of the differences actually showed greater tolerance and liberalism among White ethnics. For example, White ethnics were more in favor of welfare programs and more opposed to this country's participation in the Vietnam War.

Even when more sophisticated statistical analysis is introduced, the overall finding remains unchanged. No evidence supports the image of White ethnics as bigots. Greeley (1974a, 202) concludes, "Our argument is not that ethnics are the last bastion of liberalism in America today, but rather that it is a misrepresentation of the facts to picture them as a vanguard of conservatism." However, working-class ethnic neighborhoods have undeniably been the scene of ugly racial confrontations. If ethnics are no more bigoted than others, how have such incidents come to occur, and how has this reputation developed? For that answer, the unique relationship between White ethnic groups and African Americans must be understood.

In retrospect, it should be no surprise that one group that has been antagonistic to African Americans is the White ethnics. For many citizens, including White ethnics, the United States they remembered from the 1950s seemed to change. When politicians told people in the 1960s, "We must fight poverty and discrimination," this translated to White ethnics as, "Share your job, share your neighborhood, but pay more taxes." Whites recalled how, in several generations, they had moved from membership in a poor immigrant group to becoming a prosperous part of the working class. Government assistance to the poor was almost nonexistent then, public education was more limited, and subsidized training programs were absent. Why was it different now? Many White ethnics found it difficult to understand why African Americans seemed to be singled out as a cause for concern in the 1960s when they perceived that they, too, had real needs (Glazer and Moynihan 1970; Novak 1996; Sanders and Morawska 1975; Tyler 1972).

White ethnics went so far as to turn their backs on federal aid offered them because they did not want to have their neighborhoods marked as "poverty pockets," nor did they want to be associated with Black-oriented programs. In Newark, New Jersey, Italians successfully prevented an antipoverty office from being established and thereby cut off the jobs its programs would have created (Barbaro 1974). This ethnic opposition to publicly sponsored programs was not new. James Wilson and Edward Banfield (1964) studied elections in seven major cities between 1956 and 1963 for referenda to build new hospitals, parks, and schools. The results indicated that the least support came from White ethnics, who would have paid the least and benefited the most.

White ethnics first learned that they are not considered part of the dominant group, but in time, through assimilation, they came to be redefined to enjoy most of the White privileges we identified earlier. The case about Italian Americans looks at how the ethnic experience can change over time.

Italian Americans celebrate a religious festival in Cambridge, Massachusetts.

## Case Example: The Italian Americans

Although each European country's immigration to the United States has created its own social history, the case of Italians, though not typical of every nationality, offers insight into the White ethnic experience. Italians immigrated even during the colonial period, and they played prominent roles during the American Revolution and the early days of the republic. Mass immigration began in the 1880s, peaking in the first twenty years of the twentieth century, when Italians accounted for one-fourth of European immigration.

Italian immigration was concentrated not only in time but also by geography. The majority of the immigrants were landless peasants from rural southern Italy, the Mezzogiorno. Although many people in the United States assume that Italians are a nationality with a single culture, this is not true either culturally or economically. The Italian people recognize multiple geographic divisions reflecting sharp cultural distinctions. These divisions were brought with the immigrants to the New World.

Many Italians, especially in the early years of mass immigration in the nineteenth century, received their jobs through an ethnic labor contractor, the *padrone*. Similar arrangements have been used by Asian, Hispanic, and Greek immigrants, where the labor contractors, most often immigrants, have mastered sufficient English to mediate for their compatriots. Exploitation was common within the padrone system through kickbacks, provision of inadequate housing, and withholding of wages. By World War I, 90 percent of Italian girls and 99 percent of Italian boys in New York City were leaving school at age 14 to work, but by that time Italian Americans were sufficiently fluent in English to seek out work on their own, and the padrone system had disappeared.

Along with manual labor, the Catholic Church was a very important part of Italian Americans' lives at this time. Yet they found little comfort in a Catholic church dominated by an earlier immigrant group: the Irish. The traditions were different; weekly attendance for Italian Americans was overshadowed by the religious aspects of the *feste* (or festivals) held throughout the year in honor of saints (the Irish viewed the feste as practically a form of paganism). These initial adjustment problems were overcome with the establishment of ethnic parishes, a pattern repeated by other non-Irish immigrant groups. Thus, parishes would be staffed by Italian priests, sometimes imported for that purpose. Although the hierarchy of the church adjusted more slowly, Italian Americans were increasingly able to feel at home in their local parish church. Today, more than 70 percent of Italian Americans identify themselves as Roman Catholics (Luconi 2001).

As assimilation proceeded, Italian Americans began to construct a social identity as a nationality group, rather than viewing themselves in terms of their village or province. As shown in Figure 5.1, over time, Italian Americans shed old identities for a new one. As immigration from Italy declined, the descendants' ties became more nationalistic. This move from local or regional to national identity was followed by Irish and Greek Americans. The changing identity of Italian Americans reflected the treatment they received in the United States, where non-Italians did not make those regional distinctions. However, they were not treated well. For example, in turn-of-the-century New Orleans, Italian Americans established special ties to the Black community because both groups were marginalized in southern society. Gradually, Italian Americans became White and enjoyed all the privileges that come with it. Today it would be inconceivable to imagine that Italian Americans of New Orleans would reach out to the African American community as their natural allies on social and political issues (Guglielmo and Salemo 2003; Luconi 2001).

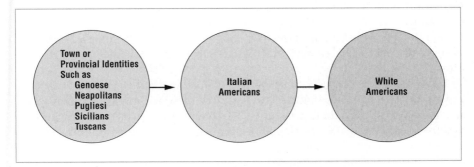

**Figure 5.1** Constructing Social Identity among Italian Immigrants

Over time Italian Americans moved from seeing themselves in terms of their provincial or village identity to their national identity, and then they successfully became indistinguishable from other Whites.

A controversial aspect of the Italian American experience involves organized crime, as typified by Al Capone (1899–1947). Arriving in U.S. society in the bottom layers, Italians lived in decaying, crime-ridden neighborhoods that became known as Little Italies. For a small segment of these immigrants, crime was a significant means of upward social mobility. In effect, entering and leading criminal activity was one aspect of assimilation, though not a positive one. Complaints linking ethnicity and crime actually began in colonial times with talk about the criminally inclined Irish and Germans, and they continue with contemporary stereotyping about such groups as Colombian drug dealers and Vietnamese street gangs. Yet the image of Italians as criminals has persisted from Prohibition-era gangsters to the view of mob families today. As noted earlier, it is not at all surprising that groups such as the Columbian Coalition have been organized to counter such negative images.

The fact that Italians often are characterized as criminal, even in the mass media, is another example of what we have called respectable bigotry toward White ethnics. The persistence of linking Italians, or any other minority group, with crime probably is attributable to attempts to explain a problem by citing a single cause: the presence of perceived undesirables. Many Italian Americans still see their image tied to old stereotypes. A 2001 survey of Italian American teenagers found that 39 percent felt the media presented their ethnic group as criminal or gang members and 34 percent as restaurant workers (Girardelli 2004; National Italian American Foundation 2001).

The immigration of Italians was slowed by the national origin system, described in Chapter 4. As Italian Americans settled permanently, the mutual aid societies that had grown up in the 1920s to provide basic social services began to dissolve. More slowly, education came to be valued by Italian Americans as a means of upward mobility. Even becoming more educated did not ward off prejudice, however. In 1930, for example, President Herbert Hoover rebuked Fiorello La Guardia, then an Italian American member of Congress from New York City, stating that "the Italians are predominantly our murderers and bootleggers" and recommending that La Guardia "go back to where you belong" because, "like a lot of other foreign spawn, you do not appreciate this country which supports you and tolerates you" (Baltzell 1964:30).

While U.S. troops, including 500,000 Italian Americans, battled Italy during World War II, some hatred and sporadic violence emerged against Italian Americans and their property. However, they were not limited to actions against individuals. Italian Americans were even confined by the federal government in specific areas of California by virtue of their ethnicity alone, and 10,000 were relocated from coastal areas. In addition, 1,800 Italian Americans who were citizens of Italy were placed in an internment camp in Montana. The internees were eventually freed on Columbus Day 1942 as President Roosevelt lobbied the Italian American community to gain full support for the impending land invasion of Italy (Department of Justice 2001a; Fox 1990).

In politics, Italian Americans have been more successful, at least at the local level, where family and community ties can be translated into votes. However, political success did not come easily because many Italian immigrants anticipated returning to their homeland and did not always take neighborhood politics seriously. It was even more difficult for Italian Americans to break into national politics.

Not until 1962 was an Italian American named to a cabinet-level position. Geraldine Ferraro's nomination as the Democratic vice presidential candidate in 1984 was every bit as much an achievement for Italian Americans as it was for women. The opposition to the nomination of Judge Samuel Alito to the Supreme Court in 2006 struck many as bordering on anti–Italian American sentiments in the manner it was advanced. Numerous critics used the phrase "Judge Scalito" in obvious reference to the sitting Italian American on the Court, Justice Antonio Scalia (Cornacchia and Nelson 1992; National Italian American Foundation 2006).

In 2000, the 15.9 million people of Italian ancestry accounted for about 6 percent of the population, although only a small fraction of them had actually been born in Italy. Italian Americans still remain the seventh-largest immigrant group. Just how ethnically conscious is the Italian American community? Although the number is declining, 1 million Americans speak Italian at home; only six languages are spoken more frequently at home (Spanish, French, Chinese, Vietnamese, Tagalog [Philippines] and German). For another 14-plus million Italian Americans, however, the language tie to their culture is absent, and depending on their degree of assimilation, only traces of symbolic ethnicity may remain. In the next section we will look at the role that language plays for many immigrants ands their children (Shin and Bruno 2003).

## The Language Divide

One evening in Chicago, Audrey Cho addressed her ten adult students holding a handout listing federal holidays, "Who is Washington?" Confused looks came on the faces of the Korean, Mexican, Peruvian and Mongolian immigrants. Finally someone raised their hand and said "February 16th?" Cho, herself having immigrated from South Korea, remains patient and states "No, it's who, not when." Learning English may not be easy but many immigrants of all ages are trying (Kaneya 2004:6).

Language is key to people's functioning in a society, and it is critical in relation to how they see themselves. But when that language is different from the dominant tongue, it can be the source of hardship and stigmatization. About 18 percent of the population speaks a language other than English, as shown in Figure 5.2 (Shin and Bruno 2003).

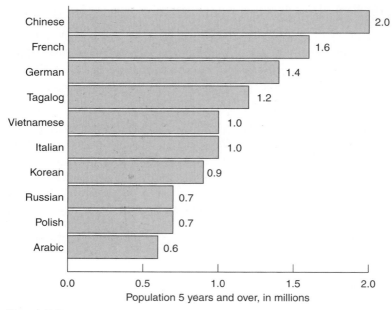

**Figure 5.2** Ten Languages Most Frequently Spoken at Home Other Than English and Spanish
*Source:* Data for 2000 released in 2003 in Shin and Bruno 2003.

As of 2002, about 23 percent of Mexican Americans are English dominant, 26 percent are bilingual, and 51 percent are Spanish dominant. Puerto Ricans in the United States tend to be more English-language oriented, with 39 percent English-dominant, 40 percent bilingual, and 21 percent Spanish dominant. At the other extreme, Salvadorans, Dominicans, Colombians, and other Central and South Americans tend to be more Spanish dominant, and they are also more likely to be more recent immigrants. Nationally, about 70 percent of Latino schoolchildren report speaking Spanish at home (Brodie et al. 2002; Bureau of the Census 2003a, 158)

The myth of Anglo superiority has rested in part on language differences. (The term *Anglo* in the following text is used to mean all non-Hispanics, but primarily Whites.) First, the criteria for economic and social achievement usually include proficiency in English. By such standards, Spanish-speaking pupils are judged less able to compete until they learn English. Second, many Anglos believe that Spanish is not an asset occupationally. Only recently, as government agencies have belatedly begun to serve Latino people and as businesses recognize the growing Latino consumer market, have Anglos recognized that knowing Spanish is not only useful but also necessary to carry out certain tasks. However, as we see in education, voting, and language practices, many people in the United States are concerned and suspicious about the public use of any language other than English.

## Bilingual Education

Until the last twenty or thirty years, there was a conscious effort to devalue Spanish and other languages and to discourage the use of foreign languages in schools. In case of Spanish, this practice was built on a pattern of segregating Hispanic schoolchildren from Anglos. In the recent past in the Southwest, Mexican Americans were assigned to Mexican schools to keep Anglo schools all White. These Mexican schools, created through *de jure* school segregation, were substantially underfunded compared with the regular public schools. Legal action against such schools dates back to 1945, but it was not until 1970 that the U.S. Supreme Court ruled, in *Cisneros v. Corpus Christi Independent School District,* that the *de jure* segregation of Mexican Americans was unconstitutional. Appeals delayed implementation of that decision, and not until September 1975 was the *de jure* plan forcibly overturned in Corpus Christi, Texas (Commission on Civil Rights 1976).

Even in integrated schools, Latino children were given separate, unequal treatment. "No Spanish" was a rule enforced throughout the Southwest, Florida, and New York City by school boards in the 1960s. Children speaking Spanish on school grounds, even on the playground, might be punished with detention after school, fines, physical reprimands, and even expulsion for repeated violations. From 1855 to as recently as 1968, teaching in any language other than English was illegal in California. Such laws existed despite a provision in the 1848 Treaty of Guadalupe Hidalgo between the United States and Mexico that guaranteed the right of Mexicans to maintain their culture. All official publications were to be bilingual, but "English only" became the social norm.

Is it essential that English be the sole language of instruction in schools in the United States? **Bilingualism** is the use of two or more languages in places of work or educational facilities, according each language equal legitimacy. Thus, a program of **bilingual education** may instruct children in their native language (such as Spanish) while gradually introducing them to the language of the dominant society (English). If such a program is also bicultural, it will teach children about the culture of both linguistic groups. Bilingual education allows students to learn academic material in their own language while they are learning a second language. Proponents believe that, ideally, bilingual education programs should also allow English-speaking pupils to be bilingual, but generally they are directed only at making non-English speakers proficient in more than one language.

Programs to teach English as a second language (ESL) have been the cornerstones of bilingual education, but they are limited in approach. For example, ESL programs tend to emphasize bilingual but not bicultural education. As a result, the method can unintentionally contribute to ethnocentric attitudes, especially if it seems to imply that a minority group is not really worthy of attention. As conflict theorists are quick to note, the interests of the less powerful—in this case, millions of non-English-speaking children—are those least likely to be recognized and respected. One alternative to the ESL approach, viewed

While research documents the value of bilingual education, funding is sparse and students are often encouraged to enter "regular" classrooms. This classroom in California accommodates both the student's home language as well as English.

with much less favor by advocates of bilingualism, is **English immersion,** in which students are taught primarily in English, using their native languages only when they do not understand their lessons. In practice, such instruction usually becomes an English-only "crash program" (Hechinger 1987).

Since its introduction into U.S. schools, bilingual education has been beset by problems. Its early supporters were disillusioned by the small number of English-speaking children participating and by the absence of a bicultural component in most programs. However, the frustration has been most clearly visible in the lack of consensus among educators on how best to implement bilingual programs. Even when a school district decides what methods it prefers, superintendents find it difficult to hire qualified instructors, although this varies depending on the language and the part of the country. The problem is further complicated by the presence of children speaking languages other than the predominant second language, so superintendents may want to mount bilingual programs in many languages.

Do bilingual programs help children to learn English? It is difficult to reach firm conclusions on the effectiveness of the bilingual programs in general because they vary so widely in their approach to non-English-speaking children. The programs differ in the length of the transition to English and how long they allow students to remain in bilingual classrooms. A major study released in 2004 analyzed more than three decades of research, combining 17 different studies, and found that bilingual education programs produce higher levels of student achievement in reading. The most successful are paired bilingual programs—those offering ongoing instruction in a native language and English at different times of day (Slavin and Cheung 2003).

Drawing on the perspective of conflict theory, we can understand some of the attacks on bilingual programs. The criticisms do not necessarily result from careful educational research. Rather, they stem from the effort to assimilate children and to deprive them of language pluralism. This view, that any deviation from the majority is bad, is expressed by those who want to stamp out foreigners, especially in our schools. Research findings have little influence on those who, holding such ethnocentric views, try to persuade policymakers to follow their thinking. This perspective does not take into account that success in bilingual education may begin to address the problem of high school dropouts and the paucity of Hispanics in colleges and universities.

As one might expect, Latinos tend to be very supportive of bilingual programs. A 2003 national survey found that 72 percent of Hispanics (and a similar proportion of African Americans) favor school districts offering such programs compared to 53 percent of non-Hispanic Whites. Nonetheless, opposition to bilingualism can be quite strong among some Hispanics. A few are very active in organized efforts to stop such programs, and some Latino parents pressure schools to keep their children out of classrooms where Spanish may be spoken out of the misguided notion that English-only education, even for the youngest children, is the key to success (Freedman 2004; Mason 2003; Soltero 2004).

## Official Language Movement

Attacks on bilingualism both in voting and in education have taken several forms and have even broadened to question the appropriateness of U.S. residents using any language other than English. Federal policy has become more restrictive. Local schools have been given more authority to determine appropriate methods of instruction; they have also been forced to provide more of their own funding for bilingual education.

In the United States, repeated efforts have been made to introduce a constitutional amendment declaring English as the nation's official language. In 2006, a congressional proposal for a national language arose during debates over immigration. Legislative leaders who were struggling to reach a compromise introduced a proposal to make English the national language. The legislation would not completely outlaw bilingual or multilingual government services. It would, however, require that such services be called for specifically as in the Voting Rights Act of 1965, which requires voting information to be multiple languages.

As shown in Figure 5.3, non-English speakers cluster in certain states, but bilingualism attracts *nationwide passions*. The release in 2006 of *Nuestro Himmo*, the Spanish-language version of *The Star-Spangled Banner*, led to a strong reaction with 69 percent of people saying it was only appropriate to be

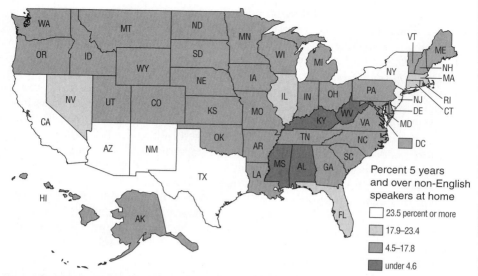

**Figure 5.3** People Who Spoke a Language Other than English at Home
*Source:* U.S. Data for 2000 released in Shin and Bruno 2003:8.

sung in English. Yet at least one Congressman decrying the Spanish version sang the anthem himself in English with incorrect lyrics. Similarly a locally famous restaurant owner in Philadelphia posted signs at his Philly steak sandwich diner he would only accept orders in English. Passions remain strong as policy makers debate how much support should be given to prople who speak other languages (Carroll 2006).

## Religious Pluralism

In popular speech, the term *pluralism* has often been used in the United States to refer explicitly to religion. Although certain faiths figure more prominently in the worship scene, there has been a history of greater religious tolerance in the United States than in most other nations. Today there are more than 1,500 religious bodies in the United States, ranging from the more than 66 million members of the Roman Catholic Church to sects with fewer than 1,000 adherents.

How do we view the United States in terms of religion? It is now more accurate to speak of the country as Judeo-Christian-Islamic or Abrahamic (referring to the historical religious leader common to the three faiths). There is an increasingly non-Christian presence in the United States. In 1900, an estimated 96 percent of the nation was Christian, just over 1 percent nonreligious, and about 3 percent all other faiths. In 2004, it is estimated that the nation is 86 percent Christian, nearly 7 percent nonreligious, and another 7 percent all other faiths. The United States has a long Jewish tradition, and Muslims number

**Figure 5.4** Predominant Christian Denominations by Counties, 2000
The diversity of Christian religious life in the United States is apparent in the figure. Many Christian denominations account for 25 percent or more of the church members in a county. Among non-Christian faiths, only Judaism figures so significantly—in New York County (Manhattan) of New York City and in Dade County, Florida (which includes Miami Beach).
*Source:* "Predominant Christian Denominations by Counties 2000" from *Churches and Church Membership in the United States, 2002* by D. Jones, et al. Reprinted with permission from Religious Congregations and Membership in the United States: 2000. (Nashville: Glenmary Research Center, 2002). © by Association of Statisticians of American Religious Bodies. All rights reserved.

close to 5 million. A smaller but also growing number of people adhere to such Eastern faiths as Hinduism, Buddhism, Confucianism, and Taoism (Barrett and Johnson 2001; Gallup 2004).

The diversity of religious life in the United States is apparent from Figure 5.4, which shows the Christian faiths that dominate various areas of the country numerically. For many nations of the world, a map of religions would hardly be useful because one faith accounts for almost all religious followers in the country. The diversity of beliefs, rituals, and experiences that characterizes religious life in the United States reflects both the nation's immigrant heritage and the First Amendment prohibition against establishing a state religion.

Sociologists use the word **denomination** for a large, organized religion that is not linked officially with the state or government. By far the largest denomination in the United States is Catholicism, yet at least 24 other Christian religious denominations have 1 million or more members (Table 5.1).

There are also at least four non-Christian religious groups in the United States whose numbers are comparable to any of these large denominations. Jews, Muslims, Buddhists, and Hindus in the United States all number more than 1 million. Within each of these groups, there are branches or sects that

**Table 5.1 Churches with More Than a Million Members**

| Denomination Name | Inclusive Membership |
| --- | --- |
| The Roman Catholic Church | 67,820,835 |
| Southern Baptist Convention | 16,267,494 |
| The United Methodist Church | 8,186,254 |
| The Church of Jesus Christ of Latter-day Saints | 5,599,177 |
| The Church of God in Christ | 5,499,875 |
| National Baptist Convention, U.S.A., Inc. | 5,000,000 |
| Evangelical Lutheran Church in America | 4,930,429 |
| National Baptist Convention of America, Inc. | 3,500,000 |
| Presbyterian Church (U.S.A.) | 3,189,573 |
| Assemblies of God | 2,779,095 |
| Progressive National Baptist Convention, Inc. | 2,500,000 |
| African Methodist Episcopal Church | 2,500,000 |
| National Missionary Baptist Convention of America | 2,500,000 |
| The Lutheran Church—Missouri Synod (LCMS) | 2,463,747 |
| Episcopal Church | 2,284,233 |
| Greek Orthodox Archdiocese of America | 1,500,000 |
| Pentecostal Assemblies of the World, Inc. | 1,500,000 |
| Churches of Christ | 1,500,000 |
| African Methodist Episcopal Zion Church | 1,432,795 |
| American Baptist Churches in the U.S.A. | 1,424,840 |
| United Church of Christ | 1,265,786 |
| Baptist Bible Fellowship International | 1,200,000 |
| Christian Churches and Churches of Christ | 1,071,616 |
| Orthodox Church in America | 1,064,000 |
| Jehovah's Witness | 1,029,092 |

Note: Most recent data as of 2006. Membership reporting year ranges from 1992 to 2004.

*Source:* "Membership Statistics in the United States" in Yearbook of American and Canadian Churches 2006 edited by Reverend Eileen W. Lindner, Ph.D. Copyright © 2006 by National Council of the Churches of Christ in the USA. Reprinted by permission [www.ncccusa.org].

distinguish themselves from each other. For example, in the United States and the rest of the world, some followers of Islam are Sunni Muslims and others are Shiites. There are further divisions within these groups, just as there are among Protestants and in turn among Baptists (Kosmin, Mayer, and Keysar 2001).

One notable characteristic of religious practice in the United States is its segregated nature at the local level. In 2006, arsonists victimized ten churches in Alabama, and some feared that these fires could be racially motivated. But state and national authorities reassured the public that since five churches were "White" and five churches were "Black," racism was unlikely to be a motivating factor. The irony is that the legacy of racism in religious expression leads to the very segregation in worship that allows churches to be easily identified as "Black" or "White" (Associated Press 2006).

Even if religious faiths have broad representation, they tend to be fairly homogeneous at the local church level. This is especially ironic, given that many faiths have played critical roles in resisting racism and trying to bring together the nation in the name of racial and ethnic harmony (Orfield and Liebowitz 1999).

Broadly defined faiths show representation of a variety of ethnic and racial groups. In Figure 5.5, we consider the interaction of White, Black, and Hispanic race with religions. Muslims, Pentecostals, and Jehovah's Witnesses are much more diverse than Presbyterians or Lutherans. Religion plays an even more central role for Blacks and Latinos than Whites. A 2004 national survey indicated that 65 percent of African Americans and 51 percent of Latinos attend a religious service every week, compared to 44 percent of non-Hispanic Whites (Winseman 2004).

About two in three Americans (66 percent) are counted as church members, but it is difficult to assess the strength of their religious commitment. A persuasive case can be made that religious institutions continue to grow stronger through an influx of new members, despite mounting secularism in society. Some observers think that, after reaching a low in the 1960s, religion is becoming more important to people again. The past upheavals in U.S. religious life are reflected on the covers of *Time* magazine, which have cried out variously, "Is God Dead?" (April 8, 1966), "Is God Coming Back to Life?" (December 26, 1969), and "The Jesus Revolution" (June 21, 1971). Much more recently, *Newsweek* proclaimed that "Science Finds God" (July 20, 1998). At present, there is little statistical support for the view that the influence of religion on society is diminishing (Moore 2002).

In "Research Focus," (see pp. 177–178) we consider how social scientists examine religious fervor in the United States and what recent studies have indicated.

It would also be incorrect to focus only on older religious organizations. Local churches that developed into national faiths in the 1990s, such as the Calvary Chapel, Vineyard, and Hope Chapel, have created a following among Pentecostal believers, who embrace a more charismatic form of worship devoid of many traditional ornaments, with pastors and congregations alike favoring informal attire. New faiths develop with increasing rapidity in what can only be called a very competitive market for individual religious faith. In addition, many people, with or without religious affiliation, become fascinated with spiritual concepts such as angels or become a part of loose-knit fellowships such as the Promise Keepers, an all-male movement of evangelical Christians founded in 1990. Religion in the United States is an ever-changing social phenomenon (Dudley and Roozen 2001; Miller and Schaefer 1998).

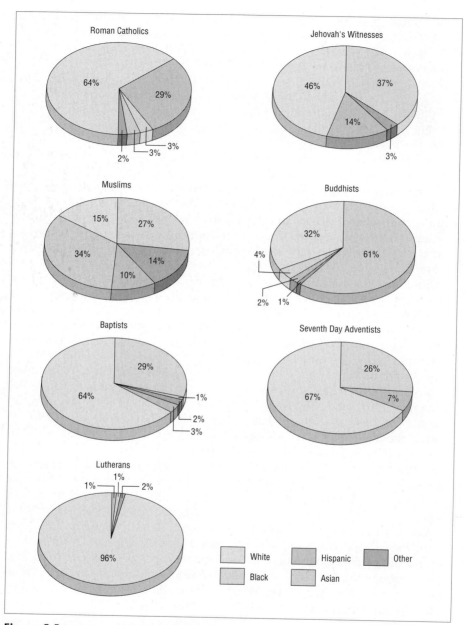

**Figure 5.5** Racial and Ethnic Makeup of Selected Religions in the United States
Note: More recent study (Latino Coalition 2006) shows 44 percent of Roman Catholics to be Hispanic. Totals do not always sum to 100 percent due to rounding.
Source: "Racial and Ethnic Make-Up of Selected Religions," in *American Religious Identification Survey, 2001* by Egon Mayer et al., The Graduate Center of the City University of New York. Reprinted with permission.

## RESEARCH FOCUS

# Measuring the Importance of Religion

Social scientists and scholars of religious behavior have tried to measure the importance that religion has for people. Studies center on the holding of religious beliefs ("Do you believe in God?"), declarations of membership, contributions of money or time, and attendance at or participation in religious services.

We will focus on how people perceive the importance of religion to themselves and to others. This is a reasonable step because it does not make any assumptions about a specific religion, as if one were to ask people whether they read the Bible or attended church. In addition, we have reliable national data covering a long period of time with the same questions being asked using largely the same survey techniques.

In Figure 5.6 we see the responses for over the last twenty-five years to two questions: how important people feel religion is to them and whether they feel religion is increasing its influence on the United States as a whole.

Two patterns emerge. First, somewhere between 53 and 61 percent of adults see religion as "very important" in their daily lives. Second, a much smaller proportion of people, usually around 35 percent, see religion's influence increasing, but this has fluctuated more widely. Of particular note across this time period is the dramatic increase in 2001. The events of September 11, 2001, had a pronounced impact on how people saw religion as influencing the nation. In February 2001, about 39 percent of the people felt religion was increasing its influence and 55 percent felt it was losing its hold on the nation—pretty typical responses for the twenty-year period. Yet by

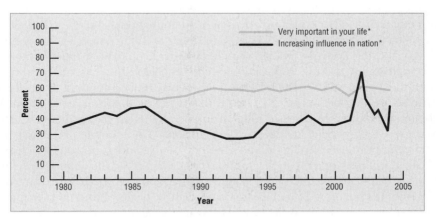

**Figure 5.6** Religion's Importance and Influence

Note: Questions were "How important would you say religion is in your own life?" and "At the present time, do you think religion as a whole is increasing its influence on American life or losing its influence?"

*Source:* Gallup 2004. Copyright 2004. The Gallup Organization. Princeton, NJ. Reprinted with permission.

December 7, 71 percent felt religion was increasing its influence and only 24 percent losing.

Will this dramatic shift in the perception of how the nation was influenced translate into people's own lives? Probably not. There was little lasting change in how people saw religion playing in their own lives: Fifty-seven percent saw it as "very important" in May 2001, 64 percent in late September after the attacks, and back down to 60 percent by December. Media accounts spoke of a possible reawakening because religious houses of worship were packed in the weeks after the September 11 terrorist attacks, but it appeared to be a short-term gathering out of a sense of grieving rather than a transformation.

These research data show the importance of not using a single measure to analyze something as complex as religion. They also show the importance of considering a broader historical perspective rather than attempting to reach a conclusion from a single snapshot.

*Sources*: Gallup 2004; Goodstein 2001; Sherkat and Ellison 1999.

## Ethnicity, Religion, and Social Class

Generally, several social factors influence a person's identity and life chances. Pioneer sociologist Max Weber described **life chances** as people's opportunities to provide themselves with material goods, positive living conditions, and favorable life experiences. Religion, ethnicity, or both may affect life chances.

Religion and ethnicity do not necessarily operate together. Sometimes, they have been studied as if they were synonymous. Groups have been described as Irish Catholic, Swedish Lutheran, Muslim Arabs, or Russian Jewish, as if religion and ethnicity had been merged into some type of national church. In the 1990s, the religion–ethnicity tie took on new meaning as Latin American immigration invigorated the Roman Catholic Church nationwide, and West Indian immigration, particularly to New York City, brought new life to the Episcopal Church.

In the 1960s, sociologists felt that religion was more important than ethnicity in explaining behavior. They based this conclusion not on data but on the apparently higher visibility of religion in society. Using national survey data, Andrew Greeley came to different conclusions. He attempted to clarify the relative importance of religion and ethnicity by measuring personality characteristics, political participation, support for civil rights, and family structure. The sample consisted of German and Irish Americans, both Protestant and Catholic. If religion was more significant than ethnicity, Protestants, whether of German or Irish ancestry, and Catholics, regardless of ethnicity, would have been similar in outlook. Conversely, if ethnicity was the key, then the similarities would be among the Germans of either faith or among the Irish as a distinct group. On 17 of the 24 items that made up the four areas measured, the differences were greater between German Catholics and Irish Catholics than between German Catholics and Protestants or between Irish Catholics and Protestants. Ethnicity was a stronger predictor of attitudes and beliefs than religion. In one area—political party allegiance—religion was more important, but this was the exception rather than the rule. In sum, Greeley found ethnicity to be generally more important than religion in predicting behavior. In reality, it is very difficult to separate the influences of religion and ethnicity on any one individual, but Greeley's research cautions against discounting the influence of ethnicity in favor of religion (Glazer and Moynihan 1970; Greeley 1974a, 1974b; Herberg 1983).

In addition, as already noted several times, social class is yet another significant factor. Sociologist Milton Gordon (1978) developed the term **ethclass** (ethnicity and class) to denote the importance of both factors. All three factors—religion, ethnicity, and class—combine to form one's identity, determine one's social behavior, and limit one's life chances. For example, in certain ethnic communities, friendships are limited, to a degree, to people who share the same ethnic background and social class. In other words, neither race and ethnicity nor religion nor class alone places one socially. One must consider several elements together, as reflected in ethclass.

Religion can provide a sense of cohesion for a people. Here overflow worshippers listen to mass on the steps of St. Matthew's Catholic Church in Washington, DC during services remembering the victims of September 11, 2001.

# Religion in the United States

Divisive conflicts along religious lines are muted in the United States compared with those in, say, Northern Ireland or the Middle East. Although not entirely absent, conflicts about religion in the United States seem to be overshadowed by civil religion. **Civil religion** is the religious dimension in U.S. life that merges the state with sacred beliefs.

Sociologist Robert Bellah (1967) borrowed the phrase civil religion from eighteenth-century French philosopher Jean-Jacques Rousseau to describe a significant phenomenon in the contemporary United States. Civil religion exists alongside established religious faiths, and it embodies a belief system incorporating all religions but not associated specifically with any one. It is the type of faith to which presidents refer in inaugural speeches and to which American Legion posts and Girl Scout troops swear allegiance. In 1954, Congress added the phrase "under God" to the Pledge of Allegiance as a legislative recognition of religion's significance. Presidents of the United States, beginning with Ronald Reagan and continuing through George W. Bush, typically concluded even their most straightforward speeches with "God Bless the United States of America," which in effect evokes the civil religion of the nation.

Functionalists see civil religion as reinforcing central American values that may be more expressly patriotic than sacred in nature. Often, the mass media, following major societal upheavals, from the 1995 Oklahoma City bombing to the 2001 terrorist attacks, show church services with clergy praying and asking for national healing. Bellah sees no sign that the importance of civil religion has diminished in promoting collective identity, but he does acknowledge that it is more conservative than during the 1970s.

In the following section, we will explore the diversity among the major Christian groups in the United States, such as Roman Catholics and Protestants. However, as already noted, significant numbers of people in the United States now practice religions long established in other parts of the world, such as Islam, Hinduism, Judaism, and Buddhism. The greater visibility of religious diversity in the United States is primarily the result of immigrants bringing their religious faith with them and not assimilating to the dominant Christian rituals.

## Diversity among Roman Catholics

Social scientists have persistently tended to ignore the diversity within the Roman Catholic Church in the United States. Recent research has not sustained the conclusions that Roman Catholics are melding into a single group, following the traditions of the American Irish Catholic model, or even that parishioners are attending English-language churches. Religious behavior has been different for each ethnic group within the Roman Catholic Church. The Irish and the French Canadians left societies that were highly competitive

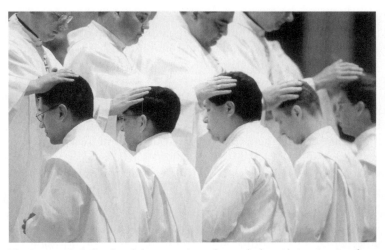

The Roman Catholic church has experienced growth through immigration from Latin America but has had difficulty recruiting men into the priesthood. Here we see an ordination ceremony at the Holy Name Cathedral in Chicago, Illinois, in 2003.

both culturally and socially. Their religious involvement in the United States is more relaxed than it was in Ireland and Quebec. However, the influence of life in the United States has increased German and Polish involvement in the Roman Catholic Church, whereas Italians have remained largely inactive. Variations by ethnic background continue to emerge in studies of contemporary religious involvement in the Roman Catholic Church (Eckstrom 2001).

Since the mid-1970s, the Roman Catholic Church in America has received a significant number of new members from the Philippines, Southeast Asia, and particularly Latin America. Although these new members have been a stabilizing force offsetting the loss of White ethnics, they have also challenged a church that for generations was dominated by Irish, Italian, and Polish parishes. Perhaps the most prominent subgroup in the Roman Catholic Church is the Latinos, who now account for one-third of all Roman Catholic parishioners. In a new class of priests ordained, nearly one-third were foreign born. Some Los Angeles churches in or near Latino neighborhoods must schedule fourteen masses each Sunday to accommodate the crowds of worshipers. By 2006, Latinos constituted 44 percent of Roman Catholics nationwide (Murphy and Banerjee 2005).

The Roman Catholic Church, despite its ethnic diversity, has clearly been a powerful force in reducing the ethnic ties of its members, making it also a significant assimilating force. The irony in this role of Catholicism is that so many nineteenth-century Americans heaped abuse on Catholics in this country for allegedly being un-American and having a dual allegiance. The history of the Catholic Church in the United States may be portrayed as a struggle within the membership between the Americanizers and the anti-Americanizers, with the former ultimately winning. Unlike the various Protestant churches that accommodated immigrants of a single nationality, the Roman Catholic Church had to Americanize a variety of linguistic and ethnic groups. The Catholic Church may have been the most potent assimilating force after the public school system. Comparing the assimilationist goal of the Catholic Church and the present diversity in it leads us to the conclusion that ethnic diversity has continued in the Roman Catholic Church despite, not because of, this religious institution.

## Diversity among Protestants

Protestantism, like Catholicism, often is portrayed as a monolithic entity. Little attention is given to the doctrinal and attitudinal differences that sharply divide the various denominations, in both laity and clergy. However, several studies document the diversity. Unfortunately, many opinion polls and surveys are content to learn whether a respondent is a Catholic, a Protestant, or a Jew. Stark and Glock (1968) found sharp differences in religious attitudes within Protestant churches. For example, 99 percent of Southern Baptists had no doubt that Jesus was the divine Son of God, as contrasted to only 40 percent of Congregationalists. We can identify four "generic theological camps":

1. Liberals: United Church of Christ (Congregationalists) and Episcopalians
2. Moderates: Disciples of Christ, Methodists, and Presbyterians
3. Conservatives: American Lutherans and American Baptists
4. Fundamentalists: Missouri Synod Lutherans, Southern Baptists, and Assembly of God

Roman Catholics generally hold religious beliefs similar to those of conservative Protestants, except on essentially Catholic issues such as papal infallibility (the authority of the spiritual role in all decisions regarding faith and morals). Whether or not there are four distinct camps is not important: The point is that the familiar practice of contrasting Roman Catholics and Protestants is clearly not productive. Some differences between Roman Catholics and Protestants are inconsequential compared with the differences between Protestant sects.

Secular criteria as well as doctrinal issues may distinguish religious faiths. Research has consistently shown that denominations can be arranged in a hierarchy based on social class. As Figure 5.7 reveals, members of certain faiths, such as Episcopalians, Jews, and Presbyterians, have a higher proportion of affluent members. Members of other faiths, including Baptists, tend to be poorer. Of course, all Protestant groups draw members from each social stratum. Nonetheless, the social significance of these class differences is that religion becomes a mechanism for signaling social mobility. A person who is moving up in wealth

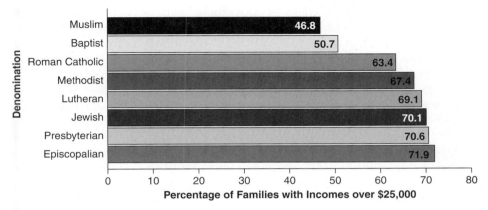

**Figure 5.7** Income and Denominations
Denominations attract different income groups. All groups have both affluent and poor members, yet some have a higher proportion of members with high incomes, and others are comparatively poor.
*Source:* General social survey, 1994 through 2004. See Davis, Smith, and Marsden 2005.

and power may seek out a faith associated with a higher social ranking. Similar contrasts are shown in formal schooling in Figure 5.8.

Protestant faiths have been diversifying, and many of their members have been leaving them for churches that follow strict codes of behavior or fundamental interpretations of Biblical teachings. This trend is reflected in the decline of the five mainline churches: Baptist, Episcopalian, Lutheran,

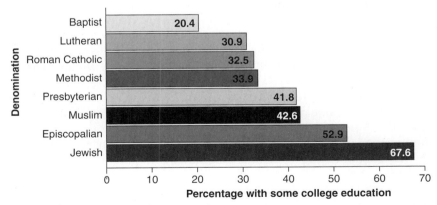

**Figure 5.8** Education and Denominations
There are sharp differences in the proportion of those with some college education by denomination.
*Source:* General social survey, 1994 through 2004. See Davis et al. 2005.

Methodist, and Presbyterian. In 2004, these faiths accounted for about 34 percent of total membership, compared with 75 percent in the 1970s. With a broader acceptance of new faiths and continuing immigration, it is unlikely that these mainline churches will regain their dominance in the near future (Davis, Smith, and Marsdren et al. 2005, 170).

Although Protestants may seem to define the civil religion and the accepted dominant orientation, some Christian faiths feel they, too, experience the discrimination usually associated with non-Christians such as Jews and Muslims. For example, representatives of the liberal and moderate faiths dominate the leadership of the military's chaplain corps. For example, there are 16 Presbyterian soldiers for every Presbyterian chaplain, 121 Full Gospel worshippers for every Full Gospel chaplain, and 339 Muslim soldiers for every Muslim chaplain (Cooperman 2005).

As another example of denominational discrimination, in 1998 the Southern Baptist Convention amended its basic theological statements of beliefs to include a strong statement on family life. However, the statement included a declaration that a woman should "submit herself graciously" to her husband's leadership. There were widespread attacks on this position, which many Baptists felt was inappropriate because they were offering guidance for their denomination's members. In some respects, Baptists felt this was a form of respectable bigotry. It was acceptable to attack them for their views on social issues even though such criticism would be much more muted for many more liberal faiths that seem free to tolerate abortion (Bowman 1998; Niebuhr 1998).

## Women and Religion

Religious beliefs have often placed women in an exalted but protected position. As religions are practiced, this position has often meant being "protected" from becoming leaders. Perhaps the only major exception in the United States is the Christian Science church, in which the majority of practitioners and readers are women. Women may be evangelists, prophets, and even saints, but they find it difficult to enter the clergy within their own congregations.

Even today, the largest denomination in the United States, Roman Catholicism, does not permit women to be priests. A 1996 Gallup survey found that 65 percent of Roman Catholics in this country favor the ordination of women, compared with only 29 percent in 1974 but the church hierarchy has continued to maintain its longstanding requirement that priests be male (Briggs 1996).

The largest Protestant denomination, the Southern Baptist Convention, has voted against ordaining women (although some of its autonomous churches have women ministers). Other religious faiths that do not allow women clergy include the Lutheran Church-Missouri Synod, the Greek Orthodox Archdiocese of North and South America, the Orthodox Church in America,

Women play a significant role as unpaid volunteers, but relatively few become members of the clergy with leadership responsibilities. Pictured is Barbara Harris as she was ordained the first female bishop in the Episcopalian Church in 1989.

the Church of God in Christ, the Church of Jesus Christ of Latter-Day Saints, and Orthodox Judaism.

Despite these restrictions, there has been a notable rise in female clergy in the last twenty years. The Bureau of the Census (2005a) shows that 6 percent of clergy were women in 1983, but that figure had increased to 14 percent in 2003. Increasingly, some branches of Protestantism and Judaism have been convinced that women have the right to become spiritual leaders. Yet a lingering question remains: Once women are ordained as spiritual leaders, do congregations necessarily accept these female ministers and rabbis? Will they advance in their calling as easily as their male counterparts, or will they face blatant or subtle discrimination in their efforts to secure desirable posts within their faiths?

It is too early to offer any definitive answers to these questions, but thus far, women clearly continue to face lingering sexism after ordination. Evidence to date indicates that women find it more difficult than men to secure jobs in larger, more prestigious congregations. Although they may be accepted as junior clergy or as copastors, women may fail to receive senior clergy appointments. In both Reform and Conservative Judaism, the largest and best-known congregations rarely hire women rabbis. Consequently, women clergy in many denominations are gathered at the low end of the pay scale and the hierarchy (Chang 1997; Religion Watch 1995).

## Religion and the U.S. Supreme Court

Religious pluralism owes its existence in the United States to the First Amendment declaration that "Congress shall make no law respecting an establishment of religion, or prohibiting the free exercise thereof." The U.S. Supreme Court has consistently interpreted this wording to mean not that government should ignore religion but that it should follow a policy of neutrality to maximize religious freedom. For example, the government may not help religion by financing a new church building, but it also may not obstruct religion by denying a church adequate police and fire protection. We will examine four issues that continue to require clarification: school prayer, secessionist minorities, creationism (including intelligent design), and the public display of religious symbols.

Despite Supreme Court rulings to the contrary, many public schools encourage children praying.

Among the most controversial and continuing disputes has been whether prayer has a role in the schools. Many people were disturbed by the 1962 Supreme Court decision in *Engel v. Vitale* that disallowed a purportedly non-denominational prayer drafted for use in the New York public schools. The prayer was "Almighty God, we acknowledge our dependence upon Thee, and we beg Thy blessings upon us, our parents, our teachers, and our country." Subsequent decisions overturned state laws requiring Bible reading in public schools, laws requiring recitation of the Lord's Prayer, and laws permitting a daily one-minute period of silent meditation or prayer. Despite such judicial pronouncements, children in many public schools in the United States are led in regular prayer recitation or Bible reading.

What about prayers at public gatherings? In 1992, the Supreme Court ruled 5–4 in *Lee v. Weisman* that prayer at a junior high school graduation in Providence, Rhode Island, violated the U.S. Constitution's mandate of separation of church and state. A rabbi had given thanks to God in his invocation. The district court suggested that the invocation would have been acceptable without that reference. The Supreme Court did not agree with the school board that a prayer at a graduation was not coercive. The Court did say in its opinion that it was acceptable for a student speaker voluntarily to say a prayer at such a program (Marshall 2001).

Several religious groups have been in legal and social conflict with the rest of society. Some can be called **secessionist minorities,** in that they reject both assimilation and coexistence in some form of cultural pluralism. The Amish are one such group that comes into conflict with outside society because of their beliefs and way of life. The Old Order Amish shun most modern conveniences, and later in this chapter we will consider them as a case study of maintaining a lifestyle dramatically different from that of larger society.

Are there limits to the free exercise of religious rituals by secessionist minorities? Today, tens of thousands of members of Native American religions believe that ingesting the powerful drug peyote is a sacrament and that those who partake of peyote will enter into direct contact with God. In 1990, the Supreme Court ruled that prosecuting people who use illegal drugs as part of a religious ritual is not a violation of the First Amendment guarantee of religious freedom. The case arose because Native Americans were dismissed from their jobs for the religious use of peyote and were then refused unemployment benefits by the State of Oregon's employment division. In 1991, however, Oregon enacted a new law permitting the sacramental use of peyote by Native Americans (*New York Times* 1991).

In another ruling on religious rituals, in 1993, the Supreme Court unanimously overturned a local ordinance in Florida that banned ritual animal sacrifice. The high court held that this law violated the free-exercise rights of adherents of the Santeria religion, in which the sacrifice of animals (including goats, chickens, and other birds) plays a central role. The same year Congress passed the Religious Freedom Restoration Act, which said the government may not enforce laws that "substantially burden" the exercise of religion. Presumably, this action will give religious groups more flexibility in practicing their faiths. However, many local and state officials are concerned that the law has led to unintended consequences, such as forcing states to accommodate prisoners' requests for questionable religious activities or to permit a church to expand into a historic district in defiance of local laws (Greenhouse 1996).

The third area of contention has been whether the biblical account of creation should be or must be presented in school curricula and whether this account should receive the same emphasis as scientific theories. In the famous "monkey trial" of 1925, Tennessee schoolteacher John Scopes was found guilty of teaching the scientific theory of evolution in public schools. Since then, however, Darwin's evolutionary theories have been presented in public schools with little reference to the biblical account in Genesis. People who support the literal interpretation of the Bible, commonly known as **creationists,** have formed various organizations to crusade for creationist treatment in U.S. public schools and universities.

In a 1987 Louisiana case, *Edwards v. Aguillard,* the Supreme Court ruled that states may not require the teaching of creationism alongside evolution in public schools if the primary purpose of such legislation is to promote a religious viewpoint. Nevertheless, the teaching of evolution and creationism has remained a controversial issue in many communities across the United States (Applebome 1996).

Beginning in the 1980s, those who believe in a divine hand in the creation of life have advanced **intelligent design** (ID). While not explicitly drawn on the biblical account, creationists fell comfortable with ID. Intelligent design is the idea that life is so complex it could only have been created by a higher intelligence. Supporters of ID advocate it is a more accurate account than Darwinism or, at the very least, that it be taught as an alternative alongside the theory of evolution. In 2005 a federal judge in *Kitzmiller v. Dove Area School District* ended a Pennsylvania school district intention to require the presentation of ID. In essence the judge found ID to be "a religious belief" that was only a subtler way of finding of God's fingerprints in nature than traditional creationism. While the issue continues to be hotly debated and agree that future courts cases will come (Clemmitt 2005; Goodstein 2005).

The fourth area of contention has been a battle over public displays that depict symbols of or seem associated with a religion. Can manger scenes be erected on public property? Do people have a right to be protected from large displays such as a cross or a star atop a water tower overlooking an entire town? In a series of decisions in the 1980s through to 1995, the Supreme Court ruled that tax-supported religious displays on public government property may be successfully challenged but are not permissible if they are made more secular. Displays that combine a crèche, the Christmas manger scene depicting the birth of Jesus, or the Hanukkah menorah and also include Frosty the Snowman or even Christmas trees have been ruled secular. These

decisions have been dubbed "the plastic reindeer rules." In 1995, the Court clarified the issue by stating that privately sponsored religious displays may be allowed on public property if other forms of expression are permitted in the same location. The final judicial word has not been heard, and all these rulings should be viewed as tentative because the Court cases have been decided by close votes, and changes in the Supreme Court composition may alter the outcome of future cases (Bork 1995; Hirsley 1991; Mauro 1995).

## Limits of Religious Freedom: The Amish

The Amish began migrating to North America early in the eighteenth century and settled first in eastern Pennsylvania, where a large settlement is still found. Those who continued the characteristic lifestyle of the Amish are primarily members of the Old Order Amish Mennonite Church. By 2003, there were about 1,400 Old Order Amish settlements in the United States and Canada. Estimates place this faith at about 180,000, with approximately 75 percent living in three states: Ohio, Pennsylvania, and Indiana.

### The Amish Way of Life

Amish practice self-segregation, living in settlements divided into church districts that are autonomous congregations composed of about 75 baptized members. If the district becomes much larger, it is again divided because the members meet in each other's homes. There are no church buildings. Amish homes are large, with the main floor often having removable walls so a household can take its periodic turn hosting the Sunday service.

Each Amish district has a bishop, two to four preachers, and an elder but there are no general conferences, mission groups, or cooperative agencies. The Amish differ little from the Mennonites in formal religious doctrine. Holy Communion is celebrated twice each year, and both groups practice washing of feet. Adults are baptized when they are admitted to formal membership in the church at about age 17 to 20. Old Order Amish services are conducted in German with a mixture of English, commonly known as Pennsylvania Dutch (from *Deutsch,* the German word for "German").

The Amish are best known for their plain clothing and their nonconformist way of life. Sociologists sometimes use the term secessionist minorities to refer to groups such as the Amish, who reject assimilation and practice coexistence or pluralism with the rest of society primarily on their own terms. The practice of *Meidung,* or shunning, persists, and sociologists view it as central to the Amish system of social control. The social norms of this secessionist minority that have evolved over the years are known as the *Ordnung.* These "understandings" specify the color and style of clothing, color and style of buggies, the use of horses for fieldwork, the use of the Pennsylvania Dutch dialect, worship services in the homes, unison singing without instruments, and marriage within the church, to name a few.

The Amish shun telephones and electric lights, and they drive horses and buggies rather than automobiles. The *Ordnung* also prohibits filing a lawsuit, entering military service, divorce, using air transportation, and even using wall-to-wall carpeting. They are generally considered excellent farmers, but they often refuse to use modern farm machinery. Concessions have been made but do vary from one Amish settlement to another. Among common exceptions to the *Ordnung* is the use of chemical fertilizers, insecticides, and pesticides, the use of indoor bathroom facilities, and modern medical and dental practice.

## The Amish and Larger Society

The Amish have made some concessions to the dominant society, but larger society has made concessions to the Amish to facilitate their lifestyle. For example, the 1972 U.S. Supreme Court, in *Yoder v. Wisconsin,* allowed Wisconsin Amish to escape prosecution from laws that required parents to send their children to school to age 18. Amish education ends at about age 13 because the community feels their members have received all the schooling necessary to prosper as Amish people. States waive certification requirements for Amish teaching staff (who are other Amish people), minimum wage requirements for the teachers, and school building requirements.

The Amish today do not totally reject social change. For example, until the late 1960s, church members could be excommunicated for being employed in other than agricultural pursuits. Now their work is much more diversified. Although

The Amish, as shown in this group of young women on a farm in Kentucky, have made relatively few accommodations with the larger culture—the culture of outsiders referred collectively to by the Amish as the "English."

you will not find Amish computer programmers, there are Amish engaged as blacksmiths, harness makers, buggy repairers, and carpenters. Non-Amish often hire these craftspeople as well.

The movement by the Amish into other occupations is sometimes a source of tension with larger society, or the "English," as the Amish refer to non-Amish people. Conflict theorists observe that as long as the Amish remained totally apart from dominant society in the United States, they experienced little hostility. As they entered the larger economic sector, however, intergroup tensions developed in the form of growing prejudice. The Amish today may underbid their competitors. The Amish entry into the commercial market-place has also strained the church's traditional teaching on litigation and insurance, both of which are to be avoided. Mutual assistance has been the historical path taken, but that does not always mesh well with the modern businessperson. After legal action taken on their behalf, Amish businesses typically have been allowed to be exempt from paying Social Security and workers' compensation, another sore point with English competitors.

The Amish entrepreneur represents an interesting variation of the typical ethnic businessperson one might encounter in a Chinatown, for example. Research on ethnic businesses often cites discrimination against minorities and immigrants as a prime force prodding the development of minority enterprises. The Amish are a very different case because their own restrictions on education, factory work, and certain occupations have propelled them into becoming small business owners. However, stratification is largely absent among the Old Order Amish. The notion of ethclass would have no meaning, as the Amish truly regard one another as equal.

Children are not sent to high schools. This practice caused the Amish some difficulty because of compulsory school attendance laws, and some Amish parents have gone to jail rather than allow their children to go to high school. Eventually, as noted earlier, the Supreme Court, in *Yoder v. Wisconsin,* upheld a lower court's decision that a Wisconsin compulsory education law violated the Amish right to religious freedom. However, not all court rulings have been friendly to Amish efforts to avoid the practices and customs of the English. In another case, the effort by the Amish to avoid using the legally mandated orange triangles for marking slow-moving vehicles (such as their buggies) was rejected. If you travel through Amish areas, you can now see their horse-drawn buggies displaying this one symbol of modernity.

Living alongside this modernity, Amish youth often test their subculture's boundaries during a period of discovery called *rumspringe,* a term that means "running around." Amish young people attend barn dances where taboos like drinking, smoking, and driving cars are commonly broken. Parents often react by looking the other way, sometimes literally. For example, when they hear radio sounds from a barn or motorcycle entering their property in the middle of the night, they don't immediately investigate and punish their offspring. Instead, they pretend not to notice, secure in the comfort that their children almost always return to the traditions of the Amish lifestyle. In 2004, UPN aired the "Amish in the City" reality program featuring five Amish youths allegedly on *rumspringe* moving in with six citywide young adults in Los Angeles. Critics on behalf of the Amish community noted that this exploitation showed how vulnerable the Amish are, since no program was developed to try to show the conversion of Muslim or Orthodox Jewish youth.

A growing area of Amish–English legal clashes is over the custom of young Amish children working as laborers. Amish families in western and central Pennsylvania in 1998 protested the federal government's enforcement of labor laws that are intended to protect children from workplace hazards. The Amish are turning to new businesses, such as sawmills and wood shops, as their available farmland begins to disappear. That means more children on the shop floor. The Amish contend that their religious and cultural traditions hold that children should work, but the U.S. Labor Department had taken a different view. The Amish argued that letting children work alongside their fathers instills core values of hard work, diligence, cooperation, and responsibility, values that they say are central to their faith. English businesses see this underage employment as another form of unfair competition by the Amish. In 2004, Congress passed the law with the Amish in mind that exempted such child labor as long as machinery is not operated and adults are present.

The Old Order Amish have developed a pluralistic position that has become increasingly difficult to maintain as their numbers grow and as they enter the economy in competition with the English, or the non-Amish (Dart 1998; *The Economist* 2004a; Kraybill 2001, 2003; Kraybill and Nolt 1995; Public Broadcasting System 1998).

## Conclusion

Considering ethnicity, and religion reinforces our understanding of the patterns of intergroup relations first presented in Chapter 1, Figure 5.9 shows the rich variety of relationships as defined by people's ethnic and religious Identity.

Any study of life in the United States, but especially one focusing on dominant and subordinate groups, cannot ignore religion and ethnicity. The two are closely related, as certain religious faiths predominate in certain nationalities. Both religious activity and interest by White ethnics in their heritage continue to be prominent features of the contemporary scene. People have been and continue to be ridiculed or deprived of opportunities solely because of their ethnic or religious affiliation. To get a true picture of people's place in society,

we need to consider both ethnicity and social class (or what has been called ethclass) in association with their religious identification.

Religion is changing in the United States. As one commercial measure, Hallmark created its first greeting card in 2003 for the Muslim holiday Eid-al-fitr, which marks the end of the month-long feast of Ramadan. The issue of the persistence of ethnicity is an intriguing one. Some people may only casually exhibit their ethnicity and practice what has been called symbolic ethnicity. However, can people immerse themselves in their ethnic culture without society punishing them for their will to be different? The tendency to put down White ethnics through respectable bigotry continues. Despite this

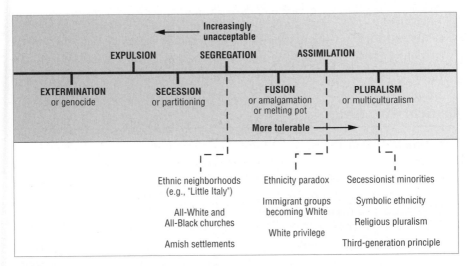

**Figure 5.9** Intergroup Relations Continuum

intolerance, ethnicity remains a viable source of identity for many citizens today. There is also the ethnicity paradox, which finds that practicing one's ethnic heritage often strengthens people and allows them to move successfully into the larger society.

The issue of religious expression in all its forms also raises a variety of intriguing questions. How can a country increasingly populated by diverse and often non-Christian faiths maintain religious tolerance? How might this change in decades ahead? How will the courts and society resolve the issues of religious freedom? This is a particularly important issue in such areas as school prayer, secessionist minorities, creationism, and public religious displays. Some examination of religious ties is fundamental to completing an accurate picture of a person's social identity.

Ethnicity and religion are a basic part of today's social reality and of each individual's identity. The emotions, disputes, and debate over religion and ethnicity in the United States are powerful indeed.

## Key Terms

bilingual education   169
bilingualism   169
civil religion   180
creationists   188
denomination   173

English immersion   170
ethclass   179
ethnicity paradox   161
intelligent design   188
life chances   178

principle of third-generation
   interest   159
respectable bigotry   162
secessionist minority   187
symbolic ethnicity   160

## Review Questions

1. In what respect are the ethnic and the religious diversity of the United States related to each other?
2. Is assimilation automatic within any given ethnic group?
3. Can "blaming the victims" be applied to prejudice among White ethnic groups?
4. To what extent has a non-Christian tradition been developing in the United States?
5. How have court rulings affected religious expression?

## Critical Thinking

1. When do you see ethnicity becoming more apparent? When does it appear to occur only in response to other people's advancing their own ethnicity? From these situations, how can ethnic identity be both positive and perhaps counterproductive or even destructive?
2. Why do you think we are so often reluctant to show our religion to others? Why might people of certain faiths be more hesitant than others?
3. How does religion reflect conservative and liberal positions on social issues? Consider services for the homeless, the need for child care, the acceptance or rejection of gay men and lesbians, and a woman's right to terminate a pregnancy versus the fetus's right to survive.

# Internet Connections—Research Navigator™

Follow the instructions found on page 42 of this text to access the features of Research Navigator™. Once at the website, enter your Login Name and Password. Then, to use the ContentSelect database, enter keywords such as "Mormons," "Amish," and "whiteness studies," and the research engine will supply relevant and recent scholarly and popular press publications. Use the New York Times Search-by-Subject Archive to find recent news articles related to sociology, and the Link Library feature to locate relevant Web links organized by the key terms associated with this chapter.

# 6

# The Nation as a Kaleidoscope

## CHAPTER OUTLINE

───────────────⟨ HIGHLIGHTS ⟩───────────────

The nation is likened to a kaleidoscope because the diverse population has not fused into a melting pot, nor is the future composition apt to be as static as a salad bowl. Racial and ethnic subordinate groups are making progress economically and educationally, but so are Whites. Even relatively successful Asian Americans are undeserving of their model-minority stereotype. We can consider the changing composition of society not only in terms of our face-to-face interaction every day but also in terms of the changing workforce.

---

What metaphor do we use to describe a nation whose racial, ethnic, and religious minorities are now becoming numerical majorities in cities coast-to-coast already in the states of California, Hawaii, and Texas (refer back to Figure 1.2)? The outpouring of statistical data and personal experience documents the racial and ethnic diversity of the entire nation. And as we see in Figure 6.1, although the mosaic may be different in different regions and different communities, the tapestry of racial and ethnic groups is always close at hand wherever one is in the United States.

Although *E Pluribus Unum* may be reassuring, it does not describe what a visitor sees along the length of Fifth Avenue in Manhattan or in Monterey Park outside Los Angeles. It is apparent in the increasing numbers of Latinos in the rural river town of Beardstown, Illinois, and the emerging Somali immigrant population in Hartford, Connecticut or Lewiston, Maine. It is not reflected in the debate that emerged in 2006 over Omaha's proposal to divide its 46,700 public school students into three districts—one largely Black, one White, and one largely Hispanic.

For several generations, the melting pot has been used as a convenient description of our culturally diverse nation. The analogy of an alchemist's cauldron was clever, even if a bit jingoistic. In the Middle Ages, the alchemist attempted to change less costly metals into gold and silver.

The phrase "melting pot" originated as the title of a 1908 play by Israel Zangwill. In this play, a young Russian Jewish immigrant to the United States composes a symphony that portrays a nation that serves as a crucible (or pot) where all ethnic and racial groups dissolve into a new, superior stock.

The belief in the United States as a melting pot became widespread in the first part of the twentieth century, particularly because it suggested that the

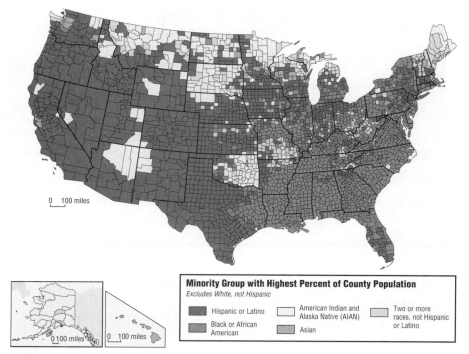

**Figure 6.1** The Image of Diversity from Census 2000
*Source*: Brewer and Suchan 2001, 20.

United States had an almost divinely inspired mission to destroy artificial divisions and create a single humankind. However, the dominant group had indicated its unwillingness to welcome Native Americans, African Americans, Hispanics, Jews, and Asians, among many others, into the melting pot.

Although the metaphor of the melting pot is still used today, observers recognize that it hides as much about a multiethnic United States as it discloses. Therefore, the metaphor of the salad bowl emerged in the 1970s to portray a country ethnically diverse. As we can distinguish the lettuce from the tomatoes from the peppers in a tossed salad, we can see the ethnic restaurants and the persistence of "foreign" language newspapers. The dressing over the ingredients is akin to the shared value system and culture, covering, but not hiding, the different ingredients of the salad.

Yet even the notion of a salad bowl is wilting. Like its melting-pot predecessor, the picture of a salad is static—certainly not what we see in the United States. It also hardly calls to mind the myriad cultural pieces that make up the fabric or mosaic of our diverse nation.

The kaleidoscope offers another familiar, yet more useful, analogy. Patented in 1817 by Scottish scientist Sir David Brewster, the kaleidoscope is both a toy and increasingly a table artifact of upscale living rooms. Users of this optical device are aware that when they turn a set of mirrors, the colors and patterns reflected off pieces of glass, tinsel, or beads seem to be endless. The growing popularity of the phrase "people of color" seems made for the kaleidoscope that is the United States. The changing images correspond to the often bewildering array of groups found in our country.

How easy is it to describe the image to someone else as we gaze into the eyepiece of a kaleidoscope? It is a challenge similar to that faced by educators who toil with what constitutes the ethnic history of the United States. We can forgive the faux pas by the *Washington Post* writer who described the lack of Hispanic-speaking (rather than Spanish-speaking) police as a factor contributing to the recent hostilities in the capital. Little wonder, given the bewildering ethnic patterns, that Chicago politicians striving to map for the first time a "safe" Hispanic congressional district find themselves scrutinized by Blacks fearful of losing their "safe" districts. We can forgive Marlon Brando for sending an Indian woman to refuse his Oscar, thus protesting Hollywood's portrayal of Native Americans. Was he unaware of Italian Americans' disbelief when his award-winning performance was in *The Godfather?* We can understand why the African Americans traumatized by Hurricane Katrina would turn their raft from the White power structure that they perceived ignoring their needs to the Latinos who took advantage of reconstruction projects in New Orleans.

It is difficult to describe the image created by a kaleidoscope because it changes dramatically with little effort. Similarly, in the kaleidoscope of the United States, we find it a challenge to describe the multiracial nature of this republic. Perhaps in viewing the multiethnic, multiracial United States as a kaleidoscope, we may take comfort that the Greek word *kalos* means "beautiful" (Schaefer 1992).

In order to develop a better understanding of the changing image through the kaleidoscope, we will first try to learn what progress has taken place and why miscommunication among our diverse peoples seems to be the rule rather than the exception.

## The Glass Half Empty

A common expression makes reference to a glass half full or half empty of water. If one is thirsty, it is half empty and in need of being replenished. If one is attempting to clear dirty dishes, it is half full. For many people, especially Whites, the progress of subordinate groups or minorities makes it difficult to understand calls for more programs and new reforms and impossible to understand when minority neighborhoods erupt in violence.

In absolute terms, the glass of water has been filling up, but people in the early twenty-first century do not compare themselves with people in the 1960s.

Significant disparities remain, but it is also impossible to ignore the gains over the last two generations. Few but growing in number, African Americans are entering positions that few people, of any color, reach. Ayana Howard, with an Electrical Engineering Ph.D., sits beside SmartNarv, a prototype for an autonomous Mars rover, on a set of the planet at NASA's Jet Propulsion Laboratory in California.

For example, Latinos and African Americans regard the appropriate reference group to be Whites today; compared with them, the glass is half empty at best.

In Figure 6.2, we have shown the present picture and recent changes by comparing African Americans and Hispanics with Whites as well as contemporary data for Native Americans (American Indians). We see that the nation's largest minority groups—African Americans and Hispanics—have higher household income, complete more schooling, and enjoy longer life expectancy today than in 1975. White Americans have made similar strides in all three areas. The gap remains and, if one analyzes it closely, has actually increased in some instances. Both Blacks and Latinos in 2004 had just edged out the income level that Whites had exceeded back in 1975. Three decades behind! Also, Black Americans today have barely matched the life expectancy that Whites had a generation earlier. Similarly, many minority Americans remain entrenched in poverty: nearly 1 out of 4 Hispanics and African Americans.

Little has changed since 1975. We have chosen 1975 because that was a year for which we have comparable data for Latinos, Whites, and African Americans. However, the patterns would be no different if we considered 1950, 1960, or 1970.

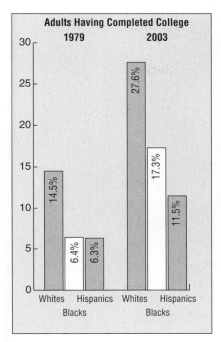

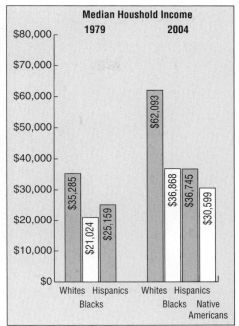

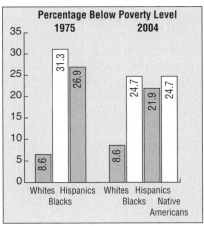

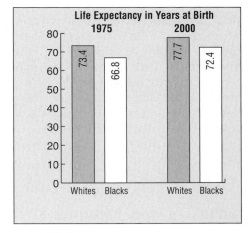

**Figure 6.2** Changes in Schooling, Income, and Life Expectancy
Note: Native American data is for 2000. Education data include people 25 and over. Hispanic education 1975 data estimated by author from data for 1970 and 1980. White data are for non-Hispanic (except in education).
*Sources*: Bureau of the Census 1988, 167, 2005a, 44; DeNavas-Walt et al. 2005, 17–20; Ogunwole 2006.

Asian Americans are subject to stereotypes such as the model-minority image.

These data provide only the broadest overview. Detailed analyses do not yield a brighter picture. For example, about 1 in 9 Whites were without health insurance in 2004 compared to 1 of 5 African Americans and 1 of 3 Latinos. Similarly, 3.9 percent of all doctorates were awarded to African Americans in 1981. By 2002, the proportion had increased only to 5.4 percent. The United States continues to rely on overseas students to fill the places on the educational ladder. The number of doctorates awarded to non-resident aliens (that is, immigrants who gained entry for schooling with no other ties to U.S. citizens) was three times that of Blacks, Asian Americans, Latinos, and American Indians *combined* (Bureau of the Census 2005a; DeNavas-Walt et al. 2005; Hoffer et al. 2001).

## Is There a Model Minority?

The desperate situation of African Americans, Latinos, and Native Americans is not the picture of Asian Americans as a group. Obviously, Asians in the United States are a diverse group, ranging from the descendants of Chinese who immigrated over 150 years ago, to Vietnamese, Laotians, and Cambodians who arrived in the United States as a result of the Vietnam War, to Indian and Pakistani physicians and teachers whose immigration is given preference by our current policy.

"Asian Americans are a success! They achieve! They succeed! There are no protests, no demands. They just do it!" This is the general image that people in the United States so often hold of Asian Americans as a group. They constitute a **model or ideal minority** because, although they have experienced prejudice and discrimination, they seem nevertheless to have succeeded economically, socially, and educationally without resorting to political or violent confrontations with Whites. Some observers point to the existence of a model minority as a reaffirmation that anyone can get ahead in the United States. Proponents of the model-minority view declare that because Asian Americans have achieved success, they have ceased to be subordinate and are no longer disadvantaged. This is only a variation of "blaming the victim"; with Asian Americans, it is "praising the victim." An examination of aspects of their socioeconomic status will allow a more thorough exploration of this view (Fong 2002; Hurh and Kim 1989; Thrupkaew 2002).

Asian Americans as a group do have impressive school enrollment rates in comparison to the total population. In 2002, 57 percent of Asian Americans 25 years or older held bachelor's degrees, compared to 32 percent of the White population. These rates vary among Asian American groups, with Asian Indians, Chinese Americans, and Japanese Americans having higher levels of educational achievement (Reeves and Bennett 2003).

This encouraging picture does have some qualifications, however, that call into question the optimistic model-minority view. According to a study of California's state university system that was released in 1991, although Asian Americans are often viewed as successful overachievers, they have unrecognized and overlooked needs and experience discomfort and harassment on campus. As a group, they also lack Asian faculty and staff members to whom they can turn for support. They confront many identity issues and have to do a sort of "cultural balancing act" along with all the usual pressures faced by college students. The report noted that an "alarming number" of Asian American students appear to be experiencing intense stress and alienation, problems that have often been "exacerbated by racial *harassment*" (Ohnuma 1991; Zhou 2004).

Even the positive stereotype of Asian American students as "academic stars" can be dysfunctional or counterproductive to people so labeled. Asian Americans who do only modestly well in school may face criticism from their parents or teachers for their failure to conform to the "whiz kid" image. In fact, some Asian American youth disengage from school when faced with these perceptions or receive little support for their interest in vocational pursuits or athletics (Kibria 2002).

Although much of the stereotyping is positive on the surface, journalist Helen Zia reminds us in "Listen to our Voices" that negative stereotypes are pervasive. In this atmosphere, immigrant parents then grapple with the decision of whether to teach their children their language or push them to become American as fast as possible.

## LISTEN TO OUR VOICES

## Gangsters, Gooks, Geishas, and Geeks

*Helen Zia*

Ah so. No tickee, no washee. So sorry, so sollee.

Chinkee, Chink. Jap, Nip, zero, kamikaze. Dothead, flat face, flat nose, slant eye, slope. Slit, mamasan, dragon lady. Gook, VC, Flip, Hindoo.

By the time I was 10, I'd heard such words so many times I could feel them coming before they parted lips. I knew they were meant in the unkindest way. Still, we didn't talk about these incidents at home, we just accepted them as part of being in America, something to learn to rise above.

The most common taunting didn't even utilize words but a string of unintelligible gobbledygook that kids—and adults—would spew as they pretended to speak Chinese or some other Asian language. It was a mockery of how they imagined my parents talked to me.

Truth was that Mom and Dad rarely spoke to us in Chinese, except to scold or call us to dinner. Worried that we might develop an accent, my father insisted that we speak English at home. This, he explained, would lessen the hardships we might encounter and make us more acceptable as Americans.

I'll never know if my father's language decision was right. On the one hand, I, like most Asian Americans, have been complimented countless times on my spoken English by people who assumed I was a foreigner. "My, you speak such good English," they'd cluck. "No kidding, I ought to," I would think to myself, then wonder: Should I thank them for assuming that English isn't my native language? Or should I correct them on the proper usage of "well" and "good"?

More often than feeling grateful for my American accent, I've wished that I could jump into a heated exchange of rapid-fire Chinese, volume high and spit flying. But with a vocabulary limited to *"Ni hao?"* (How are you?) and *"Ting bu dong"* (I hear but don't understand), meaningful exchanges are woefully impossible. I find myself smiling and nodding like a dashboard ornament. I'm envious of the many people I know who grew up speaking an Asian language yet converse in English beautifully.

Armed with standard English and my flat New Jersey "a," I still couldn't escape the name-calling. I became all too familiar with other names and faces that supposedly matched mine—Fu Manchu, Suzie Wong, Hop Sing, Madame Butterfly, Charlie Chan, Ming the Merciless—the "Asians" produced for mass consumption. Their faces filled me with shame whenever I saw them on TV or in the movies. They defined my face to the rest of the world: a sinister Fu, Suzie the whore, subservient Hop Sing, pathetic Butterfly, cunning Chan, and warlike Ming. Inscrutable Orientals all, real Americans none.

That Asian Americans as a group work in the same occupations as Whites suggests that they have been successful, and many have. The pattern, however, shows some differences. Asian immigrants, like other minorities and immigrants before them, are found disproportionately in the low-paying service occupations. At the same time, they are also concentrated at the top in professional and managerial positions. Yet, as we will see, they rarely reach the very top. They hit the "glass ceiling" (as described in Chapter 3) or, as some others say, try to "climb a broken ladder," before they reach management. In 2002, there were only 176 Asian Americans on any of the boards of the *Fortune* 1,000 corporations—that amounts to less than 2 percent. In California, where the Asian American presence is very visible, the situation is a bit better (Strauss 2002).

Another misleading sign of the apparent "success" of Asian Americans is their high incomes as a group. Like other elements of the image, however, this deserves closer inspection. Asian American family income approaches parity with that of Whites because of their greater achievement than Whites in formal schooling. If we look at specific educational levels, Whites earn more than their Asian counterparts of the same age. Asian Americans' average earnings increased by at least $2,300 for each additional year of schooling, whereas Whites gained almost $3,000 (Wu 2002; Zhou and Kamo 1994).

There are striking contrasts among Asian Americans. For every Asian American family with an annual income of $75,000 or more, another earns less than $10,000 a year. In New York City's Chinatown neighborhood, about one-quarter of all families live below the poverty level. In San Diego, dropout rates were close to 60 percent among Southeast Asians in 1997. Even relatively successful Asian Americans continue to face obstacles because of their racial heritage. According to a study of three major public hospitals in Los Angeles, Asian Americans account for 34 percent of all physicians and nurses but fill only 11 percent of management positions at these hospitals (Dunn 1994; Reeves and Bennett 2003; Sengupta 1997).

At first glance, one might be puzzled to see criticism of a positive generalization such as "model minority." Why should the stereotype of adjusting without problems be a disservice to Asian Americans? The answer is that this incorrect view helps to exclude Asian Americans from social programs and conceals unemployment and other social ills. When representatives of Asian groups do seek assistance for those in need, they are resented by those who are convinced of the model-minority view. If a minority group is viewed as successful, it is unlikely that its members will be included in programs designed to alleviate the problems they encounter as minorities. The positive stereotype reaffirms the United States system of mobility: New immigrants as well as established subordinate groups ought to achieve more merely by working within the system. At the same time, viewed from the conflict perspective outlined in Chapter 1, this becomes yet another instance of "blaming the victim"; if Asian Americans have succeeded, Blacks and Hispanics must be responsible for their own low status (Committee of 100 2001; Ryan 1976).

## Persistence of Inequality

Progress has occurred. Indignities and injustices have been eliminated, allowing us to focus on the remaining barriers to equity. But why do the gaps in income, living wages, education, and even life expectancy persist? Especially perplexing is this glass half full or half empty given the numerous civil rights laws, study commissions, favorable court decisions, and efforts by nonprofits and private sectors.

In trying to comprehend the persistence of inequality among racial and ethnic groups, sociologists and other social scientists have found it useful to think in terms of the role played by social and cultural capital. Popularized by the French sociologist Pierre Bourdieu, these concepts refer to assets that are not necessarily economic but do impact economic capital for one's family and future. Less cultural and social capital may be passed on from one generation to the next, especially when prejudice and discrimination make it difficult to overcome deficits. Racial and ethnic minorities reproduce disadvantage while Whites are more likely to reproduce privilege (Bourdieu 1983; Bourdieu and Passeron 1990).

**Cultural capital** refers to noneconomic forces such as family background, past investments in education that is then reflected in knowledge about the arts, and language. It is not necessarily book knowledge but the kind of education valued by the elites. African Americans and Native Americans have in the past

Racial and ethnic minorities may not have the cultural and social capital of privileged Whites, but they treasure their rich heritage. Education on reservations stresses American Indian and tribal culture more than in the past. Pictured is a classroom on the Crow Reservation in Montana.

faced significant restrictions in receiving a quality education. Immigrants have faced challenges because English was not being spoken at home. Muslim immigrants face an immediate challenge in functioning in a culture that advantages a different form of spirituality and lifestyle. The general historical pattern have been for immigrants, especially those who came in large numbers and settled in ethnic enclaves, to take two or three generations to reach educational parity. Knowledge of hip-hop and familiarity with Polish cuisine is culture, but it is not the culture that is valued and prestigious. Society privileges or values some lifestyles over others. This is not good but it is social reality. Differentiating between pirogis will not get you to the top of corporate America as fast as will differentiating among wines. This is, of course, not unique to the United States. Someone settling in Japan would have to deal with cultural capital that includes knowledge of Noh Theatre and tea ceremonies. In most countries, you are much better off following the run-up to the World Cup rather than the contenders for the next Super Bowl (DiMaggio 2004).

**Social capital** refers to the collective benefit of durable social networks and their patterns of reciprocal trust. Much has been written about the strength of family and friendship networks among all racial and ethnic minorities. Family reunions are major events. Family history and storytelling is rich and full. Kinfolk are not merely acquaintances but truly living assets upon which one depends or at the very least feels comfortable to call upon repeatedly. Extrafamily networks are critical to coping in a society that often seems to be determined to keep anyone who looks like you down. But given past as well as current discrimination and prejudice, these social networks may help you become a construction worker but they are less likely to get you into a board room. Residential and school segregation make developing social capital more difficult. Immigrant professionals find their skills or advanced degrees devalued and are shut out of networks of the educated and influential. Working-class Latino and Black workers have begun to develop informal social ties with their White coworkers and neighbors. Professional immigrants, in time, become accepted as equals, but racial and ethnic minority communities continue to resist institutional marginalization (Coleman 1988).

As the ranks of the powerful and important have been reached by all racial and ethnic groups, social capital is more widely shared, but this process has proven to be slower than advocates of social equality would wish. Perhaps the process will be accelerated by the tendency for successful minority members to be more likely to network with up-and-coming members of their own communities, while Whites are more likely to be more comfortable—even complacent—with the next generation's making it on their own. We are increasingly appreciative the importance of aspirations and motivation that are often much more present among people with poor or immigrant backgrounds than those born of affluence. We know that bilingualism is an asset, not a detriment. Children who have translated for their parents develop "real-world" skills at a much earlier age than their monolingual English counterparts (Bauder 2003; Monkman, Ronald, and Théraméne 2005; Portes 1998; Yosso 2005).

People of different races, religions, and ethnic backgrounds talk to each other, but do we talk past one another?


Considering cultural and social capital does leave room for measured optimism. Racial and ethnic groups have shared their cultural capital, whether it be the music we dance to or the food we eat. As the barriers to privilege weaken and eventually fall, people of all colors will be able to advance. The particular strength that African Americans, tribal people, Latinos, Asian Americans, and arriving immigrants bring to the table is that they also have the ability to resist and to refuse to accept second-class status. The roles that cultural and social capital play also point to the need to embrace strategies of intervention that will increasingly acknowledge the skills and talents found in a pluralistic society.


## Talking Past One Another

African Americans, German Americans, Korean Americans, Puerto Ricans, Native Americans, Mexican Americans, and many others live in the United States and interact on a daily basis, sometimes directly face to face and constantly through the media. But communication does not mean we listen to, much less understand, one another. Sometimes, we assume that, as we become a nation educated, we will set aside our prejudices. Yet our college campuses have been the scenes in recent years of tension, insults, and even violence. Fletcher Blanchard, Teri Lilly, and Leigh Ann Vaughn (1991) conducted an experiment at Smith College and found that even overheard statements can influence expressions of opinion on the issue of racism.

The researchers asked a student who said she was conducting an opinion poll for a class to approach seventy-two White students as each was walking across the campus. Each time she did so, she also stopped a second White student—actually a confederate working with the researchers—and asked her to participate in the survey as well. Both students were asked how Smith College should respond to anonymous racist notes actually sent to four African American students in 1989. However, the confederate was always instructed to answer first. In some cases, she condemned the notes; in others, she justified them. Blanchard and his colleagues (1991) concluded that "hearing at least one other person express strongly antiracist opinions produced dramatically more strongly antiracist public reactions to racism than hearing others express equivocal opinions or opinions more accepting of racism" (pp. 102–103). However, a second experiment demonstrated that when the confederate expressed sentiments justifying racism, the subjects were much less likely to express antiracist opinions than were those who heard no one else offer opinions. In this experiment, social control (through the process of conformity) influenced people's attitudes and the expression of those attitudes.

Why is there so much disagreement and tension? There is a growing realization that people do not mean the same thing when they are addressing problems of race, ethnicity, gender, or religion. A husband regularly does the dishes and feels he is an equal partner in doing the housework, not recognizing that the care of his infant daughter is left totally to his wife. A manager is delighted that he has been able to hire a Puerto Rican salesperson but makes no effort to see that the new employee will adjust to an all-While, non-Hispanic staff.

We talk, but do we talk past one another? Surveys regularly show that different ethnic and racial groups have different perceptions, whether on immigration policies, racial profiling, or whether discrimination occurs in the labor force. Sociologist Robert Blauner (1989, 1992) contends that Blacks and Whites see racism differently. Minorities see racism as central to society, as ever present, whereas Whites regard it as a peripheral concern and a national concern only when accompanied by violence or involving a celebrity. African Americans and other minorities consider racist acts in a broader context: "It is racist if my college fails to have Blacks significantly present as advisers, teachers, and administrators." Whites would generally accept a racism charge if there had been an explicit denial of a job to an appropriately qualified minority member. Furthermore, Whites would apply the label racist only to the person or the few people who were actually responsible for the act. Members of minority groups would be more willing to call most of the college's members racist for allowing racist practices to persist. For many Whites, the word *racism* is a red flag, and they are reluctant to give it the

wide use typically employed by minorities, that is, those who have been oppressed by racism (Lichtenberg, 1992).

Is one view correct—the broader minority perspective or the more limited
White outlook? No, but both are a part of the social reality in which we all
live. We need to recognize both interpretations.

As we saw when we considered Whiteness in Chapter 5, the need to confront racism, however perceived, is not to make Whites guilty and absolve
Blacks, Asians, Hispanics, and Native Americans of any responsibility for their
present plight. Rather, to understand racism, past and present, is to understand how its impact has shaped both a single person's behavior and that of
the entire society (Duke, 1992).

## Conclusion

Joe Muskrat (1972), while working for the
United States Commission on Civil Rights,
declared that Native Americans could assimilate or remain Indian and starve. Martin
Luther King, Jr., told thousands assembled
before the Lincoln Memorial that he had a
dream of a day when all people could
work, play, and live together.

Assimilation, even when strictly followed, does not necessarily bring with
it acceptance as an equal, nor does it
even mean that one will be tolerated.
Segregation persists. Efforts toward pluralism can be identified, but we can
also easily see the counter efforts,
whether they be the legal efforts to

make English the official language or
acts of intimidation by Klansmen, skin-
heads, and others. However, the sheer
changing population of the United States
guarantees that we will learn, work, and
play in a more diverse society.

The task of making this kaleidoscope
image of diverse cultures, languages, colors, and religions into a picture of harmony is overwhelming. But the images of
failure in this task, some of which we
have witnessed in our news media, are
even more frightening. We can applaud
success and even take time to congratu-
late ourselves, but we must also review
the unfinished agenda.

## Key Terms

cultural capital   206             model or ideal minority          social capital   207
                                   203

## Review Questions

1. What contributes to the changing image of diversity in the United States?
2. Pose views of some issue facing contemporary society that takes the position of "half full" and then "half empty."
3. Why is it harmful to be viewed as a model minority?
4. Is one view of racism the correct one?
5. Why are White Americans less likely to be concerned with social and
   cultural capital?

# Critical Thinking Questions

1. Helen Zia feels that Asian Americans experience significant stereotyping. Reconcile this perspective with the notion of Asian Americans' being regarded as a model minority.

2. Consider conversations you have with people very different than yourself. Why do you feel those people are very different? To what degree did you talk to them or past them? To what degree do they talk to you or past you?

3. How have places you worked, even part-time, been different from those of your parents or grandparents in terms of diversity of the workforce? What explains these changes?

# Internet Connections—Research Navigator™

Follow the instructions found on page 42 of this text to access the features of Research Navigator™. Once at the website, enter your Login Name and Password. Then, to use the ContentSelect database, enter keywords such as "model minority" and "inequality," and the research engine will supply relevant and recent scholarly and popular press publications. Use the New York Times Search-by-Subject Archive to find recent news articles related to sociology and the Link Library feature to locate relevant Web links organized by the key terms associated with this chapter.

# Internet Resource Directory

The following is a sample of the thousands of websites that offer information on topics discussed in this book. Most of these sites have links to other resources.

## GENERAL

**Hate Crimes Laws**

http://www.adl.org/99hatecrime/intro.asp

**U.S. Citizenship and Immigration Services**

http://www.uscis.gov/graphics/

**Race Traitor (constructing whiteness)**

http://www.racetraitor.org

**Southern Poverty Law Center (tolerance education)**

http://splccenter.org and www.tolerance.org

**U.S. Census Bureau**

http://www.census.gov

and specifically www.census.gov/pubinfo/www/hotlinks.html

**U.S. Commission on Civil Rights**

http://www.usccr.gov

## AFRICAN AMERICANS

**Black Collegian Online**

http://www.black-collegian.com/

**Kwanzaa Information Center**

http://www.melanet.com/kwanzaa/

**MelaNET (The UnCut Black Experience)**

http://www.melanet.com/

## ASIAN AMERICANS

**Asian American Network**

http://www.aan.net/

**Hmong Home Page**

http://www.stolaf.edu/people/cdr/hmong/

## HISPANICS AND LATINOS

**Latin American National Information Center**

http://lanic.utexas.edu

**Mexican American Studies and Research Center (University of Arizona)**

http://masrc.arizona.edu/

## JEWS AND JUDAISM

**American Jewish Committee**

http://www.ajc.org

**Anti-Defamation League**

http://www.adl.org

**Jewish culture**

http://myjewishlearning.com

**Judaism and Jewish Resources**

http://shamash.org

## MUSLIM AND ARAB AMERICANS

**Arab American Institute**

http://www.aaiusa.org/

**American-Arab Anti-Discrimination Committee**

http://www.adc.org

**Muslim Students' Association**

http://msa-natl.org

## NATIVE AMERICANS

**Bureau of Indian Affairs**

http://www.doi.gov/bureau-indian-affairs.html

**Nation of Hawai'i**

http://hawaii-nation.org/

**Native Web**

http://www.nativeweb.org

**Smithsonian National Museum of the American Indian**

http://www.nmai.si.edu

## WOMEN AND MEN

**National Organization for Women**

http://www.now.org

**National Women's History Project**

http://www.nwhp.org/

**Womensnet**

http://www.igc.apc.org/

## OUTSIDE THE UNITED STATES

**Abya Yala Net (South and Meso American Indian Rights Center)**

http://abyayala.nativeweb.org

**African National Congress (South Africa)**

http://www.anc.org.za/

**Information (general) on countries (CIA World Factbook)**

http://www.odci.gov/cia/publications/factbook

**Peace People (Northern Ireland)**

http://www.peacepeople.com

# ETHNIC GROUPS AND OTHER SUBORDINATE GROUPS

**Administration on Aging**

http://www.aoa.dhhs.gov

**American Institute of Polish Culture**

http://www.ampolinstitute.org

**American Irish Historical Society**

http://www.aihs.org

**Catholics for a Free Choice**

http://www.cath4choice.org

**Disability Social History Project**

http://www.disabilityhistory.org

**German Americans (German Embassy site)**

http://www.germany-info.org/

**Human Rights Web**

http://www.hrweb.org

**Interracial Voice (people of mixed racial background)**

http://www.webcom.com/~intvoice

**Polish American Association**

http://www.polish.org

**SeniorLink**

http://www.seniorlink.com/

**Society and Culture: Disabilities (Yahoo)**

http://www.yahoo.com/Society_and_Culture/Disabilities/

**Sons of Norway**

http://www.sofn.com

# THE AUTHOR

**Richard T. Schaefer (for email correspondence)**

schaeferrt@aol.com

www.schaefersociology.net

# Glossary

Parenthetical numbers refer to the pages on which the term is introduced.

**absolute deprivation** The minimum level of subsistence below which families or individuals should not be expected to exist. (88)

**affirmative action** Positive efforts to recruit subordinate group members, including women, for jobs, promotions, and educational opportunities. (108)

**Afrocentric perspective** An emphasis on the customs of African cultures and how they have pervaded the history, culture, and behavior of Blacks in the United States and around the world. (39)

**amalgamation** The process by which a dominant group and a subordinate group combine through intermarriage to form a new group. (30)

**assimilation** The process by which a subordinate individual or group takes on the characteristics of the dominant group. (31)

**asylees** Foreigners who have already entered the United States and now seek protection because of persecution or a well-founded fear of persecution. (147)

**authoritarian personality** A psychological construct of a personality type likely to be prejudiced and to use others as scapegoats. (53)

**bilingual education** A program designed to allow students to learn academic concepts in their native language while they learn a second language. (169)

**bilingualism** The use of two or more languages in places of work or education and the treatment of each language as legitimate. (33, 169)

**biological race** The mistaken notion of a genetically isolated human group. (13)

**blaming the victim** Portraying the problems of racial and ethnic minorities as their fault rather than recognizing society's responsibilities. (20)

**Bogardus scale** Technique to measure social distance toward different racial and ethnic groups. (62)

**brain drain** Immigration to the United States of skilled workers, professionals, and technicians who are desperately needed by their home countries. (134)

**civil religion** The religious dimension in American life that merges the state with sacred beliefs. (180)

**class** As defined by Max Weber, people who share similar levels of wealth. (18)

**colonialism** A foreign power's maintenance of political, social, economic, and cultural dominance over people for an extended period. (25)

**conflict perspective** A sociological approach that assumes that the social structure is best understood in terms of conflict or tension between competing groups. (20)

**contact hypothesis** An interactionist perspective stating that intergroup contact between people of equal status in noncompetitive circumstances will reduce prejudice. (73)

**creationists** People who support a literal interpretation of the biblical book of Genesis on the origins of the universe and argue that evolution should not be presented as established scientific thought. (188)

**cultural capital** Noneconomic forces such as family background and past investments in education that are then reflected in knowledge about the arts and language. (206)

**denomination** A large, organized religion not officially linked with the state or government. (173)

**discrimination** The denial of opportunities and equal rights to individuals and groups because of prejudice or for other arbitrary reasons. (49)

**double jeopardy** The subordinate status twice defined, as experienced by women of color. (99)

**dual labor market** Division of the economy into two areas of employment, the secondary one of which is populated primarily by minorities working at menial jobs. (96)

**dysfunction** An element of society that may disrupt a social system or decrease its stability. (19)

**emigration** Leaving a country to settle in another. (23)

**English immersion** Teaching in English by teachers who know the students' native language but use it only when students do not understand the lessons. (170)

**environmental justice** Efforts to ensure that hazardous substances are controlled so that all communities receive protection regardless of race or socioeconomic circumstances. (106)

**ethclass** The merged ethnicity and class in a person's status. (179)

**ethnic cleansing** Policy of ethnic Serbs to eliminate Muslims from parts of Bosnia. (26)

**ethnic group** A group set apart from others because of its national origin or distinctive cultural patterns. (9)

**ethnicity paradox** The maintenance of one's ethnic ties in a way that can assist with assimilation in larger society. (152, 161)

**ethnocentrism** The tendency to assume that one's culture and way of life are superior to all others. (45)

**ethnophaulism** Ethnic or racial slurs, including derisive nicknames. (49)

**exploitation theory** A Marxist theory that views racial subordination in the United States as a manifestation of the class system inherent in capitalism. (54)

**functionalist perspective** A sociological approach emphasizing how parts of a society are structured to maintain its stability. (18)

**fusion** A minority and a majority group combining to form a new group. (30)

**genocide** The deliberate, systematic killing of an entire people or nation. (26)

**glass ceiling** The barrier that blocks the promotion of a qualified worker because of gender or minority membership. (114)

**glass escalator** The male advantage experienced in occupations dominated by women. (116)

**glass wall** A barrier to moving laterally in a business to positions that are more likely to lead to upward mobility. (116)

**globalization** Worldwide integration of government policies, cultures, social movements, and financial markets through trade, movements of people, and the exchange of ideas. (23, 145)

**hate crimes** Criminal offense committee because of the offender's bias against a race, religion, ethnic/national origin group or sexualorientation group. (46)

**ideal minority** See model minority. (203)

**immigration** Coming into a new country as a permanent resident. (23)

**informal economy** Transfers of money, goods, or services that are not reported to the government. Common in inner-city neighborhoods and poverty-stricken rural areas. (95)

**institutional discrimination** A denial of opportunities and equal rights to individuals or groups resulting from the normal operations of a society. (92)

**intelligence quotient (IQ)** The ratio of a person's mental age (as computed by an IQ test) to his or her chronological age, multiplied by 100. (13)

**intelligent design** Idea that life is so compex it can only have been created by higher intelligence. (188)

**internal colonialism** The treatment of subordinate peoples as colonial subjects by those in power. (25)

**irregular economy** See informal economy. (95)

**labeling theory** A sociological approach introduced by Howard Becker that attempts to explain why certain people are viewed as deviants and others engaging in the same behavior are not. (20)

**life chances** People's opportunities to provide themselves with material goods, positive living conditions, and favorable life experiences. (178)

**marginality** The status of being between two cultures at the same time, such as the status of Jewish immigrants in the United States. (37)

**melting pot** Diverse racial or ethnic groups or both, forming a new creation, a new cultural entity. (30)

**migradollars (or remittances)** The money that immigrant workers send back to families in their native societies. (144)

**migration** A general term that describes any transfer of population. (23)

**minority group** A subordinate group whose members have significantly less control or power over their own lives than do the members of a dominant or majority group. (6)

**model or ideal minority** A group that, despite past prejudice and discrimination, succeeds economically, socially, and educationally without resorting to political or violent confrontations with Whites. (203)

**nativism** Beliefs and policies favoring native-born citizens over immigrants. (125)

**naturalization** Conferring of citizenship on a person after birth. (132)

**normative approach** The view that prejudice is influenced by societal norms and situations that encourage or discourage the tolerance of minorities. (55)

**panethnicity** The development of solidarity between ethnic subgroups, as reflected in the terms Hispanic or Asian American. (37)

**pluralism** Mutual respect between the various groups in a society for one another's cultures, allowing minorities to express their own culture. (32)

**prejudice** A negative attitude toward an entire category of people, such as a racial or ethnic minority. (48)

**principle of third-generation interest** Marcus Hansen's contention that ethnic interest and awareness increase in the third generation, among the grandchildren of immigrants. (159)

**racial formation** A sociohistorical process by which racial categories are created, inhibited, transformed, and destroyed. (17)

**racial group** A group that is socially set apart because of obvious physical differences. (8)

**racial profiling** Any arbitrary police-initiated action based on race, ethnicity, or natural origin rather than a person's behavior. (60)

**racism** A doctrine that one race is superior. (16)

**redlining** The pattern of discrimination against people trying to buy homes in minority and racially changing neighborhoods. (104)

**refugees** People living outside their country of citizenship for fear of political or religious persecution. (147)

**relative deprivation** The conscious experience of a negative discrepancy between legitimate expectations and present actualities. (88)

**remittances (or migradollars)** The monies that immigrants return to their country of origin. (144)

**respectable bigotry** Michael Lerner's term for the social acceptance of prejudice against White ethnics, when intolerance against non-White minorities is regarded as unacceptable. (152, 162)

**reverse discrimination** Actions that cause better-qualified White men to be passed over for women and minority men. (113)

**scapegoating theory** A person or group blamed irrationally for another person's or group's problems or difficulties. (52)

**secessionist minority** Groups, such as the Amish, that reject both assimilation and coexistence. (187)

**segregation** The physical separation of two groups, often imposed on a subordinate group by the dominant group. (28)

**self-fulfilling prophecy** The tendency to respond to and act on the basis of stereotypes, a predisposition that can lead one to validate false definitions. (21)

**sinophobes** People with a fear of anything associated with China. (128)

**social capital** Collective benefits of durable social networks and their patterns of reciprocal trust. (207)

**social distance** Tendency to approach or withdraw from a racial group. (62)

**sociology** The systematic study of social behavior and human groups. (17)

**states' rights** The principle, reinvoked in the late 1940s, that holds that each state is sovereign and has the right to order its own affairs without interference by the federal government. (103)

**stereotypes** Unreliable, exaggerated generalizations about all members of a group that do not take individual differences into account. (21, 56)

**stratification** A structured ranking of entire groups of people that perpetuates unequal rewards and power in a society. (17)

**symbolic ethnicity** Herbert Gans's term that describes emphasis on ethnic food and ethnically associated political issues rather than deeper ties to one's heritage. (160)

**total discrimination** The combination of current discrimination with past discrimination created by poor schools and menial jobs. (89)

**transnationals** Immigrants who sustain multiple social relationships linking their societies of origin and settlement. (146)

**underground economy** See informal economy. (95)

**world systems theory** A view of the global economic system as divided between nations that control wealth and those that provide natural resources and labor. (25)

**xenophobia** The fear or hatred of strangers or foreigners. (125)

# References

AARP. 2003. AARP Home. Accessed May 12, 2003, at www.aarp.org

———. 2004. *Civil rights and labor relations.* Princeton, NJ: Gallup Organization.

ADORNO, T. W., ELSE FRENKEL-BRUNSWIK, DANIEL J. LEVINSON, AND R. NEVITT SANFORD. 1950. *The authoritarian personality.* New York: Wiley.

ALLPORT, GORDON W. 1979. *The nature of prejudice* (25th Anniversary Edition). Reading, MA: Addison-Wesley.

ALONSO-ZALDIVAR, RICHARDO OLDHAM, AND JENNIFER OLDHAM. 2002. New airport screener jobs going mostly to whites. *Los Angeles Times* (September 24): A18.

ANTI-DEFAMATION LEAGUE (ADL). 2001. *Audit of anti-Semitic incidents 2000.* New York: Anti-Defamation League.

APPELBAUM, RICHARD, AND PETER DREIER. 1999. The campus anti sweatshop movement. *The American Prospect* (September–October): 71–78.

APPLEBOME, PETER. 1996. 70 years after Scopes trial, creation debate lives. *New York Times* (March 10): 1, 22.

ASANTE, MOLEFI KETE. 2000. *All American: How To Cover Asian America.* San Francisco: AAJA.

ASSOCIATED PRESS. 2006. Church blaze—Alabama's 10th—"definitely arson," official says. *Chicago Tribune* (February 14): 3.

BADGETT, M. V. LEE, AND HEIDI I. HARTMANN. 1995. The effectiveness of equal employment opportunity policies. In *Economic perspectives in affirmative action,* ed. Margaret C. Simms, 55–83. Washington, DC: Joint Center for Political and Economic Studies.

BALTZELL, E. DIGBY. 1964. *The Protestant establishment: Aristocracy and caste in America.* New York: Vintage Books.

BAMSHAD, MICHAEL J., AND STEVE E. OLSON. 2003. Does race exist? *Scientific American* (December): 78–85.

BARBARO, FRED. 1974. Ethnic resentment. *Society* 11 (March–April): 67–75.

BARLETT, DONALD L., AND JAMES B. STEELE. 2004. Who left the door open? *Time* 164 (September 20): 51–66.

BARNES, EDWARD. 1996. Can't get there from here. *Time* 147 (February 19): 33.

BARRETT, DAVID B., AND TODD M. JOHNSON. 2001. Worldwide adherents of all religions by six continental areas, mid-2000. In *Britannica Book of the Year 2001,* p. 302. Chicago: Encyclopedia Britannica.

BARRINGER, FELICITY. 2004. Bitter division for Sierra Club on immigration. *New York Times* (March 14): A1, A16.

BASH, HARRY M. 1979. *Sociology, race and ethnicity.* New York: Gordon & Breach.

———. 2001. *If I'm so white, why ain't I right?: Some methodological misgivings on taking identity ascriptions at face value.* Paper presented at the Annual Meeting of the Midwest Sociological Society, St. Louis.

BAUDER, HARALD. 2003. "Brain Abuse," or the devaluation of immigrant labour in Canada. *Antipode* 35 (September): 699–717.

BEAN, FRANK D., JENNIFER LEE, JEANNE BATALOVA, AND MARK LEACH. 2004. *Immigration and fading color Lines in America.* New York: Russell Sage Foundation.

BELL, DERRICK. 1994. The Freedom of Employment Act. *The Nation* 258 (May 23): 708, 710–714.

BELL, WENDELL. 1991. Colonialism and internal colonialism. In *The encyclopedic dictionary of sociology* (4th ed., edited by Richard Lachmann. pp. 52–53). Guilford, CT: Dushkin Publishing Group.

BELLAH, ROBERT. 1967. "CIVIL RELIGION IN AMERICA." *DAEDALUS,* WINTER, 96: 1–21.

BENDYNA, MARY E., AND PAUL M. PEARL. 2000. *Political preferences of American Catholics at the time of election 2000*. Washington, DC: Center for Applied Research in the Apostolate, Georgetown University.

BENNETT, PHILLIP. 1993. Ethnic labels fail to keep up with reality. *The Cincinnati Enquirer* (November 18): A10.

BERTRAND, MARIANE, AND SENDHIL MULLAINATHAN. 2003. *Are Emily and Greg more employable than Lakisha and Jamal? A field experiment on labor market discrimination*. Cambridge, MA: National Bureau of Economic Research.

BEST, JOEL. 2001. Social progress and social problems: Toward a sociology of gloom. *Sociological Quarterly* 42 (1):1–12.

BILLSON, JANET MANCINI. 1988. No owner of soil: The concept of marginality revisited on its sixtieth birthday. *International Review of Modern Sociology* 18 (Autumn): 183–204.

BLANCHARD, FLETCHER A., TERI LILLY, AND LEIGH ANN VAUGHN. 1991. Reducing the expression of racial prejudice. *Psychological Science* 2 (March): 101–5.

BLAUNER, ROBERT. 1969. Internal colonialism and ghetto revolt. *Social Problems* 16 (Spring): 393–408.

———. 1972. *Racial oppression in America*. New York: Harper & Row.

———. 1989. *Black lives, white lives: Three decades of race relations in America*. Berkeley: University of California Press.

———. 1992. THE TWO LANGUAGES OF RACE. *THE AMERICAN PROSPECT* (SUMMER): 55–64.

BLOCH, HANNAH. 1996. Cutting off the brains. *Time* 147 (February 5):46.

BLOOM, LEONARD. 1971. *The social psychology of race relations*. Cambridge, MA: Schenkman.

BOBO, LAWRENCE, JAMES R. KLUEGEL, AND RYAN A. SMITH. 1997. Laissez-faire racism: The crystallization of a kinder, gentler, antiblack ideology. In *Racial Attitudes in the 1990s: Continuity and Change*, ed. Steven A. Tuch and Jack K. Martin, 15–42. Westport, CT: Praeger.

BOGARDUS, EMORY. 1968. Comparing racial distance in Ethiopia, South Africa, and the United States. *Sociology and Social Research* 52 (January):149–56.

BONACICH, EDNA. 1972. A theory of ethnic antagonism: The split labor market. *American Sociological Review* 37 (October): 547–59.

———. 1976. Advanced capitalism and black/white race relations in the United States: A split labor market interpretation. *American Sociological Review* 41 (February): 34–51.

———, AND RICHARD APPELBAUM. 2000. *Behind the label: Inequality in the Los Angeles apparel industry*. Berkeley: University of California Press.

BONILLA-SILVA, EDUARDO. 1996. Rethinking racism: Toward a structural interpretation. *American Sociological Review* 62 (June): 465–80.

———. 2002. The linguistics of color blind racism: How to talk nasty about blacks without sounding racist. *Critical Sociology* 28 (1–2): 41–64.

BORDT, REBECCA L. 2005. Using a research article to facilitate a deep structure understanding of discrimination. *Teaching Sociology* 33 (October): 403–410.

BORK, ROBERT H. 1995. What to do about the First Amendment. *Commentary* 99 (February):23–29.

BOURDIEU, PIERRE. 1983. The forms of capital." In *Handbook of theory and research for the sociology of education,* ed. J.G. Richardson, 241–58. Westport, CT: Greenwood.

——— AND JEAN-CLAUDE PASSERON. 1990. *Reproduction in education, society and culture*. 2d ed. London: Sage (Originally published as *La Reproduction* 1970).

BOWLES, SCOTT. 2000. Bans on racial profiling gain steam. *USA Today* (June 2): 3A.

BOWMAN, TOM. 1998. Evangelicals allege bias in U.S. Navy, Marine Chaplain Corps. *Baltimore Sun* (August 23): A12.

BOWSER, BENJAMIN, AND RAYMOND G. HUNT, EDS. 1996. *Impacts of racism on white Americans*. Beverly Hills, CA: Sage Publications.

BOXALL, BETTINA. 2001. Asian Indians remake Silicon Valley. *Los Angeles Times* (July 6): A1, A26.

BOYER, EDWARD J. 1996. Life in a new land: Illegal immigrant who fled deputies reaches goal: A job in U.S. *Chicago Tribune* (May 7):131, B8.

BRACHEAR, MANYA A. 2003. Muslim-Run Food Pantry Feeds Body and Soul. *New York Times* (December 14):sect. 4, 1, 5.

BRADDOCK, D., AND BACHELDER, L. 1994. *The glass ceiling and persons with disabilities*. Washington, DC: The Glass Ceiling Commission.

BRANNON, RUTH. 1995. The use of the concept of disability culture: A historian's view. *Disability Studies Quarterly* 15 (Fall):3–15.

BRAXTON, GREG. 1999. A mad dash for diversity. *Los Angeles Times* (August 9): F1, F10.

BREWER, CYNTHIA A., AND TRUDY A. SUCHAN. 2001. *Mapping census 2000: The geography of U.S. diversity*. Washington, DC: U.S. Government Printing Office.

BRIGGS, DAVID. 1996. Greeley poll says Catholics want democratic church. *Chicago Tribune* (May 31): sect. 2, 9.

BRIMMER, ANDREW. 1995. "The Economic Cost Of Discrimination Against Black Americans." Pp. 9–29 *In Economic Perspectives In Affirmative Action,* Edited By Margaret C. Simms. Washington, DC: Joint Center For Political And Economic Studies.

BRITTINGHAM, ANGELA, AND G. PATRICIA DE LA CRUZ. 2004. *Ancestry 2000*. Census 2000 Brief c2kbr-35. Washington, DC: U.S. Government Printing Office.

BRODER, JOHN M. 2006 "Immigrants and the Economics of Hard Work." *New York Times* (April 2): Section wk, p. 3.

BRODIE, MOLLYANN, ANNIE STEFFENSON, JAMIE VALDEZ, REBECCA LEVIN, AND ROBERTO SURO. 2002. *2002 national survey of Latinos.* Menlo Park, CA: Henry J. Kaiser Foundation and Pew Hispanic Center.

BROOKS-GUNN, JEANNE, PAMELA K. KLEBANOV, AND GREG J. DUNCAN. 1996. Ethnic differences in children's intelligence test scores: Role of economic deprivation, home environment, and maternal characteristics. *Child Development* 67 (April): 396–408.

BROWNSTEIN, ANDREW. 2001. A battle over a name in the land of the Sioux. *Chronicle of Higher Education* 47 (February 23): A46–A49.

BUDIG, MICHELLE J. 2002. Male advantage and the gender composition of jobs: Who rides the glass escalator. *Social Problems* 49(2): 258–77.

BULLARD, ROBERT D. 1990. Ecological Inequalities and the New South: Black Communities under Siege. *Journal of Ethnic Studies* 17 (Winter):101–15.

BUNCHE CENTER. 2003. Prime time in black and white: Not much is new for 2002. *Bunche Research Report* 1 (1).

BUREAU OF THE CENSUS. 1988. *Statistical abstract of the United States, 1988.* Washington, DC: U.S. Government Printing Office.

————. 2001a. *Profile of the foreign-born population in the United States.* Washington, DC: U.S. Government Printing Office.

————. 2001b. Census 2000 PHC-T.6., *Population by race and Hispanic or Latino origin in the United States.* Accessed February 5, 2001, at http://www.census.gov.

————. 2001c. *March 2001 Current Population Survey.* From Table HINC-01. Accessed February 1, 2002 (www.census.gov/hhes/www/Income.html).

————. 2003a. *Statistical Abstract of the United States, 2003.* Washington, DC: U.S. Government Printing Office.

————. 2003b. *Characteristics of American Indians and Alaska Natives by tribe and language: 2000.* Washington, DC: U.S. Government Printing Office.

————. 2004. *U.S. interim projections by age, sex, race, and Hispanic origin.* Released March 18, 2004 at www.census.gov/ipc/www/usinterimproj.

————. 2005a. *Statistical abstract of the United States 2004–2005.* Washington, DC: U.S. Printing Office.

————. 2005b. *Texas becomes nation's newest "majority-minority" State, Census Bureau Announces.* CBO5-118. Washington, DC: U.S. Printing Office.

BUREAU OF CITIZENSHIP AND IMMIGRATION SERVICES. 2003. *Fiscal Year 2002 Yearbook of Immigrant Statistics.* Accessed January 16, 2006. www.bcis.gov.

————. 2006. *Civics flash cards.* Accessed February 3, 2006 at http://uscis.gov/graphics/citizenship/flashcards/questionaire.htm.

BUREAU OF JUSTICE STATISTICS. 2004. *First release from state prisons 2001.* Washington, DC: Bureau of Justice Statistics.

Bush, George W. 2005 "President, Lieutenant General Honere Discuss Hurricane Relief In Louisiana." September 12. Accessed January 31, 2006 (\www.whitehouse.gov).

BUSTILLO, MIGUEL. 2006. Remarks leave Nagin in a not-so-sweet spot. *Los Angeles Times* (January 22):

CAPPS, RANDY, KU LEIGHTON, AND MICHAEL FIX. 2002. *How are immigrants faring after welfare reform? Preliminary evidence from Los Angeles and New York City.* Washington, DC: Urban Institute.

CARBERRY, MAEGAN. 2006 "MULLTICULTI CHIC." (CHICAGO) *RED EYE* (FEBRUARY 16). P. 4–5.

CARD, DAVID, JOHN DINARDO, AND EUGENA ESTES. 1998. *The more things change: Immigrants and the children of immigrants in the 1940s, the 1970s, and the 1990s.* Paper presented at the Joint Center for Poverty Research, Northwestern University of Chicago, April 9.

CARLSON, DARREN K. 2004. *Racial profiling seen as pervasive, unjust,* July 30, at http://www.gallup.com.

CARRELL, MICHAEL R., NORBERT F. ELBERT, AND ROBERT D. HATFIELD. 2000. *Human resource management: Strategies for managing a diverse and global workforce.* 6th ed. Orlando, FL: Dryden Press.

CARRIER, JIM. 2000. *Ten ways to fight hate,* 2d ed. Montgomery, AL: Tolerance.org.

Carrol, Joseph. 2006. "Public National Anthem Should Be Sung in English". The Gallop Poll (May 3).

CARTER, BILL. 2001. "Los Simpsons": Don't have a vaca, man. *New York Times* (February 18): sec. WK, 3.

CARVAJAL, DOREEN. 1996. Diversity pays off in a babel of yellow pages. *New York Times* (December 3): 1, 23.

CATALYST. 2001. *Women satisfied with current job in financial industry but barriers still exist.* Press Release July 25, 2001. Accessed January 31, 2002, at http://www.catalystwomen.org.

CBS NEW YORK. 2003. *Shame on you: Rockstar Video Games.* Accessed November 15, 2003, at cbsnewyork.com.

CHANG, PATRICIA M. Y. 1997. Female clergy in the contemporary protestant church: A current assessment. *Journal for the Scientific Study of Religion* 36 (December): 565–73.

CHEN, DAVID W. AND SOMINI SENGUPTA. 2001. "Not Yet Citizens But Eager To Fight For The U.S." *New York Times,* October 22, A1, B2.

CHILDREN NOW. 1998. *A different world: Children's perceptions of race, class, and the media.* Oakland, CA: Author.

———. 2004. *2003-04 Fall colors prime time diversity report*. Oakland, CA: Author.

CHIROT, DANIEL, AND JENNIFER EDWARDS. 2003. Making Sense of the Senseless: Understanding Genocide. *Contexts* (Spring): 12–19.

CHU, JEFF, AND NADIA MUSTAFA. 2006. Between two worlds. *Time* (January 16) 167:64–68.

CLARK, KENNETH B., AND MAMIE P. CLARK. 1947. Racial identification and preferences in Negro children. In *Readings in Social Psychology*, ed. Theodore M. Newcomb and Eugene L. Hartley, 169–78. New York: Holt, Rinehart & Winston.

COATES, RODNEY D. 2004. Critical racial and ethnic studies—profiling and reparations. *American Behavioral Scientist* 47 (March):873–78.

COGNARD-BLACK, ANDREW J. 2004. Will they stay, or will they go? Sex—atypical among token men who teach. *Sociological Quarterly* 45(1):113–39.

COLEMAN, JAMES S. 1988. Social capital in the creation of human capital. *American Journal of Sociology* 94 (Supplement):S95–S120.

COMMISSION ON CIVIL RIGHTS. 1977. *Window dressing on the set: Women and minorities in television*. Washington, DC: U.S. Government Printing Office.

———. 1981. *Affirmative action in the 1980s: Dismantling the process of discrimination*. Washington, DC: U.S. Government Printing Office.

COMMITTEE OF 100. 2001. *American attitudes towards Chinese Americans and Asian immigrants*. New York: Author.

COOPER, MARY H. 2004. Voting rights. *CQ Researcher* 14 (October 29): 901–24.

COOPERMAN, ALAN. 2005. One way to pray? *Washington Post National Weekly Edition* 22 (September 5):10–11.

CORNACCHIA, EUGENE J., AND DALE C. NELSON. 1992. Historical differences in the political experiences of American Blacks and White Ethnics: Revisiting an unresolved controversy. *Ethnic and Racial Studies* 15 (January):102–24.

CORNELIUS, WAYNE A. 1996. Economics, Culture, and the Politics of Restricting Immigration. *Chronicle of Higher Education* 43 (November 15):B4–B5.

CORRELL, JOSHUA ET AL. 2002. The police officer's dilemma: Using ethnicity to disambiguate potentially threatening individuals. *Journal of Personality and Social Psychology* 83(6):1314–29.

COSE, ELLIS. 1993. *The rage of a privileged class*. New York: HarperCollins.

COX, OLIVER C. 1942. The modern caste school of social relations. *Social Forces* 21 (December): 218–226.

DAHLBURG, JOHN-THOR. 2001. A new world for Haitians. *Los Angeles Times* (September 4):A1, A9.

DART, BOB. 1998. Preserving America: Lancaster County, PA. *Atlanta Journal and Constitution* (June 28)

DAVIS, JAMES AND TOM W. SMITH. 2001. *General Social Surveys, 1972–2000*. Storrs, CT: The Roper Center.

DAVIS, JAMES A., TOM W. SMITH, AND PETER V. MARSDEN. 2005. *General social surveys, 1972–2004: Cumulative codebook*. Chicago: NORC.

DE LA GARZA, RODOLFO O., LOUIS DESIPIO, F. CHRIS GARCIA, JOHN GARCIA, AND ANGELO FALCON. 1992. *Latino Voices: Mexican, Puerto Rican, And Cuban Perspectives On American Politics*. Boulder, CO: Westview Press.

DEL OLMO, FRANK. 2003. Slow motion carnage at the border. *Los Angeles Times* (May 18): M5.

DENAVAS-WALT, CARMEN, BERNADETTE PROCTOR, AND ROBERT J. MILLS. 2005. *Income, poverty, and health insurance 2004*. Washington, DC: U.S. Government Printing Office.

DEPARTMENT OF JUSTICE. 2001a. *Report to the Congress of the United States: A review of restrictions on persons of Italian ancestry during World War II*. Accessed February 1, 2002 at http://www.house.gov/judiciary/Italians.pdf.

DEPARTMENT OF JUSTICE. 2001b. *Uniform Crime Reports 2000*. Washington, DC: U.S. Government Printing Office.

———. 2005. *Uniform Crime Reports 2005*. Washington, DC: U.S. Government Printing Office.

DEUTSCHER, IRWIN, FRED P. PESTELLO, AND H. FRANCES PESTELLO. 1993. *Sentiments and acts*. New York: Aldine de Gruyter.

DIAMOND, JARED. 2003. Globalization, then. *Los Angeles Times* (September 14): M1, M3.

DIMAGGIO, PAUL. 2005. Cultural capital. In *Encyclopedia of Social Theory*, ed. George Ritzer, 167–70. Thousand Oaks, CA: Sage Publications.

DOLAN, MAURA. 2000. "State Justices Deal New Set Back To Affirmative Action." *Los Angeles Times*, December 1.

DU BOIS, W. E. B. 1903. *The souls of black folks: Essays and sketches*. Reprinted in 1961 by New York: Facade Publications.

———. 1969a. *An ABC of color*. New York: International Publications.

———. 1969b. *The suppression of the African slave-trade to the United States of America, 1638–1870*. New York: Schocken.

———. 1970. *The negro American family*. Cambridge, MA: MIT Press.

DUDLEY, CARL S., AND DAVID A. ROOZEN. 2001. *Faith communities today*. Hartford, CT: Hartford Seminary.

DUFF, JOHN B. 1971. *The Irish in the United States*. Belmont, CA: Wadsworth.

DUKE, LYNNE. 1992. You See Color-Blindness, I See Discrimination. *Washington Post National Weekly Edition* 9 (June 15):33.

DUNN, ASHLEY. 1994. Southeast Asians Highly Dependent on Welfare in U.S. *New York Times* (May 19):A1, A20.

EARLY, GERALD. 1994. Defining Afrocentrism. *Journal of Blacks in Higher Education* 1 (Winter):46.

ECHAVESTE, MARIA. 2005. Target employees. *American Prospect* (November):A10–A11.

ECKSTROM, KEVIN. 2001. "New, Diverse Take Spot On Catholic Altars." *Chicago Tribune,* August 31, 8.

THE ECONOMIST. 2004B. "Who's Winning The Fight?" (July): 3, 38.

EL NASSER, HAYA. 1997. Varied heritage claimed and extolled by millions. *USA Today* (May 8):1A, 2A.

ENG, MONICA. 1998. Chinese-Americans have their own ways of paying respect. *Chicago Tribune* (May 28):sec. 5, 1, 2.

ESPIRITU, YEN LE. 1992. *Asian American panethnicity: Bridging institutions and identities.* Philadelphia: Temple University Press.

FARKAS, STEVE. 2003. *What immigrants say about life in the United States.* Washington DC: Migration Policy Institute.

FEAGIN, JOE AND EILEEN O'BRIEN. 2003. *White men on race, power, privilege, and the shaping of cultural consciousness.* Boston, Beacon Press.

FEAGIN, JOE R., HERNÁN VERA, AND PINAR BATUR. 2000. *White racism.* 2d ed. New York: Routledge.

Fine, Gary Alan 2004 "Forgotten Classic: The Robbers Cave Experiment." *Sociological Forum,* (December) 19: 663–666.

FIX, MICHAEL, WENDY ZIMMERMAN, AND JEFFERY S. PASSEL. 2001. *The integration of immigrant families in the United States.* Washington, DC: The Urban Institute.

FOERSTER, AMY. 2004. Race, identity, and belonging: "Blackness" and the struggle for solidarity in a multi-ethnic labor union. *Social Problems* 51(3):386–409.

FONG, STANLEY L. M. 2002. *The contemporary Asian American experience: Beyond the model minority.* 2d ed. Upper Saddle River, NJ: Prentice Hall.

FOX, STEPHEN. 1990. *The unknown internment.* Boston: Twayne.

FREEDMAN, SAMUEL G. 2004. Latino parents decry bilingual programs. *New York Times.* (July 14): A21.

FULLER, CHEVON. 1998. Service redlining. *Civil Rights Journal* 3 (Fall):33–36.

GALLAGHER, MARI. 2005. *Chain reaction: Income, race, and access to Chicago's major player grocers.* Chicago: Metro Chicago Information Center.

GALLUP. 2004. *Poll topics and trends: Religion.* Accessed August 2, 2004, at www.gallup.com.

GANS, HERBERT J. 1979. Symbolic ethnicity: The future of ethnic groups and cultures in America. *Ethnic and Racial Studies* 2 (January):1–20.

GERBER, DAVID A. 1993. *Nativism, anti-Catholicism, and anti-Semitism.* New York: Scribner's.

GERTH, H. H., AND C. WRIGHT MILLS. 1958. *From Max Weber: Essays in sociology.* New York: Galaxy Books.

GERSTENFELD, PHYLLIS B., AND DIANA R. GRANT. 2003. Hate online: A content analysis of extremist Internet sites. *Analysis of Social Issues and Public Policy* 3(1):29–44.

GILENS, MARTIN. 1996. "Race coding" and white opposition to welfare. *American Political Science Review* 90 (September):593–604.

GIRARDELLI, DAVIDE. 2004. Commodified identities: The myth of Italian food in the United States. *Journal of Communication Inquiry* 28 (October):307–24.

GLADWELL, MALCOLM. 1996. Discrimination: It's just a bus stop away. *Washington Post National Weekly Edition* 13 (February 19):33.

GLANCY, DIANE. 1998. When the boats arrived. Hungry Mind Review. *The National Book Magazine* 7 (Spring).

GLAZER, NATHAN. 1971. The issue of cultural pluralism in America today. In *Pluralism beyond the Frontier: Report of the San Francisco consultation on ethnicity,* 2–8. San Francisco: American Jewish Committee.

———, AND DANIEL PATRICK MOYNIHAN. 1970. *Beyond the melting pot: The Negroes, Puerto Ricans, Jews, Italians, and Irish of New York City.* 2d ed. Cambridge, MA: MIT Press.

GLEASON, PHILIP. 1980. American identity and Americanization. In *Harvard Encyclopedia of American Ethnic Groups,* ed. Stephen Therstromm, 31–58. Cambridge, MA: Belknap Press of Harvard University Press.

GOERING, JOHN M. 1971. The emergence of ethnic interests: A case of serendipity. *Social Forces* 48 (March):379–384.

GOMPERS, SAMUEL, AND HERMAN GUSTADT. 1908. *Meat vs. rice: American manhood against Asiatic coolieism: Which shall survive?* San Francisco: Asiatic Exclusion League.

GOODSTEIN, LAURIE. 2001. As attacks' impact recedes a return to religion as usual. *New York Times* (November 26): A1, B6.

———. 2005. Issuing rebuke, judge rejects teaching of intelligent design. *New York Times* (December 21): A1, A21.

GORDON, MILTON M. 1964. *Assimilation in American life: The role of race, religion, and national origins.* New York: Oxford University Press.

———. 1978. *Human nature, class, and ethnicity.* New York: Oxford University Press.

———. 1996. Liberal versus corporate pluralism. *Society* 33 (March/April):37–40.

GRAHAM, LAWRENCE OTIS. 1995. *Member of the club: Reflections on life in a racially polarized world.* New York: HarperCollins.

GRAY-LITTLE, BERNADETTE AND ADAM R. HAFDAHL. 2000. "Factors Influencing Racial Comparisons Of Self-Esteem: A Qualitative Review." *Psychological Bulletin* 126(1):26–54.

GREELEY, ANDREW M. 1974a. *Ethnicity in the United States: A preliminary reconnaissance.* New York: Wiley.

———. 1974b. Political participation among ethnic groups in the United States: A preliminary reconnaissance. *American Journal of Sociology* 80 (July): 170–204.

———. 1977. *The American Catholic.* New York: Basic Books.

GREENHOUSE, LINDA. 1996. Case on government interface in religion tied to separation of powers. *New York Times* (October 16): C23.

———. 2003. Justices back affirmative action by 5–4. But wider vote bans a racial point system. *New York Times* (June 24): A1, A25.

GREENWALD, ANTHONY G., MARK A. OAKES, AND HUNTER HOFFMAN. 2003. Targets of discrimination: Effects of race on responses to weapon holders. *Journal of Experimental Social Psychology* 39 (July):399–405.

GRIECO, ELIZABETH M., AND RACHEL C. CASSIDY. 2001. *Overview of race and Hispanic origin.* Current Population Reports Ser. CENBR/01-1. Washington, DC: U.S. Government Printing Office.

GUGLIELMO, JENNIFER, AND SALVATORE, SALERNO, EDS. 2003. *Are Italians white?* New York: Routledge.

HAGENBAUGH, BARBARA. 2006. "Sending Money Back Has Vital Role." *USA TODAY* (APRIL 11, 2006), P. 2B.

HANDLIN, OSCAR. 1951. *The uprooted: The epic story of the great migrations that made the American people.* New York: Grossett and Dunlap.

HANSEN, MARCUS LEE. 1952. The third generation in America. *Commentary* 14 (November): 493–500.

HARLOW, CAROLINE WOLF. 2005. Hate Crime Reported By Victims And Police. *Bureau Of Justice Statistics Special Report* (November).

HECHINGER, FRED M. 1987. Bilingual programs. *New York Times* (April 7): C10.

HERBERG, WILL. 1983. *Protestant–Catholic–Jew: An essay in American religious sociology.* Rev. ed. Chicago: University of Chicago Press.

HERRNSTEIN, RICHARD J., AND CHARLES MURRAY. 1994. *The bell curve: Intelligence and class structure in American life.* New York: Free Press.

HERSKOVITS, MELVILLE J. 1930. *The anthropometry of the American negro.* New York: Columbia University Press.

———. 1941. *The myth of the Negro past.* New York: Harper.

HILL, HERBERT. 1967. The racial practices of organized labor: The age of Gompers and after. In *Employment, race, and poverty,* ed. Arthur M. Ross and Herbert Hill, 365–402. New York: Harcourt, Brace & World.

HIRSCHMAN, CHARLES. 1983. America's melting pot reconsidered. In *Annual Review of Sociology 1983,* ed. Ralph H. Turner, 397–423. Palo Alto, CA: Annual Reviews.

HIRSLEY, MICHAEL. 1991. Religious Display Needs Firm Count. *Chicago Tribune* (December 20): Sect. 2, 10.

HOCHSCHILD, JENNIFER L. 1995. *Facing up to the American dream: Race, class, and the soul of the nation.* Princeton, NJ: Rutgers University Press.

HOFFER, THOMAS B. et al. 2001. *Doctorate recipients from United States universities: Summary report 2000.* Chicago: National Opinion Research Center.

HUGHES, MICHAEL. 1998. Symbolic racism, old-fashioned racism, and whites' opposition to affirmative action. In *Racial Attitudes in the 1990s: Continuity and Change,* ed. Steven A. Tuch and Jack K. Martin, 45–75. Westport, CT: Praeger.

HURH, WON MOO, AND KWANG CHUNG KIM. 1989. The "success" image of Asian Americans: Its validity, and its practical and theoretical implications. *Ethnic and Racial Studies* 12 (October):512–38.

IGNATIEV, NOEL. 1994. Treason to whiteness is loyalty to humanity. Interview with Noel Ignatiev. *Utne Reader* (November/December): 83–86.

———. 1995. *How the Irish became white.* New York: Routledge.

IMMIGRATION AND NATURALIZATION SERVICE. 2002. *1999 statistical yearbook of the Immigration and Naturalization Service.* Washington, DC: United States Government Printing Office.

IMMIGRATION AND REFUGEE SERVICES OF AMERICA. 2004. *Refugees Admitted to the United States* 31 (December): 25.

INSTITUTES OF MEDICINE. 1999. *Towards environmental justice.* Washington, DC: National Academy Press.

JOHNSON, KEVIN. 1992. German ancestry is strong beneath Milwaukee surface. *USA Today* (August 4): 9A.

JOHNSON, PETER C. 2001. Minorities lose time on network news. *USA Today* (February 28): 4D.

JONES, CHARISSE. 2003. Newcomers give old city a look at itself. *USA Today* (February 7): 13A.

JONES, DALE E., SHERRI DOTY, JAMES E. HORSCH, RICHARD HOUSEAL, MAC LYNN, JOHN P. MARCUM, KENNETH M. SANCHAGRIN, AND RICHARD H. TAYLOR. 2002. *Religious congregations and membership in the United States*

*2000: An enumeration by region, state, and county based on data reported by 149 religious bodies.* Nashville, TN: Glenmary Research Center.

JONES, JEFFREY M. 2003. *Nearly half of Americans say immigration levels should be decreased.* Poll Analysis, July 10, 2003. Accessed August 6, 2003, at www.gallup.com.

JONES, NICHOLAS, AND AMY SYMENS SMITH. 2001. *The two or more races population: 2000.* Series C2KBR/01-6. Washington, DC: U.S. Government Printing Office.

KAGAN, JEROME. 1971. The magical aura of the IQ. *Saturday Review of Literature* 4 (December 4):92–93.

KAHNG, ANTHONY. 1978. EEO in America. *Equal Opportunity Forum* 5 (July):22–23.

KANEYA, RUI. 2004. "NATIVE TONGUE." *The Chicago Reporter* 7(November): 6–7.

Kao, Grace and Kara Joyner. 2004. Do race and ethnicity matter among friends? *Sociological Quarterly* 45 (3):557–73

KAPUR, DEUESH, AND JOHN McHALE. 2003. Migration's new payoff. *Foreign Policy* (November/December): 48–57.

KATEL, PETER. 2005. Illegal immigration." *CQ Researcher* 15 (May 6):393–420.

KELLY, KIMBRIELL. 2005. Retail runaround. *Chicago Reporter* 14 (November/December):8–12.

KIBRIA, NAZLI. 2002. *Becoming Asian American: Second-generation Chinese and Korean American identities.* Baltimore, MD: Johns Hopkins Press.

KILSON, MARTIN. 1995. Affirmative action. *Dissent* 42 (Fall):469–70.

KIM, T.C. 2005. Electronic storm. *Intelligence Report.* (Summer):50–57.

KINLOCH, GRAHAM C. 1974. *The Dynamics Of Race Relations: A Sociological Analysis.* New York: Mcgraw-Hill.

KOSMIN, BARRY A., EGON MAYER, AND ARIELA KEYSAR. 2001. *American religious identification survey 2001.* New York: Graduate Center of the City University of New York.

KRAYBILL, DONALD B. 2001. *The riddle of Amish culture.* Rev. ed. Baltimore, MD: Johns Hopkins University Press.

———, ed. 2003. *The Amish and the state.* 2d ed. Baltimore, MD: John Hopkins University Press.

———, AND STEVEN M. NOLT. 1995. *Amish enterprises: From plows to profits.* Baltimore, MD: Johns Hopkins Press.

KRUEGER, BROOKE. 2004. "When a Dissertation Makes a Difference." Accessed January 15, 2005 (www.racematters.rrg/devahpager.html).

KRUEGER, ALAN B. 2002. Economic scene. *New York Times* (December 11): C2.

LAL, BARBARA BALLIS. 1995. Symbolic interaction theories. *American Behavioral Scientist* 38 (January):421–41.

LAPIERE, RICHARD T. 1934. Attitudes vs. actions. *Social Forces* 13 (October):230–37.

———. 1969. Comment of Irwin Deutscher's looking backward. *American Sociologist* 4 (February):41–42.

LARSON, LAKE J. 2004. The Foreign-Born Population in the United States: 2003. *Current Population Reports,* p20 No. 551. Washington, DC: U.S. Government Printing Office.

LATINO COALITION. 2006. *2005 National Latino survey topline.* Washington, DC: Author.

LEAVITT, PAUL. 2002. Bush calls agent kicked off flight "honorable fellow." *USA Today* (January 8): . . . .

LEE, SHARON M., AND BARRY EDMONSTON. 2005. New marriages, new families: U.S. racial and Hispanic intermarriages. *Population Bulletin,* 60 (2):1–36.

LEEHOTZ, ROBERT. 1995. Is concept of race a relic? *Los Angeles Times* (April 15): A1, A14.

LERNER, MICHAEL. 1969. RESPECTABLE BIGOTRY. *American Scholar* 38 (August):606–17.

LEWIS, AMANDA E. 2004. "What group?" Studying whites and whiteness in the era of "color-blindness." *Sociological Theory* 22 (December):623–46.

LEWIS MUMFORD CENTER. 2001. *Ethnic diversity grows, neighborhood integration is at a standstill.* Albany, NY: Author.

LICHTBLAU, ERIC. 2003. Bush issues racial profiling ban but exempts security information. *New York Times* (June 18): A1, A16.

———. 2005. Profiling report leads to a clash?? and a demotion? *New York Times* (August 24): A1, A9.

LICHTENBERG, JUDITH. 1992. Racism in the head, racism in the world. *Report from the Institute for Philosophy and Public Policy* 12 (Spring–Summer): 3–5.

LINDNER, EILEEN, ED. 2006. *Yearbook of American and Canadian churches 2006.* Nashville, TN: Abingden Press.

LINDSLEY, SHERYL L. 1998. Organizational interventions to prejudice. In *Communicating prejudice,* ed. Michael L. Hecht, 302–10. Thousand Oaks, CA: Sage Publications.

LODDER, LEEANN, SCOTT McFARLAND, AND DIANA WHITE. 2003. *Racial preference and suburban employment opportunities.* Chicago: Chicago Urban League.

LOPATA, HELENA ZNANIECKA. 1993. *Polish Americans.* Rutgers, NJ: Transaction Books.

LOPEZ, JULIE AMPARANO. 1992. Women face glass walls as well as ceilings. *Wall Street Journal* (March 3) pp. B1–B2: . . .

LUCONI, STEFANO. 2001. *From paesani to white ethnics: The Italian experience in Philadelphia.* Albany: State University Press of New York.

MACK, RAYMOND W. 1996. Whose affirmative action? *Society* 33 (March/April):41–43.

MACRAE, NEIL C., CHARLES STANGOR, AND MILES HEWSTONE. 1996. *Stereotypes and stereotyping*. New York: Guilford Press.

MALONE, TARA. 2005. Student rebuked for sitting during the Mexican anthem. *Daily Herald* (October 6): . . . .

MANING, ANITA. 1997. Troubled waters: Environmental racism suit makes waves. *USA Today* (July 31): A1.

MANNING, ROBERT D. 1995. "Multiculturalism In The United States: Clashing Concepts, Changing Demographics, And Competing Cultures." *International Journal Of Group Tensions*, Summer, 117–168.

MARSHALL, PATRICK. 2001. Religion in Schools. *CQ Research* 11 (July 12):1–24.

MARX, KARL, AND FREDERICK ENGELS. 1955. *Selected works in two volumes*. Moscow: Foreign Languages Publishing House.

MASON, HEATHER. 2003. *Does bilingual education translate to success?* Accessed July 8, 2003, at http://www.gallup.com.

MASSEY, DOUGLAS. 2004. "Reparations Segregation And Stratification: A Biosocial Perspective." *Dubois Review* 1(1): 7–25.

MASSEY, DOUGLAS S., AND NANCY A. DENTON. 1993. *American apartheid: Segregation and the making of the underclass*. Cambridge, MA: Harvard University Press.

———— JORGE DURAND, And NOLAN MALONE 2002. *Beyond Smoke And Mirrors: Mexican Immigration In An Age Of Economic Integration*. NEW YORK: RUSSELL SAGE FOUNDATION.

MATZA, DAVID. 1964. *Delinquency and drift*. New York: Wiley.

MAURO, TONY. 1995. Ruling helps communities set guidelines. *USA Today* (December 21): A1, A2.

MAYER, EGON. 2001. *American religious identification survey*. New York: The Graduate Center of the City University of New York.

McINTOSH, PEGGY. 1988. *White privilege: Unpacking the invisible knapsack*. Wellesley, MA: Wellesley College Center for Research on Women.

McKINNEY, K.D. 2003. I feel "whiteness" when I hear people blaming whites: Whiteness as cultural victimization. *Race and Society* 6:39–55.

MERTON, ROBERT K. 1949. Discrimination and the American creed. In *Discrimination and National Welfare*, ed. Robert M. MacIver, 99–126. New York: Harper & Row.

————. 1976. *Sociological ambivalence and other essays*. New York: Free Press.

MEYERS, DOWELL, JOHN PITKIN, AND JULIE PARK. 2004. *California's immigrants turn the corner*. Urban Initiative Policy Brief. Los Angeles: University of Southern California.

MILLER, DAVID L., and RICHARD T. SCHAEFER. 1998. *Promise Keepers and race: The stand in the gap rally, Washington, DC, 1997*. Paper presented at the annual meeting of the Midwest Sociological Society, April, Kansas City, MO.

MILLER, NORMAN. 2002. Personalization and the promise of contact theory. *Journal of Social Issues* 58 (Summer):387–410.

MOFFAT, SUSAN. 1995. Minorities found more likely to live near toxic sites. *Los Angeles Times* (August 30): B1, B3.

MONKMAN, KAREN, MARGARET RONALD, AND FLORENCE DÉLIMON THÉRAMÉNE. 2005. Social and cultural capital in an urban Latino school community. *Urban Education* 40 (January):4–33.

MONTAGU, ASHLEY. 1972. *Statement On Race*. New York: Oxford University Press.

MOORE, DAVID W. 2002. *Americans' view of influences of religion settling back to pre-September 11th levels*. Gallup Poll Tuesday Briefly, December 31, 2002. Accessed at http://www.gallup.com.

MOORE, STEPHEN. 1998. *A fiscal report of the newest Americans*. Washington, DC: National Immigration Forum and Cato Institute.

MORSE, SAMUEL F. B. 1835. *Foreign conspiracy against the liberties of United States*. New York: Leavitt, Lord.

MOULDER, FRANCES V. 1996. *Teaching about race and ethnicity: A message of despair or a message of hope?* Paper presented at the Annual Meeting of the American Sociological Association, New York City.

MULLAN, FITZHUGH. 2005 "The Metrics Of The Physician Brain Drain." *New England Journal of Medicine* 353 (October 27):1810–18.

MURPHY, DEAN. 2004. Imagining life without illegal immigrants. *New York Times* (January 11): . . .

MUSKRAT, JOE. 1972, "Assimilate or Starve." *Civil Rights Digest* 5 (October), PP. 27–34.

————, AND NEELA BANERJEE. 2005. Catholics in U.S. keep faith but live with contradictions. *New York Times* (April 11): A1, A16.

MYRDAL, GUNNAR. 1944. *An American dilemma: The negro problem and modern democracy*. New York: Harper.

NASH, MANNING. 1962. Race and the ideology of race. *Current Anthropology* 3 (June):285–88.

NATIONAL COLLEGIATE ATHLETIC ASSOCIATION (NCAA). 2005. *NCAA Executive Committee issues guidelines for use of Native American mascots at championship events*. August 5, 2005. Accessed February 1, 2006 at www.ncaa.org

NATIONAL CONFERENCE OF CHRISTIANS AND JEWS (NCCJ). 1994. *Taking America's pulse.* New York: Author.

NATIONAL ITALIAN AMERICAN FOUNDATION. 2006. Stop Ethnic Bashing. *New York Times* (January . . . .):

NAVARRO, MIREYA. 1998. With a vote for "None of the Above," Puerto Ricans endorse island's status quo. *New York Times* (December 14):A12.

NETWORK OMNI. 2006. *Anywhere, anytime, any language.* Accessed January 11, 2006 at www. networkomni.com

*NEW YORK TIMES.* 1917a. Illiteracy is not all alike. (February 8):12.

———. 1917b. The immigration bill veto. (January 31): 210.

———. 1991. FOR 2, An Answer To Years of Doubt on Use of Peyote In Religious Rite, (July 9), P. A14.

———. 2001. *How race is lived in America.* New York: New York Times Books/Henry Holt & Co.

———. 2005a. U.S. panel backs nuclear dump on Indian reservation in Utah. (September 10):A10.

———. 2005b. Warnings raised about exodus of Philippine doctors and nurses. (November 27):13.

NEWMAN, WILLIAM M. 1973. *American pluralism: A study of minority groups and social theory.* New York: Harper & Row.

NIE, NORMAN H., BARBARA CURRIE, AND ANDREW M. GREELEY. 1974. Political attitudes among American ethnics: A study of perceptual distortion. *Ethnicity* 1 (December):317–43.

NIEBUHR, GUSTAV. 1998. Southern Baptists declare wife should "submit" to her husband. *New York Times* (June 10):A1, A20.

NOBLE, BARBARA PRESLEY. 1995. A level playing field, for just $121. *New York Times* (March 5):F21.

NOEL, DONALD L. 1972. *The origins of American slavery and racism.* Columbus, OH: Charles Merrill Publishing Co.

NOVAK, MICHAEL. 1996. *Unmeltable ethnics: Politics and culture in American life.* 2d ed. New Brunswick, NJ: Transaction Books.

OFFICE OF IMMIGRATION STATISTICS. 2006. *2004 YEARBOOK OF IMMIGRATION STATISTICS.* WASHINGTON, DC: US GOVERNMENT PRINTING OFFICE.

OGUNWOLE, STELLA. 2006. *We the people: American Indians and Alaska Natives in the United States.* CENSR-28. Washington, DC: U.S. Government Printing Office.

OHNUMA, KEIKO. 1991. Study finds Asians unhappy at CSU. *AsianWeek* 12 (August 8):5.

OMI, MICHAEL, AND HOWARD WINANT. 1994. *Racial formation in the United States.* 2d ed. New York: Routledge.

ORFIELD, GARY, AND HOLLY J. LIEBOWITZ, EDS. 1999. *Religion, race, and justice in a changing America.* New York: The Twentieth Century Fund.

OTTAVIANO, GIANMARCO, AND GIOVANNI PERI. 2005. *Rethinking the gains from immigration theory and evidence from the U.S.* Accessed November 5, 2005 at http://www.ottavian@economia.unibo.it

OZDEN, CAGLAR, AND MAURICE SCHIFF, EDS. 2006. *International migration, remittances and the brain drain.* New York: World Bank and Palgrave Macmillan.

PAGER, DEVAH. 2003. The mark of a criminal. *American Journal of Sociology* 108:937–75.

———, AND LINCOLN QUILLIAN. 2005. Walking the talk? What employers say versus what they do. *American Sociological Review* 70 (3):355–80.

PARK, ROBERT E. 1928. Human migration and the marginal man. *American Journal of Sociology* 33 (May):881–93.

———. 1950. *Race and culture: Essays in the sociology of contemporary man.* New York: Free Press.

———. AND ERNEST W. BURGESS. 1921. *Introduction To The Science Of Sociology.* Chicago: University Of Chicago Press.

PARKER, LAURA. 2001. USA just wouldn't work without immigrant labor. *USA Today* (July 23):A1, A2.

PASSEL, JEFFERY S. 2005. *Unauthorized migrants: Numbers and characteristics.* Washington, DC: Pew Hispanic Center.

PASSEL, JEFFREY S. 2006. *The Size and Characteristics Of The Unauthroized Migrant Population in the US.: Estimates Based on the March 2005 Current Population Survey.* Washingotn, DC: Pew Hispanic Center.

PEASE, JOHN, AND LEE MARTIN. 1997. Want ads and jobs for the poor: A glaring mismatch. *Sociological Forum* 12(4):545–64.

PEDDER, SOPHIE. 1991. *Social isolation and the labour market: Black Americans in Chicago.* Paper presented at the Chicago Urban Poverty and Family Life Conference, Chicago.

PEW RESEARCH CENTER. 2005. *Huge racial divide over Katrina and its consequences.* Washington, DC: Author.

POLAKOVIC, GARY. 2001. Latinos, poor live closer to sources of air pollution. *Los Angeles Times* (October 18):B1, B12.

PORTER, EDUARDO. 2005. Illegal immigrants are bolstering social security with billions. *New York Times* (April 5): A1, C6.

PORTES, ALEJANDRO. 1998. Social capital: Its origins and applications in modern society. In *Annual Review of Sociology 1998,* 1–24. Palo Alto, CA: Annual Review.

POWELL-HOPSON, DARLENE, AND DEREK HOPSON. 1988.

Implications of doll color preferences among black preschool children and white preschool children. *Journal of Black Psychology* 14 (February):57–63.

PRESSER, HARRIET B. 2003. Race-ethnic and gender differences in nonstandard work shifts. *Work and Occupations* 30 (November):412–39.

PUBLIC BROADCASTING SYSTEM. 1998. Weekend Edition: National Public Radio with Eric Westervelt and Scott Simon, May 30.

PURDY, MATTHEW. 2001. Ignoring and Then Embracing the Truth about Racial Profiling. *New York Times* (March 11): p. 37.

REEVES, TERRANCE AND CLAUDETTE BENNETTE. 2003. "The Asian People and Pacific Islander Population in the United States: March 22." *Current Population Reports.* Ser. P20. No. 540. Washington, DC: US Government Printing Office.

RELIGION WATCH. 1995. Women religious leadership facing mainline decline, conservative growth. 11 (November):1–3.

RESKIN, BARBARA F. 1998. *The Realities Of Affirmative Action In Employment.* Washington, DC: American Sociological Association.

RICHMOND, ANTHONY H. 2002. Globalization: Implications for Immigrants and Refugees. *Ethnic and Racial Studies* 25 (September):707–27.

RIVLIN, GARY. 2005. Hate messages on Google site draw concern. *New York Times* (February 7): C1, C7.

ROBERTS, D. F. 1955. The dynamics of racial intermixture in the American negro: Some anthropological considerations. *American Journal of Human Genetics* 7 (December):361–67.

ROEDIGER, DAVID R. 1994. *Towards the abolition of whiteness: Essays on race, politics, and working class history* (Haymarket). New York: Verso Books.

ROSE, ARNOLD. 1951. *The roots of prejudice.* Paris: UNESCO.

ROSENBAUM, JAMES E., AND PATRICIA MEADEN. 1992. *Harassment and acceptance of low-income black youth in white suburban schools.* Paper presented at the Annual Meeting of the American Sociological Association, Pittsburgh.

RUSK, DAVID. 2001. *The "segregation tax": The cost of racial segregation to black homeowners.* Washington, DC: Brookings Institution.

RYAN, WILLIAM. 1976. *Blaming the victim.* Rev. ed. New York: Random House.

RYO, EMILY. "Through The Back Door: Applying Theories of Legal Compliance to Illegal Immigration during the Chinese Exclsuion Era." *Law And Social Inquiry* 31 (Winter): 109–146.

SAAD, LYDIA. 1998. America divided over status of Puerto Rico. *Gallup Poll Monthly* 390 (March):278.

SANDERS, IRWIN T., AND EWA T. MORAWSKA. 1975. *Polish-American community life: A survey of research.* Boston: Community Sociology Training Program.

SAVAGE, DAVID G. 1995. Plan to boost firms owned by minorities is assailed. *Los Angeles Times* (April 2): A14.

SCHAEFER, RICHARD T. 1976. *The extent and content of racial prejudice in Great Britain.* SAN FRANCISCO: R & E RESEARCH ASSOCIATES.

———. 1986. Racial Prejudice in a Capitalist State: What Has Happened to the American Creed? *Phylon* 47 (September):192–8.

———. 1992. People of color: The kaleidoscope may be a better way to describe America than the "melting pot." *Peoria Journal Star* (January 19): A7.

———. 1996. Education and prejudice: Unraveling the relationship. *Sociological Quarterly* 37 (January): 1–16.

SCHWARTZ, ALEX. 2001. *The state of minority access to home mortgage lending: A profile of the New York metropolitan area.* Washington: Brooking Institution Center on Urban and Metropolitan Policy.

SCOTT, JANNY. 2003. Debating White Private Clubs Are Acceptable and Private. *New York Times* (December 8): Sect. 7, 5.

SENGUPTA, SOMINI. 1997. Asians' advances academically are found to obscure a need. *New York Times* (November 9):17.

SHANKLIN, EUGENIA. 1994. *Anthropology and race.* Belmont, CA: Wadsworth.

SHERIF, MUSAFER, AND CAROLYN SHERIF. 1969. *Social psychology.* New York: Harper & Row.

SHERKAT, DARREN E., AND CHRISTOPHER G. ELLISON. 1999. Recent developments and current controversies in the sociology of religion. In *Annual Review of Sociology 1999,* ed. Karen S. Cook and John Hagan, 363–94. Palo Alto, CA: Annual Reviews.

SHIN, HYON S., AND ROSALIND BRUNO. 2003. *Language use and English-speaking ability: 2000.* C2KBR-29. Washington, DC: U.S. Government Printing Office.

SIGELMAN, LEE, AND STEVEN A. TUCH. 1997. Metastereotypes: Blacks' perception of whites' stereotypes of blacks. *Public Opinion Quarterly* 61 (Spring): 87–101.

SILVERMAN, ROBERT MARK. 2003. "Race, Consumer Characteristics, And Hiring Preferences: The South Side Of Chicago." *Research In Community Sociology* 8: 159–79.

SIMPSON, JACQUELINE C. 1995. "Pluralism: The Evolution Of A Nebulous Concept." *American Behavioral Scientist,* January, 38: 459–477. STARK, RODNEY AND CHARLES GLOCK. 1968. *American Piety: The Nature Of Religious Commitment.* Berkeley: University Of California Press.

SINGER, AUDREY. 2004. *The rise of new immigrant gateways*. Washington, DC: The Brookings Institute.

SKRENTNY, JOHN DAVID. 1996. *The ironies of affirmative action*. Chicago: University of Chicago Press.

SKULL VALLEY GOSHUTES. 2006. *Home page*. Accessed February 2, 2006 at http://www.skullvalleygoshutes.org

SLAVIN, ROBERT E., AND ALAN CHEUNG. 2003. *Effective reading programs for English language learners*. Baltimore, MD: Center for Research on the Education of Students Placed at Risk, Johns Hopkins University.

SMITH, JAMES P., AND BARRY EDMONSTON, EDS. 1997. *The new americans: Economic, demographic, and fiscal effects of immigration*. Washington, DC: National Academy Press.

SMITH, TOM W. 2000. *Taking America's pulse II: A survey of intergroup relations*. New York: National Conference for Community and Justice.

SNIDERMAN, PAUL M., AND EDWARD G. CARMINES. 1997. *Reaching beyond race*. Cambridge, MA: Harvard University Press.

SOCIETY FOR HUMAN RESOURCE MANAGEMENT. 2002. Diversity aspects covered in corporate America. *New York Times Magazine* (August 15): 100.

SOLTERO, SONIA WHITE. 2004. *Dual language: Teaching and learning in two languages*. Boston: Allyn and Bacon.

SONG, TAE-HYON. 1991. *Social contact and ethnic distance between Koreans and the U.S. whites in the United States*. Paper, Western Illinois University, Macomb.

SOUTHERN, DAVID W. 1987. *Gunnar Myrdal and black–white relations*. Baton Rouge: Louisiana State University.

SOUTHERN POVERTY LAW CENTER. 2006. *Intelligence project: Top hate watch headlines*. Accessed February 12, 2006 at http://www.splcenter.org.

Steinberg, Stephen. 2005. "Immigration, African Americans, And Race Discourse." *New Politics* 10 (Winter).

STONEQUIST, EVERETT V. 1937. *The marginal man: A study in personality and culture conflict*. New York: Scribner's.

STRAUSS, GARY. 2002. Good Old Boys' Network Still Rules Corporate Boards. *USA Today* (November 1): B1, B2.

STRETESKY, PAUL B., AND MICHAEL J. LYNCH. 2002. Environmental hazards and school segregation in Hillsborough County, Florida, 1987–1999. *Sociology Quarterly* 43 (4): 553–73.

SULLIVAN, KEITH. 2005. Desperate moves. *Washington Post National Weekly Edition* (March 14): 9–10.

TAFOYA, SONYA M., HANS JOHNSON, AND LAURA E. HILL. 2004. *Who chooses to choose two?* New York: Russell Sage Foundation and Population Reference Bureau.

TAKAKI, RONALD. 1989. *Strangers from a different shore: A history of Asian Americans*. Boston: Little, Brown.

TAYLOR, STUART, JR. 1987. High court backs basing promotion on a racial quota. *New York Times* (February 26): 1, 14.

———. 1988. Justices back New York law ending sex bias by big clubs. *New York Times* (June 21): A1, A18.

THERRIEN, MELISSA, AND ROBERTO R. RAMIREZ. 2001. *The Hispanic population in the United States, March 2000*. Current Population Reports Ser. P20, No. 535. Washington, DC: U.S. Government Printing Office.

THOMAS, WILLIAM ISAAC. 1923. *The Unadjusted Girl*. Boston: Little, Brown.

THORNBURGH, NATHAN. 2005. Serving up a conflict. *Time* 166 (August 1): 33.

THRUPKAEW, NOY. 2002. The myth of the model minority. *The American Prospect* 13 (April 8): 38–47.

TOOSSI, MITRA. 2005. Labor force projections to 2014: Retiring boomers. *Monthly Labor Review*. (November): 25–44.

TUMULTY, KAREN. 2006. "Should they Stay or Should They GO?" *Time* (April 10), 28–41.

TURE, KWAME, AND CHARLES HAMILTON. 1992. *Black power: The politics of liberation*. New York: Vintage Books.

TURNER, MARGERY AUSTIN, FRED FREIBURG, ERIN GODFREY, CLARK HERBIG, DIANE K. LEVY, AND ROBIN R. SMITH. 2002. *All other things being equal: A paired testing study of mortgage lending institutions*. Washington, DC: Urban Institute.

TYLER, GUS. 1972. White Worker/Blue Mood. *Dissent* 190 (Winter): 190–6.

UNITED JEWISH COMMUNITIES. 2003. *The National Jewish Population Survey 2000–01*. New York: Author.

U.S. COMMITTEE FOR REFUGEES. 2003. *World Refugee Survey 2003*. Washington, DC: Author.

U.S. ENGLISH. 2006. *Official English: States with official English laws*. Accessed January 28, 2006 at http://www.us-english.org.

USDANSKY, MARGARET L. 1992. Old ethnic influences still play in cities. *USA Today* (August 4):9A.

VERHOVEK, SAM HOWE. 1997. Racial tensions in suit slowing drive for "environmental justice." *New York Times* (September 7): 1, 16.

WAGLEY, CHARLES, AND MARVIN HARRIS. 1958. *Minorities in the New World: Six case studies*. New York: Columbia University Press.

WALLERSTEIN, IMMANUEL. 1974. *The modern world system*. New York: Academic Press.

———. 2004. *World-systems analysis: An introduction*. Durham, NC: Duke University Press.

WALLIS, CLAUDIA. 2005. The evolution wars. *Time* (August 15):26–35.

WARNER, SAM BASS, JR. 1968. *The private city: Philadelphia in three periods of its growth*. Philadelphia: University of Pennsylvania Press.

WARNER, W. LLOYD, AND LEO SROLE. 1945. *The social systems of American ethnic groups*. New Haven, CT: Yale University Press.

WATERS, MARY. 1990. *Ethnic options. Choosing identities in America*. Berkeley: University of California Press.

WEBER, MAX [1913–1922]. 1947. *The theory of social and economic organization*. Trans. A. Henderson and T. Parsons. New York: Free Press.

WERNICK, ROBERT. 1996. The Rise, and Fall, of a Fervid Third Party. *Smithsonian* 27 (November): 150–152, 154–158.

WESSEL, DAVID. 2001. Hidden costs of brain drain. *Wall Street Journal* (March 1):1.

WHITE, JACK E. 1997. "I'm Just Who I Am." *Time,* May 5, 149: 32–34, 36.

WICKHAM, DEWAYNE. 1993. "Subtle Racism Thrives." *USA Today,* October 25, 2A.

WILLIAMS, PATRICIA J. 1997. *Of race and risk*. The Nation Digital Edition, December 12, 1997. Accessed at http://www. thenation.com.

WITHROW, BRIAN L. 2006. *Racial profiling: From rhetoric to reason*. Upper Saddle River, NJ; Prentice-Hall.

WILSON, JAMES Q., AND EDWARD C. BANFIELD. 1964. Public regardingness as a value premise in voting behavior. *American Political Science Review* 58 (December): 876–87.

WINANT, HOWARD. 1994. *Racial conditions: Politics, theory, comparisons*. Minneapolis: University of Minnesota Press.

WINSEMAN, ALBERT L. 2004. *U.S. churches looking for a few white men*. Accessed July 27, 2004, at http://www. gallup.com.

WRONG, DENNIS H. 1972. How important is social class? *Dissent* 19 (Winter):278–85.

WU, FRANK M. 2002. *Yellow: Race in America beyond black and white*. New York: Basic Books.

WYMAN, MARK. 1993. *Round-trip to America. The immigrants return to Europe, 1830–1930*. Ithaca, NY: Cornell University Press.

YANCEY, GEORGE. 2003. *Who Is White? Latinos, Asians, and the new black-nonblack divide*. Boulder, CO: Lynne Rienner.

YINGER, JOHN. 1995. *Closed doors, opportunities lost: The continuing costs of housing discrimination*. New York: Russell Sage Foundation.

YOSSO, TARA J. 2005. Whose culture has capital? A critical race theory discussion of community cultural wealth. *Race Ethnicity and Education* 8 (March): 69–91.

YOUNG, JEFFREY R. 2003. Researchers change racial bias on the SAT. *Chronicle of Higher Education* (October 10): A34–A35.

ZERNIKE, KATE. 2005. Cultural differences complicate a Georgia drug sting operation. *New York Times* (August 4): A1, A16.

ZHOU, MIN. 2004. Are Asian Americans becoming "white?" *Contexts* (Winter): 29–37.

———, AND YOSHINORI KAMO. 1994. An analysis of earnings patterns for Chinese, Japanese, and non-Hispanic white males in the United States. *Sociological Quarterly* 35 (4):581–602.

ZIA, HELEN. 2000. *Asian American dreams: The emergence of an American people*. New York: Farrar, Straus & Giroux.

ZOGBY, JAMES J. 2003. *Arab pendulum swings on civil liberties*. Accessed July 20, 2004, at http://www.aaiusa. org/wwatch/112403.htm.

# Photo Credits

**Chapter 1 Page 1:** Ariel Skelley © Ariel Skelley/Corbis; **10:** Getty Images Inc.—Hulton Archive Photos; **12:** Cartoon by Don Wright. Copyright 2006 Tribune Media Services. Reprinted with Permission; **16:** Tony Freeman, PhotoEdit Inc.; **24:** Getty Images, Inc—Liaison; **31:** Chuck Pefley, Stock Boston; **34:** Tribune Media Services TMS Reprints; **38:** Getty Images, Inc.

**Chapter 2 Page 43:** Kai Pfaffentach, Corbis-NY; **46:** Artists Rights Society, Inc., © 2006 The Jacob and Gwendolyn Lawrence Foundation, Seattle/Artists Rights Society (ARS), New York; **52:** Bernard J. "Barney" Gallagher, **54:** Jennifer Warburg; **56:** Joe Heller/Green Bay Press-Gazette; **57:** Arab American Institute; **60:** AP Wide World Photos; **63:** AP Wide World Photos; **65:** AP Wide World Photos; **71:** JEFF STAHLER reprinted by permission of Newspaper Enterprise Association, Inc.; **75:** [Photographer]/Image Bank/Getty Images; **80:** AP Wide World Photos.

**Chapter 3 Page 84:** Mark Peterson, Corbis—NY; **86:** Ted Hardin; **87:** Courtesy of the Library of Congress; **90:** Columbia Law School; **94:** APJ. Pat Carter, Wide World Photos; **95:** Judy Gelles, Stock Boston; **102:** Bachmann, Stock Boston; **105:** Copley News Service/Steve Breen; **106:** The Image Works; **107:** AP Wide World Photos; **112:** Signe Wilkinson, Cartoonists & Writers Syndicate/cartoonweb.com

**Chapter 4 Page 119:** Corbis/Bettmann, © David H. Wells/Corbis; **127:** Corbis/Bettmann, © Bettmann/Corbis; **130:** Courtesy of the Library of Congress; **135:** Takeshi Takahara, Photo Researchers, Inc.; **137:** King Features Syndicate (NAS) North America Syndicate; **137:** Courtesy of The New York Times Company; **142:** Copley News Service/Bruce Beattie; **145:** Corbis/Bettmann; **146:** AP Wide World Photos.

**Chapter 5 Page 151:** Corbis/Bettmann, © Bettmann/Corbis; **155:** Diane Glancy; **157:** Corbis—NY; **160:** Joel Gordon Photography; **164:** Woodfin Camp & Associates; **170:** PhotoEdit Inc.; **179:** Agence France Presse/Getty Images; **181:** Chicago Tribune; **185:** AP Wide World Photos; **186:** Corbis/Sygma; **189:** King Features Syndicate NAS North America Syndicate; **191:** AP Wide World Photos.

**Chapter 6 Page 196:** PhotoEdit Inc.; **200:** Michael Grecco/Icon International; **202:** Corbis Royalty Free, © Chris Carroll/Corbis; **204:** AP Wide World Photos; **206:** Lawrence Migdale, Stock Boston; **208:** Randy Matusow.

# Author Index

# Subject Index